The Design Quality Manual

The Design Quality Manual

Improving building performance

Martin Cook
Building Research Establishment Ltd

Blackwell
Publishing

Editorial offices:
Blackwell Publishing Ltd, 9600 Garsington Road, Oxford OX4 2DQ, UK
  Tel: +44 (0)1865 776868
Blackwell Publishing Inc., 350 Main Street, Malden, MA 02148-5020, USA
  Tel: +1 781 388 8250
Blackwell Publishing Asia Pty Ltd, 550 Swanston Street, Carlton, Victoria 3053, Australia
  Tel: +61 (0)3 8359 1011

First published 2007 by Blackwell Publishing Ltd

ISBN-13: 978-14051-3088-2
ISBN-10: 1-4051-3088-1

Library of Congress Cataloging-in-Publication Data
Cook, Martin, 1959–
    The design quality manual : improving building performance / Martin Cook.
        p.   cm.
    Includes bibliographical references and index.
    ISBN-13: 978-1-4051-3088-2 (hardback : alk. paper)
    ISBN-10: 1-4051-3088-1 (hardback : alk. paper)
    1. Building–Quality control.   2. Public buildings–Purchasing.   3. Public architecture.
4. Architecture, Domestic.   5. Building designers.   6. Dwellings.   7. Public housing.   I. Title.
    TH438.2.C66 2006
    720–dc22

                                                                    2006011203

A catalogue record for this title is available from the British Library

Set in 11 on 13.5 pt Avenir
by SNP Best-set Typesetter Ltd., Hong Kong
Printed and bound in Singapore
by Markono Print Media Pte Ltd

The publisher's policy is to use permanent paper from mills that operate a sustainable forestry policy, and which has been manufactured from pulp processed using acid-free and elementary chlorine-free practices. Furthermore, the publisher ensures that the text paper and cover board used have met acceptable environmental accreditation standards.

For further information on Blackwell Publishing, visit our website:
www.blackwellpublishing.com

Contents

3 Schools 61

4 Hospitals 135

The colour plate section is to be found after page 116

Acknowledgements

The author would like to express sincere gratitude to all who have contributed to the production of this publication. I am particularly grateful to all those who contributed their time, knowledge and experience during the post-occupancy evaluations of their buildings, and to the auditing bodies who commissioned the research. Several of my colleagues at the Building Research Establishment (BRE) were consistently involved in the Design Quality Method (DQM) projects in schools, hospitals and housing. Colin Ashford was involved in all of the DQM projects and helped to draft the DQM matrices. He also took extensive measurements of building performance indicators such as lighting levels; heating and temperature levels; acoustics and air quality levels across the total sample of nearly a hundred buildings that were evaluated using the Method.

> *'All truth passes through three stages. First it is ridiculed, second it is violently opposed, and third it is accepted as being self-evident.'*

Arthur Schopenhauer, German philosopher, 1788–1860.

Abbreviations and acronyms

ACA	Association of Consultant Architects
APM	Association of Project Managers
BEC	Building Employers Confederation
BEDC	Building Economic Development Council
BPF	British Property Federation
B of Q	Bill of Quantities
BRE	Building Research Establishment
BRT	Business Round Table
BUILD	Building Users' Insurance against Latent Defects
CABE	Commission for Architecture and the Built Environment
CAD	Computer Aided Design
CCMI	Centre for Construction Market Information
CIB	International Research Council for Building Research Studies and Documentation
CIC	Construction Industry Council
CIOB	Chartered Institute of Building
CIRIA	Construction Industry Research and Information Association
CMF	Construction Management Forum
CPM	Critical Path Method
CRT	Construction Round Table
CSSC	Centre for Strategic Studies in Construction (Reading)
CUP	Central Unit for Procurement (DoE)
DoE	Department of the Environment
FIDIC	International Federation of Consulting Engineers
GDP	Gross Domestic Product
GMP	Guaranteed Maximum Price
HBS	Harvard Business School
HMSO	Her Majesty's Stationery Office
ICE	Institution of Civil Engineers
IOD	Institute of Directors
IT	Information Technology
JCT	Joint Contracts Tribunal
MIT	Massachusetts Institute of Technology
MMC	Modern Methods of Construction
NASA	National Aeronautics and Space Administration (USA)
NCC	New Construction Contract (proposed by Latham)
NEC	New Engineering Contract
NEDO	National Economic Development Office

NJCC	National Joint Consultative Committee for Building
PCP	Project Client Consultants
PERT	Programme Evaluation and Review Technique
PSA	Property Services Agency (DoE) [now defunct]
QS	Quantity Surveyor
QUANGO	Quasi-autonomous non-governmental organisation
RIBA	Royal Institute of British Architects
RICS	Royal Institution of Chartered Surveyors
USM	Unlisted Securities Market
WBS	Work Breakdown Structure

Chapter 1

Introduction

1.1 Overview of design quality and building performance

The design quality of buildings and their subsequent performance is a pre-occupation of humankind stretching back to ancient times. And not just expressed in aesthetic terms, such as the Roman architect, Vitruvius', three principles of *firmitas*, *utilitas* and *venustas* – later interpreted as firmness, commodity and delight in the architectural treatise of Sir Henry Wooton, *The elements of architecture*, published in 1624. But Marco Vitruvius was also a highly practical Roman military engineer and his ten books on architecture, the only surviving ancient writings on the subject, also contain sound advice on the construction of military hardware such as catapults and other siege machinery. Functionality is implicit in the search for optimum design quality – and although it may not entirely follow form, it is obviously an integral and essential part of the whole architectural solution. The three ancient principles of design quality still hold true, and I suspect that they always will. A building must certainly have firmness, or strength, to resist the forces of gravity and other natural forces such as those of the wind, not to mention being robust enough to age and weather gracefully with optimal maintenance and repair, to fulfil its designed life-cycle, and beyond. It must be commodious, or functional, or fit for purpose, otherwise what is the point of building it at all? Even seemingly minor functional shortfalls can escalate into serious and long-term failings which plague a building's life and those of its users. Finally, it should certainly be delightful or beautiful – capable of lifting human spirits in regular users and visitors alike, if it is truly to be called architecture, and not merely utilitarian 'building'. Pevsner's simplistic description of a cathedral as architecture and a bicycle shed as building, useful in establishing diametric extremes, is less helpful when assessing the subtle shades of grey between them – and the place of individual structures in the continuum.

The subsequent performance of a building over its lifetime is inevitably bound-up with, and begins with, its design parameters, programme, or brief. Vitruvius' ancient advice focused on aesthetic matters, and centred around detailed explanations of architectural orders and column proportions. He was espousing the virtues of Greek architecture mainly for the purpose of temple building – the aesthetic impact of a religious structure on its worshippers was the paramount criterion of his design brief. But such symbolic architecture was closely linked to the continued political power of such a building's clients and funders. A tradition continued well into the Middle Ages with cathedral building, and beyond, to the present day in secular architecture. A religious, or other such symbolic structure, is performing if it wields power over worshippers and visitors. User comfort, for example, was certainly secondary, in terms of performance criteria, to inspiring awe and fear among worshippers, and probably irrelevant as the initiated did not even enter ancient temples. Fortunately, building users have become more demanding, and nowadays even a brief, weekly, foray into an uncomfortable place of worship is largely unacceptable.

Building performance in more complex, modern times, with a plethora of different building types, is not quite as simple as in ancient precedents. But, the basic physical dictates of shelter from the elements, ventilation, sunlight, acoustics and daylight remain the same. Some would say that we have allowed scientific principles too much reign at the expense of spiritual, symbolic and human aspects. Le Corbusier's definition of the house as 'a machine for living in' certainly does nothing to dispell this view of contemporary architecture and helps to explain the burgeoning membership of heritage organisations, as well as the general public's choice of buildings such as the Houses of Parliament and St Paul's as the most popular, confirming the 'performance' success of such political and religious symbols in the population's consciousness. Or, possibly, the failure of modern architecture, made more poignant at a time when the public building estate is being rebuilt in the United Kingdom – which only happens once in a generation. However, in a scientific age there are still doubts over the physical performance of buildings and their ability to provide comfort for all users, and perform in other areas such as energy efficiency or environmental sustainability. Our architecture is a reflection of the state of society at the time of construction and society's conventions, contracts and methods of procuring buildings will always have a strong influence over the results in terms of design quality – for better or worse. In the words of Winston Churchill, referring to the Houses of Parliament, '. . . first we shape our buildings and then they shape us'.

The eighteenth century was a simpler time than our own, but even then there was an urge for a simpler form of society, expressed in the literaure of Jean-Jacques Rousseau, but also in the architectural theory of M. A. Laugier (1713–69). Laugier's *Essai sur l'architecture* (1755), like most previous writers on the subject, again invoked Vitruvius in the form of an iconic image of architectural theory (Figure 1.1 left). The primitive hut was used by Vitruvius to prove that Greek architecture had transposed the principles of timber-constructed architecture directly into stone construction. The functions of the carpentry joints were honestly expressed and contained the ubiquitous architectural elements of column, pediment and entablature. These are formal elements which express function in any and every form of architecture. Laugier's ideas influenced the development of neoclassicism and further perpetuated Vitruvius' theories. The revival of classical architecture was a search for perfect forms, usually inspired by Andrea

Figure 1.1 Laugier's primitive hut from *Essai sur l'architecture* (1755), and modern stripped-down portico. Reproduced with permission RIBA Library Photographs Collection.

Palladio's Renaissance villas and his treatise, *Quatro libri*, or *The four books of architecture* (1570). The four books are partly a theoretical and partly a practical manual, as Palladio was originally a stonemason who rapidly became a popular architect to the villa-building classes in and around Venice. The books are well illustrated with Palladio's completed works and idealised versions of unimplemented projects, establishing a 'pattern book' format that became essential for all future manuals on architecture. Palladio's acknowledged debt to Vitruvius, and the four books' subsequent popularity, further enshrined the ancient Roman's principles in all ages of Western architecture. Palladianism took a strong hold on architecture in the British Isles, first with Inigo Jones, Christopher Wren and Vanbrugh. Later, the patronage of Lord Burlington ensured that British Palladianism was popular well into the nineteenth century. Although, doubts over the suitability of a form of architecture conceived in a Mediterranean climate, echoed by later doubts over such continental imports, led Alexander Pope to satirise architects' choice in verse:

> *Shall call forth the Winds through long arcades to roar,*
> *Proud to catch cold at a Venetian door,*
> *Conscious to act a true Palladian part.*[1]

However, the timeless power of the classical symbolism of columns and porticos is shown by the reliance on this device to produce dramatic entrances to banks, colleges, and other building types. And it is still in use today, although usually in a stripped down form (Figure 1.1 right).

Figure 1.2 The Casino at Marino, Dublin, by Sir William Chambers, 1764. The urn is a chimney.

The search for the perfect building continued in the eighteenth century, under the patronage of Lord Charlemont and his architect Sir William Chambers – leaving Ireland with a strong symbol of neo-classicism. Charlemont was inspired by his grand tour of the classical world which ultimately lasted nine years, including his long residence in Rome. He did, however, venture further east to Greece, Turkey and Egypt.[2] The Casino at Marino, sited in a park between the centre of Dublin and the airport to the north, is predominantly informed by Roman classical architecture (Figure 1.2 left, right). Charlemont's architect, Chambers, was also a writer, and his *Treatise on civil architecture* (1759) was highly influential, focused on decorative elements and provided an accessible guide to the use of column orders. Chambers also presaged the Gothic revival of the nineteenth century when he called for the preservation and appreciation of medieval architecture. The Casino is an architectural gem, which, through ingenious devices, appears externally as a single-roomed, single-storey, Greek temple. It is, in fact, a sixteen-roomed, three-storeyed, functional belvedere, or as the name suggests, a small ornamental house. That most famous of Georgian architects working in Ireland, James Gandon, is also thought, by some, to have had a hand in the Casino, as he was Chamber's pupil in the mid-eighteenth century. It is likely that he executed the working drawings for the Casino and the composition contains many motifs uncommon to Chamber's other work (e.g. Somerset House, 1776–86), but symbolic of Gandon's, such as a surfeit of externally visible windows – most being top-lights or clerestorys. These are ingeniously hidden by the entablature in this case, along with other devices such as small convex panes of glass to the windows to disguise the deceit behind, and naturally light each of the sixteen rooms.[3]

British architecture became a battle of the styles in the nineteenth century, with neo-classicism largely holding sway for public buildings early in the century, such as the National Gallery (1834–8) by William Wilkins (1778–1839), who was also the architect of another neo-classical portico at

University College London (1826). Wilkins, in common with other architects of this era, although largely a committed neo-classicist employed other architectural styles, such as Tudor-Gothic for the New Court of Corpus Christi College, Cambridge. This is in contrast to his neo-classical essay at Downing College (1806); the latter was virtually a green-field site, while the former was adjacent to the oldest, medieval Court in Cambridge. Gothic and Classic styles battled it out throughout the century for public building commissions, while an Italianate style became popular for villas; all the while the search for a British 'national style' continued. Ironically, many of these variegated examples of stylism have become treasured national icons, but buildings such as the Houses of Parliament were as controversial in their day as other new national parliament buildings are today. Modernist architecture claims many roots in the freestyle experiments of the later nineteenth century, such as the stripped, whitewash rendering of Charles Voysey's domestic architecture, to the rationalism of Philip Webb's Red House for William Morris.

Architecture and design quality is rarely without controversy, as it is largely viewed as subjective. One person's 'carbuncle on the face of a much loved friend' is often another's idea of design perfection. Benchmarks to help achieve consensus are essential. However, there is invariably a route back to the ancient treatise of Vitruvius, even if it is sometimes through the enduring legacy of modern architects such as the American, Robert Venturi, who often chooses to refract neo-classicism through the lens of Pop Art, and the popularism of Las Vegas.[4] His architecture is in many ways a backlash against the simplifications of Modernism, and he uses architectural history to regain a 'complexity and contradiction' in the built environment – centred, once more, around symbolism and meaning in architecture.[5] But, it is a difficult task to find such meaning in a largely secular society, and possibly the only way to seek it is through popularism. The 'architectural joke', such as games with scale and proportion of the one-lined meaning, is rarely enduring, but even this can contain more symbolism than the bland and meaningless structures that tend to make up most of our modern built environment. Venturi actually argues for 'ordinariness' which he symbolises as the 'decorated shed', as it provides a contrast for the 'duck' – the former containing its meaning in its, often commercially inspired, façade, with a shed behind it, while the latter subverts its architectural form into the message or symbol of its function – the building as sign (Figure 1.3 left, right).* Venturi also invokes Vitruvius' three principles, but famously changes the formula Firmness + Commodity + Delight = Architecture, into a criticism of Modernism's 'form follows function' dictact which implies that Firmness + Commodity = Delight. Design quality in architecture must ensure the first two ingredients and also integrate the third and final ingredient to achieve a high quality of architecture.[6]

---

*The 'duck' is named after a roadside eatery in Long Island, New York – literally built in the shape of a duck as an implicit advertisement of its wares.

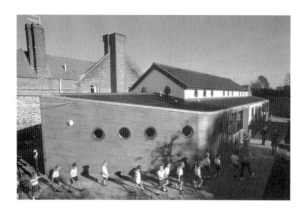

Figure 1.3 Imaginative buildings for young children – 'ducks'. The boat and waves are primary schools. Copyright Joe Low/Architectural Association. This figure is also reproduced in colour in the colour plate section.

1.2 Building procurement systems

The method or system by which a building is procured is crucial to consequent design and building performance quality. Defined as the entire approach to creating the building, including initial approaches to the construction industry, briefing, designing, contract choice, communications systems, and consultant and client involvement. All too often this choice of approach is made by default, too late, or simply by choosing the currently fashionable method from a burgeoning array of alternatives. Unfortunately, the choice is also often dictated by political or organisational circumstances, and approaches dubbed mere 'funding mechanisms' have a crucial impact on subsequent design quality and functionality. Inexperienced clients in particular are often unsure about how to approach the construction industry, and ill-advised decisions at the early stages can have disastrous consequences.

The Royal Academy of Engineering's rule of thumb concerning the proportional effect of different stages of a building's life estimates that the capital cost is in a ratio of $1:5:200$ when compared to operational costs and business costs. Even if this ratio is lower, such as $1:2:100$, it is still undeniable that the capital cost of a building is invariably smaller than its operational costs, and minute against the impact of the building in use for an average life span of 60 years. Design costs must be an even smaller fraction of this ratio, and if added as an interpolation would probably give the ratio $0.1:1:5:200$ (Figure 1.4). Even seemingly minor functionality problems, such as narrow corridors or inadequate daylight, will have negative business, educational or health impacts over the life of the facility. The whole life context of a building places early decisions, such as choice of procurement route or system, in a crucial light.

1.3 Chequered history of building procurement systems

The construction industry, like most other industries, has always had its problems – no doubt these were solved relatively easily in a slave-based

0.1 : 1 : 5 : 200

Typical office building

KEY
0.1	Design cost
1	Construction cost
5	Maintenance and building operating costs
200	Business operating costs

Figure 1.4 Design influences performance over time.

society such as that of the Egyptians building the pyramids, or for that matter, the Greeks and Romans with their monumental architectural achievements. Many critics of the industry would hazard that it has not changed much since those days, and is still 'brick upon brick' or 'stone upon stone'. A conservative industry, construction has responded slowly to technological and social change – but the industry was never short of, usually external, pundits highlighting problems and putting forward, sometimes simplistic, solutions. Exhortations to emulate other, seemingly more efficient industries, are among the more recent suggestions. But a long line of such reports litter the history of the UK construction industry in the late twentieth century, dating back to the Simon Report in 1944, an era in which there were still some social and technological certainties, and there was still only, really, one acceptable route of procuring a building – or preferably 'architecture'.

There was only one form of building procurement system that was really respectable at the beginning of the twentieth century. This 'traditional system', which remained essentially unchanged into the 1960s, retained sharp vestiges of social stratification. Cultured clients would use no other system. It was approved by architects and they were recognised as head of the hierarchy. However, increasing social, economic, and technological change heralded by post-war rebuilding began to show up flaws in the system. This led Bowley to comment:

> It is difficult to see how any system more wasteful of technical knowledge, intellectual ability, and practical and organising experience could have been invented.[7]

The traditional system persisted, despite the technical advances of industrialisation. It was the social agenda of the welfare state, with the need for a rapid rebuilding programme, that led to the recommendations arising from successive government reports into the 'problems' of the construction industry. Among the first was the Simon Report (1944), which abhorred the use of open tendering as 'contrary to the interests both of the building owner and of the building industry'. Selective tendering was advocated in this and later reports, which culminated in its detailed formalisation in various NJCC codes of procedure.[8] Other shortcomings of the traditional system were variously identified by reports, such as Emmerson's in 1962.[9] He contended that, '. . . in no other industry is the responsibility for design so far removed from the responsibility for production.' Such a state of affairs has obviously been exacerbated by the sociological evolution of the system in which increased status and influence accrued to the design professionals. Architects could further their vested interests by divorcing design from construction, and increase their influence with the client at the earliest stages of the project. This schism between design and construction was not improved by educational initiatives of the late 1950s – the infamous Oxford conference required architects to completely abandon articles, or apprenticeships, in favour of full-time academic training; followed by a few years practical experience.

Emmerson also recommended that unconventional types of contract, which integrated design and construction, should be carefully considered by public bodies. The Banwell Committee (1964) went on to advocate openly the use of such variants of the traditional system as negotiated contracts. Banwell's main message was that:

> . . . the various sections of the industry have long acted independently. We consider that the most urgent problem which confronts the construction industry is the necessity of thinking and acting as a whole.[10]

However, such well meaning platitudes belie the inherently fragmented nature of the building industry. Any attempt to integrate design and construction has to contend with the disparate socio-economic and organisational objectives of the various protagonists. The client is clearly the key participant, and increasingly a catalyst for change.[11] In the post-war period up to the early 1970s the majority of building work was implemented using the traditional procurement system. This was in spite of all the recommendations to use relatively unconventional systems, such as negotiation, serial tendering and package deals. The economic impact of the oil shocks of the mid- to late-1970s created a plethora of alternative building procurement systems – making informed and rational selection of an appropriate system increasingly difficult. However, there are really only a few generic systems, and correct selection of an appropriate one is made simpler by classifying them in terms of their organisational structure (i.e. communications, functions and responsibilities).[12]

Poor or biased client guidance often leads to inappropriate procurement systems being selected: even between the three generic systems of 'traditional', 'design and build' and 'management'. The choice of building procurement system is too often made by default, too late, or by choosing the currently fashionable process which is being lauded in journals and other publicity vehicles. The National Economic Development Office (NEDO) also found that customers of the industry 'lacked sources of information or impartial advice about the options or alternative courses of action open to them' and that, 'projects were often organised traditionally by default rather than as a result of a conscious decision'.[13]

The traditional system relies on the architect 'taking a brief from his client'. But the concept of one individual communicating his requirements to another individual, derived from older professions such as law, was condemned as obsolete as long ago as the mid-1960s.[14] The main grounds for this judgement were that the client is seldom an individual, and they rarely deal with a single member of the building industry. As traditionally organised, the system does at least provide the client with an adviser, in the form of an architect as lead consultant. In this traditional role the architect is presumed impartial, and acts as a quasi-arbitrator between the client and contractor later in the project. As other consultants are appointed directly by the client the lines of communication can become unwieldy. This led to the search for a system with a single point of responsibility, which in turn encouraged building professionals to laud themselves as proponents of the ideal system. Inexperienced clients are inevitably influenced by marketing or other claims that possibly unsuitable systems are appropriate for their proposed projects.

Successive research consistently stresses the importance of clients accurately choosing an appropriate procurement path to suit their primary objectives, to facilitate project success. Surveys by the RICS of contracts in use identified an increasing diversity of building procurement methods. But the traditional method remains the most familiar, and often preferred, procurement route – and is design-led. A trend has grown, particularly for complex projects, in the use of management-based arrangements. While different procurement arrangements will suit different circumstances, some systems are successively lauded as universal panaceas. Many of these, often transitory, systems seem to suit the vested interests of their main proponents, rather than the best interests of value-for-money for the client. Many commentators have observed that clients of the construction industry lack impartial sources of advice about the services available to them. This problem was first identified by the seminal Tavistock Institute research study, *Communications in the building industry*.[15] They contended that many prospective customers do not know enough about the range of services to make an appropriately informed first approach to the industry's marketplace; and that the industry should communicate information about itself. Largely as a result of these findings a client guide was commissioned by NEDO in 1974 – the importance of the client's role in the building process is the central theme of this guide.[16] Other client guides were also produced at this time, most notably the CIRIA guides to discrete procurement routes.

Despite these early attempts to provide the client with guidance, subsequent research continued to indicate that customers still lacked sources of impartial information. The NEDO report, *Faster building for industry* (1983), led to the production of a guide aimed at inexperienced clients, *Thinking about building* (1985). However, this and earlier guides were not widely disseminated among clients, possibly due to a reliance on inappropriate dissemination routes, such as via construction professionals. The Latham Report reiterated the central role of the client. Latham asserted that clients are the key to the whole construction process; as they fund it, their wants and needs should be paramount. While this is largely undeniable, the absence of civic-minded patronage and trends towards 'form follows profit' has led to much lamentation of the quality of buildings, townscape, and architecture. Clients have a pivotal role to play in these areas as well. Another problem identified by the Higgin and Jessop report in 1965,[15] that

Project Objectives / Parameters	Traditional	Design and build	Management
Time	Time consuming. Design must be complete before tender stage and construction. Negotiation quicker.	Faster method. Construction time reduced because design and building proceed in parallel. ■	Early start on site possible, before works package tenders. Design and construction in parallel. ■
Cost	Price and time certainty before building. Risk of claims due to delayed design information. ■	Virtually guaranteed price and completion date. ■	Client is committed to build on the basis of target costs. Cost plan, drawings and specification only.
Quality	Client's standards explicit in completed documents. Contractor responsible for achieving quality on site. ■	Client cannot control detailed design, contractor's performance or the selection of specialist subcontractors.	Client controls design standards and selection of works contractors. Construction manager responsible for site quality. ■
Complexity	Suitable for medium technology and complexity. Familiar to many clients.	Appropriate for standard technology and low complexity. Simple buildings.	Most appropriate for high technology and complexity. Sophisticated management. ■
Competition	Highly competitive tenders for all items, easy to evaluate. Negotiation reduces competition. ■	Proposals difficult for client to evaluate. No direct benefit to client for subcontractors competition.	Limited competition for appointment of management team. Competition can be retained for works contractors. ■
Flexibility	Client controls design. Variations during construction are possible, at a price. Medium flexibility.	Virtually none for the client, after contract is signed. Later variations will mean heavy cost penalties. Low flexibility.	Client can modify design during construction, without compromising cost control. High flexibility. ■
Risk	Risk is apportioned equally between the client and the contractor.	Contractor bears almost all the risk. ■	Client bears most of the risk – almost all for construction management.
Responsibility	Usually clear cut division between design and construction. Familiar roles. ■	Single point responsibility. Can be confused when client's requirements are detailed. ■	Success depends on the manager's skills. Team must be well coordinated.
Size	Most appropriate for small–medium projects. ■	Applicable to projects of varying sizes.	Most suitable for large, complex projects. Extremely large for project management. ■
Summary	Benefits in **cost** and **quality** – but at the expense of **time**.	Benefits in **cost** and **time** – but at the expense of quality.	Benefits in **time** and **quality** – but at the expense of cost.

KEY ■ = Usually most appropriate; dependent upon specific project objectves.

Figure 1.5 Summary matrix to aid choice of building procurement method at the early stages of a project.

of communications between prospective clients and advisors, was further investigated a decade ago. The conclusion was that all disciplines of advisor proffered advice on procurement options at initial meetings, but this advice was obviously much constrained by their education, training and experience. It is also likely that initial advice was biased by the consultants' vested interests in the future of the potential project. Recommendations included the need for guidance for inexperienced clients, before they committed themselves to a particular procurement option or professional. The dissemination of guidance to clients at the very early stages of their projects needs improvement. The objective choice of an appropriate procurement approach should be a major decision for the building client, as it may have extensive effects on the subsequent project (Figure 1.5).[17]

1.4 Cultural context of building procurement systems – public v. private?

Jane Jacobs, the author of *The death and life of great American cities* (1961), proposed opposing schools of thought for what she terms commercial and guardian 'moral syndromes', in the early 1990s (Figure 1.6). They effectively relate to simplistic notions of behaviour in the public (guardian) and private (commercial) sectors of our economy, respectively. Simplistic because divisions between the two sectors are increasingly blurred. Jacobs contends that while the two cultures are not mutually exclusive, and fusion can reap harmony in some cases, 'monstrous hybrids' represented by organised crime and the Mafia (practices commerce in accord with guardian precepts) can also result.[18]

Commercial *moral syndrome principles*	Guardian *moral syndrome principles*
• Shun force	• Shun trading
• Come to voluntary agreements	• Exert prowess
• Be honest	• Be obedient and disciplined
• Collaborate easily with strangers and aliens	• Adhere to tradition
• Compete	• Respect hierarchy
• Respect contracts	• Be loyal
• Use initiative and enterprise	• Take vengeance
• Be open to inventiveness and novelty	• Deceive for the sake of the task
• Be efficient	• Make rich use of leisure
• Promote comfort and convenience	• Be ostentatious
• Dissent for the sake of the task	• Dispense largesse
• Invest for productive purposes	• Be exclusive
• Be industrious	• Show fortitude
• Be thrifty	• Be fatalistic
• Be optimistic	• Treasure honour

Figure 1.6 Commerical and guardian moral syndrome principles – according to Jane Jacobs.

1.5 Architects and social status

One of the most profound paradoxes of modern architectural practice stems from the beginning of the eighteenth century: when the title architect was a pretension claimed by those aspiring to a higher social status, and a more literary and academic vocation, than the master-builder or surveyor. Many architects conceive of themselves primarily as artists. Beginning with the Romantic tradition, avant-garde artists did not expect to get rich. It was partly because architecture was perceived as an art for which remuneration at commercial values was unlikely to occur, that it became a proper pursuit for a gentleman.[19]

As the industrial revolution greatly expanded, the building market catered for many new clients, such as developers, industrialists, public corporations and others. Occupations which were formerly the province of the upper streams of society began to expand to meet these burgeoning supply and technological opportunities. Architects, in an attempt to maintain their professional image, decided upon exclusion as a way of combating unscrupulous developers and builders; who also offered design services. The role of the architect as the independent, educated, gentleman designer became the model of the nineteenth century. They eschewed speculation and fee competition, and claimed the independent status permitting action as an impartial arbiter between client and contractor. Associated professions, who also had concern for status, identified their own professional roles, exacerbating the process of fragmentation of the industry. However, during the nineteenth century the role and definition of the architect was undefined. Many architects acted as developers and designed, constructed and financed vast areas of new housing in the industrial cities. Men such as Cubbitt (1788–1855) and Nash (1752–1835) proved that architects could retain stature as designers while involving themselves in the business of construction. A tradition possibly revived by architects such as John Portman in the United States, who acted as architect and developer for hotel projects.

The registrationalists' more prosaic intentions were to provide for architects a particular social status, and economic benefits, deriving from a 'closed shop' which controlled the market for their services.[20] The architects who saw themselves as artists had opposing ambitions, more akin to fine artists of the turn of the century; concisely described by Tom Wolfe:

> . . . the modern picture of The Artist (sic) began to form: the poor but free spirit, plebeian but aspiring only to be classless, to cut himself forever free from the bonds of the greedy and hypocritical bourgeoisie, to be whatever the fat burghers feared most, to cross the line wherever they drew it, to look at the world in a way they couldn't see, to be high, live low, stay young forever – in short, to be the bohemian.[21]

To transpose this artistic analogy to architectural practice seems unrealistic, as the architect's creative ambitions are immutably bound to capital and patronage. As, 'Painters and authors can execute their work in haughty isolation. An architect can only build at somebody else's expense . . .'.[22] However, the vestiges of this bohemian urge sometimes lead to clients' assertions that architects are arrogant and oblivious to, or ignorant of, their needs.[23] The architectural equivalent of the artistic bohemian ideal was elucidated by a group of 'artist–architects'; in response to the increasing professionalisation of architecture, at the turn of the century:

> Legislation has at last reached the domain of art . . . It is not likely that any one . . . who knows what Art (sic) really means will be taken in by this chimeral project. To a true artist his art is an individual matter purely between himself and his artistic conscience . . . He must go his own way; his art must be absolutely free, unfettered save by the canons of truth and nature, the limitations of human sense, and the possibilities of his instruments and his materials.[24]

More recently, those architects who choose to practise in the realm of architectural concepts rather than the mundanities of building, are able to pursue the bohemian ideal. This line of practitioners can be traced from the Futurists and Constructivists of the early twentieth century through to Archigram in the 1960s. Some would contend that Archigram epitomised the visionary spirit of the architect. The 'vision' of Archigram heralded the 'high-tech' architecture of the late twentieth century; in buildings such as the Lloyd's building. In that sense they could be perceived to have created an almost 'future' surplus value – or predicted a largely self-fulfilling prophesy, as some members of the group went on to build their visions. But not everyone perceives this vision:

> The underlying tone of Archigram was one of educated, apolitical and anarchic satire. There is a parallel here with the line in British comedy that led from the Goons to Monty Python. Both tendencies relied heavily on cartoon graphics, surrealist imagery, and an over-riding desire to mock and shock the values of bourgeois, suburban England. Together, Archigram and the Pythons could well have devised a Ministry of Funny Walking Buildings.[25]

1.6 Architecture: art, profession or commercial enterprise?

The separation of architecture as an art from the business of architecture has a long tradition. In the first century BC Vitruvius praised the 'gentleman' architect in contrast to the suspect architect of wealth: 'But for my part, Caesar, I have never been eager to make money by my art, but have gone on the principle that slender means and a good reputation are preferable to wealth and disrepute'. Vitruvius also described the tremendous range of knowledge an architect needs; the burden of such an unwieldy bundle of expertise weighs heavily upon the profession:

> Let him be educated, skillful with the pencil, instructed in geometry, know much history, have followed the philosophers with attention, understand music, have some knowledge of medicine, know the opinions of the jurists, and be acquainted with astronomy and the theory of the heavens.[26]

This burden is certainly not lightened by the great Victorian John Ruskin's later invocations of the ideal architect in *Lectures on architecture and painting* (circa 1850):

> No person who is not a great sculptor or painter can be an architect. If he is not a sculptor or painter, he can only be a builder.

The architect's primary expertise, as epitomised by the École des Beaux-Arts, was design as art. This has created a legacy for architecture distinct from other professions, and partly explains why medicine and law are more fully developed. Art, or design as conceptual work, has been a difficult commodity to sell in a pragmatic marketplace. Since at least the late nineteenth century, architects have decried the public's ambivalence toward aesthetic concerns. For architects as for other professions, the emphasis on academic training was a means of preserving professional activity for those of social status. Two forces operated in tandem: educational movements were established to raise the status of the profession, and professional activity was kept in the hands of those with status.[27] Despite the radical changes to the context of the architect as the servant of an enlightened patron, to that of a high grade technician or 'technocrat': the fundamental role of the architect as a conceiver of buildings remains unchanged. This notion of enhanced social status accruing to the architect, when compared with other construction professionals, continued into the nineteenth and twentieth centuries.

The architect's traditional role of the mediator between the client or patron and the builder, however, is obviously challenged by a proliferation of alternative procurement methods. This role of quasi-arbitrator under the JCT forms of contract was first challenged by the Latham review, which recommended the adoption of a hybrid form of the New Engineering Contract (NEC) for all construction projects. The NEC contains the premise that a project manager is appointed, and that an adjudicator is the first arbiter of disputes. The NEC explicitly adopts the traditional legal model of two parties, and two parties only, to the typical bilateral contract (i.e. the employer and the contractor). Unfortunately, the complex role of the modern construction professional, with its enhanced dispute resolution function to avert litigation, has often rendered this traditional contractual model inadequate.[28] That clients now undertake, on their own behalf, activities that many architects believe are in their domain, is a relatively recent development in the industry. The competition between architects and other professions for domination of the building process, however, is a contest with a long history, extending over centuries.[29] Courtney Blackmore asks why architects have not safeguarded their professional position in the way that solicitors, doctors or accountants clearly have. He suggests the answer lies in the nature of the relationship between client and professional adviser. In professions such as law and medicine the client has little option but to accept the advice given; as to do otherwise could render him or her in an illegal or life threatening position. In architecture the consequences of ignoring advice are rarely as fearful. Additionally, the necessary one-to-one nature of the professional to client is often lost with larger practices, and the burgeoning array of specialists necessary to procure a complex modern building. Finally, everyone has an opinion concerning an aesthetic judgement: and increasing commercialism has led to predominantly pecuniary evaluations. The demands of increasingly sophisticated and commercial clients are now playing a central role in reducing the architect's influence – not to mention the arrangement of Private Finance Initiative (PFI) contracts.

However, there are rarely any universal panaceas to the problems of the construction industry, as they are usually deeply historically rooted in its practices. It is all too easy to make architects the scapegoats for general conditions within the industry. It is even easier if such accusations will increase the influence of other protagonists and enhance their vested interests. Some larger clients have also expressed disquiet over the loose controls of management contracting, design-and-build and other procurement methods. There have been some dramatic examples of inappropriate 'alternative' procurement forms being used for complex buildings (possibly combined with under-specification), which have resulted in costly remedial work. Assertations that the public sector brought design–build into disrepute by adopting it for the wrong buildings for the wrong reasons are not uncommon, as are claims that the system was not the right way to commission high-profile, prestige buildings or buildings on prominent sites. If speed is essential, that can be achieved in other ways. Many clients are determined to expand their reliance on the traditional open market tender. The central role of the client is increasingly recognised, and solutions could well become client led:

> Clients are the key to the whole construction process . . . But they are distrustful of other sectors of the construction process. They feel the need to hire consultants to defend their interests, even when they have chosen the procurement route of contractor-led design, or even if they have commissioned original designs and then novated the design practice to the design–build contractor.

Architects design most of the major public and institutional buildings in the United States, such as schools, universities, museums, city halls, and airports; but are involved in the design of no more than 50 per cent of the housing units and only about 30 per cent of the commercial buildings.[30] These proportions are probably quite similar in the UK. RIBA past-president, Frank Duffy, articulated the shift in architects' workload; from public sector, socially conscious patronage to private sector market forces a decade or so ago:

> We have not recovered from the trauma of having been so important in the 1950s and 1960s as handmaidens of the welfare state. Until the 1970s architects working for commerce were despised. We haven't found a comparable commercial apparatus to get us into the 1980s and the 1990s.[31]

Duffy also acknowledged that the architectural profession was an economic failure due to a lack of commercial nous. He reiterates the familiar refrain that the decline stems from philistinism and lack of patronage, epitomised by, 'this wretched government and this deal-saturated, unthinking, cheapo culture'. He goes on to argue that the 'supply side' (construction and property companies) has a prevailing mentality to get things built as quickly as possible to ensure instant gratification for shareholders; many on the supply side regard design as a luxury. He views architecture as primarily about 'defining the future' through knowledge about invention, design and understanding patterns of use (i.e. 'vision').

The implications of the dictates of the supply side, and increasingly the demand side, trends towards contractor-led procurement methods are sobering for architects. They get less money, far less status and next to no control over the quality of the finished building. The prospect of architects being responsible for less in the building process, and consequently earning less fees would seem to push the profession to the very edge of economic viability. Historic comparison of professional incomes dating back to the 1960s show architects as relatively under-remunerated (Figure 1.7).[32] This was at a time when the profession's role was clearly identified as 'handmaidens of the welfare state' and should have been valued by society. It seems strange that architects have consistently earned less than engineers

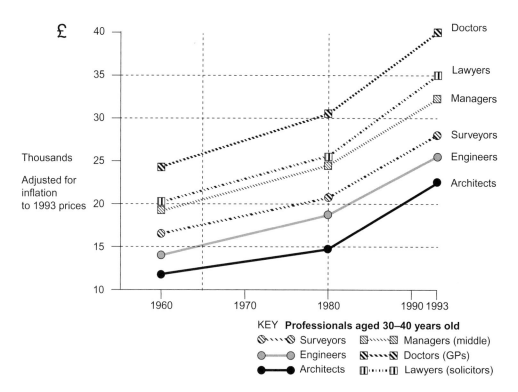

£

40 ···································· Doctors

35 ···································· Lawyers

Thousands   30 ···································· Managers

Adjusted for
inflation
to 1993 prices   25 ···································· Surveyors
                                            Engineers
                 20 ···································· Architects

15

10

1960   1970   1980   1990 1993

KEY **Professionals aged 30–40 years old**
Surveyors   Managers (middle)
Engineers   Doctors (GPs)
Architects   Lawyers (solicitors)

Figure 1.7 Professionals' median annual incomes, 1960–93.

and surveyors – yet arguably have higher social status. Suggesting that this status was originally derived from their historical role, and maintained by their position as 'leader of the design team' under the traditional method of building procurement. However, alternative procurement systems have undoubtedly eroded this status. Perhaps levels of remuneration have improved over the past decade due to the opportunities presented by the present rebuilding of the public estate – or are architects still heeding Vitruvius' ancient advice on pecuniary matters?

Some commentators find it hard to believe that young people are attracted to pay levels in the architectural profession. For most professions there is a clustering of positive attributes, so that a profession that ranks highly in prestige also pays better. This principle applies to the legal and medical professions, but not in architecture; resulting in very able graduates of some of the top architecture schools going on to study law, business, and medicine, even after obtaining professional degrees.[33] The economic crisis among architects reached such a point at the time of the Latham review in the early 1990s, that he remarked upon it quite candidly:

> But the morale of the professions, and especially of architects, has been severely affected by the economic pressures upon them . . . Professions which feel under-remunerated, marginalised, and with their historic and proud role changed to that of design services subcontractors, will be sucked further into adversarial stances.[34]

The mandatory fee scale for architects was abolished in 1983, in the wake of criticism from the Office of Fair Trading. But, the restrictions on architects' advertising were lifted, following a Monopolies Commission Report on advertising by solicitors, vets and accountants. The 'directors rule', whereby architects could not be directors of limited companies (particularly construction companies), was also abolished. Theoretically, architects had returned to the status of master-builders and, after a lapse of one hundred years, could be totally involved in the production of buildings again in the 1980s. However, architecture is still regarded as a profession in which there are good opportunities for self-expression and individual creativity. But, this myth was dented by American sociological research:

> The problem is that architecture's self-proclaimed mission is successful in that it attracts and trains vast numbers of aspiring artists who define architecture in aesthetic terms. The paradox is that with its exclusive emphasis on individual expression and in the absence of many opportunities to be designers, most architects are anonymous craftworkers; yet they lack the dignity accorded some craftworkers in earlier times.[35]

This view is reiterated by Gutman (1988); although he does not confine this syndrome to architecture, but claims that the downgrading of work responsibilities of individuals with professional degrees is a major concern in many professions, including medicine, the profession with the most powerful position in the marketplace. Apparently a large number of physicians who have been licensed as specialists are forced, because of lack of suitable openings, to practice family medicine (i.e. General Practice):

> However, the distressing feature of the current system is that many architects with professional degrees may remain locked in relatively routine, menial, and low-paying jobs for most of their careers.[36]

In achieving its economic ambition it is crucial to the success of any profession that it persuades society to value its services and the benefits deriving from its expertise. Status is thus crucial to gaining market control and generating a flow of income by means of strategies of closure which exclude the unqualified. However, professionalism generates a consequent propensity for arrogance, condescension and a mutual disdain between various professions themselves – especially when they compete in similar markets. In America the high failure rate in architectural practice is consistent with the high bankruptcy rate in the construction industry generally (a similar situation pertains in the UK). Even offices that survive the cyclical recessions and depressions in construction typically lose money on a quarter of their jobs. Perhaps the architectural profession can take solace from Adam Smith's commentary on another profession over two centuries ago:

> In a profession where twenty fail for one that succeeds, that one ought to gain all that should have been gained by the unsuccessful twenty . . . The lottery of the law, therefore, is very far from being a perfectly fair lottery; and, that, as well as many other liberal and honourable professions, are, in point of pecuniary gain, evidently under-recompensed.[37]

The profitable architectural practices are generally the larger ones, which have to resort to bureaucratic management and a corresponding division of labour. However, such organisational structures are the opposite of the informal, organic teams necessary for creative and 'thinking' activities, which will engender high-quality design:

> . . . that very structure on which (architectural) ideas depend (in order) to have consequence is composed of the main conditions that disadvantage firms in the market economy.[38]

This link is also borne out by seminal research in the UK.[39] Most British architects still cling to the notion that their future lies in building original works of art, to last for ever. The reality looks different. A handful of distinguished partnerships – what the Americans call 'signature architects', with enough clout to dominate their big projects – will no doubt prosper. But the rest of the profession can expect a future more in line with life elsewhere in the world. Working below or alongside contractors and putting up (relatively temporary) homes for large companies – rather than artistic statements that will become part of Britain's built heritage.

A decade ago researchers used a framework for industrial analysis to understand the competitive context of architectural practices, which considers the following five elements of industry structure:

- Competitive rivalry.
- The threat of substitutes.
- The threat of new entrants.
- The bargaining power of suppliers.
- The bargaining power of buyers.[40]

They concluded that as a result of these competitive pressures, the architect's position in the 'value chain' had changed from being the client's representative, located between the client and all the other members of the project coalition, to that of reporting to a project manager in that position. In some cases, architecture was little more than just another works package. This is not helped by the fact that the architectural service is intangible – what is purchased is a capacity to produce, rather than a product. Ultimately, only the client can judge whether their objectives have been met in terms of their subjective criteria for project performance.[41]

Many commentators asserted that to retain a lead role architects must broaden their education, so they understand areas like project management. The need for architects to widen the professional practice syllabus to include management theory and practice was a main conclusion of a RIBA report nearly half-a-century ago.[42] But the inherent conflict between managers' and professionals' value systems makes such integration difficult (Figure 1.8).

The reason that architects have not trained to deal with strategic management issues is probably because of the stigma attached to the management role. Management is usually defined as office administration – something carried out by an individual with a lower status. It was also

Managers' value	Professionals' value
Hierarchy	Participation
Respect for authority	Defiance of authority
Corporate efficiency	Social justice
Team player	Individual initiative
Career	Quality of life

Figure 1.8 Differences in managers' and professionals' value systems. Source: Allinson 1993 (ref. 20).

Managers' project view	Professionals' project view
Means to an end	Opportunity to design
Non-routine	Routine to practice
To be managed	To be administered
Providing a facility	Creating a building
Needs orientated	Disinterested service
Corporate criteria	Peer group criteria
Risks to success	Risk of liability

Figure 1.9 Differences in managers' and architects' attitudes to projects. Source: Allinson 1993 (ref. 20).

something of a dirty word, and seen as the antithesis of professionalism. But the dilemma is that architects' best claim to a professional ethic is artistic, which risks marginalisation – while a claim to managerial competence could undermine professional status (Figure 1.9).[43]

The emergence of large scale and complex buildings is setting the standard for the skills architects must present to clients – and the manner in which they organise and present these skills as a means of constituting a practice. During the 1930s, when the volume of construction work went down precipitously, applications and architectural enrolments dwindled too. The process was the result of market decisions by prospective students – rather than policy decisions by the profession.

1.7 Client's changing needs and objectives

The age of the client was announced at least two decades ago in the wake of NEDO's investigation into *Faster building for industry*. Latham and Egan again stressed the central importance of the client's role in architectural and building procurement. Viewed philosophically, the client's era is continuous – it is merely a question of discerning what type of client is in the ascendant. The problem so often then becomes how the industry responds to clients' identified needs and objectives. In a notably conservative industry, resistant to change, the period of transition from one client's reign to another is invariable traumatic.[44]

The development of the architectural profession was fostered by clients pursuing a guardian culture – successively from members of the aristocracy to the post-war emergence of the 'cradle to grave' welfare state. A halcyon turning point was the lead up to the turn of the nineteenth century, when English domestic architecture was celebrated throughout Europe. The patrons of the time were the *nouveau riche* industrialists emulating the aristocracy by commissioning country houses, as well as early commercial and industrial buildings. The demand for architects' services was undoubtedly fuelled by notions of *conspicuous consumption* and *pecuniary emulation*.[45] Architecture became a public service in post-war reconstruction, with the demand for schools, housing and health buildings driven by social responsibility and Keynesian economics. Architects perceived themselves as firmly ensconced in the guardian culture.[46]

The rise of modern commercialism in the construction industry is founded in Conservative post-war legislation, designed to encourage real estate activity. An era which saw the making of property millionaires in a period of lax planning laws and the need for building licences swinging back and forth. Property becomes a financial asset determined by profitability rather than social necessity which resulted in the Labour Party calling for the nationalisation of development land in 1973. The more commercially astute architects made a premium out of their most vital function, as far as the property developer was concerned – negotiating the most favourable terms for, and obtaining planning permission.[47] Leading Richard Rogers to expand upon his 'thesis' that 'form follows profit' and emphasises the key role of clients in terms of selection:

> No one blames the artist if a museum has a bad collection, or the author if the library has a bad selection. As long as there are good painters and writers the blame must fall on those responsible for selection. The same is true regarding architecture ... Most contemporary architecture is therefore the product of stark economic forces rather than the work of a designer; it represents the logical product of a society which sees the environment in terms of profit ... The brilliant, single-minded efficiency of modern business is endangering both our culture and our universe.[48]

1.8 References

1 Rybczynski, W. (2002) *The perfect house: A journey with the Renaissance Master, Andrea Palladio.* London: Scribner.
2 O'Connor, C. (1999) *The pleasing hours: The Grand Tour of James Caulfeild, First Earl of Charlemont (1728–1799), traveller, connoisseur and patron of the arts.* Cork: The Collins Press.
3 Duffy, H. (1999) *James Gandon and his times.* Kinsale: Gandon Editions.

4 Venturi, R. *et al.* (1977) *Learning from Las Vegas: The forgotten symbolism of architectural form.* Cambridge, Massachusetts: MIT Press.

5 Venturi, R. (1967) *Complexity and contradiction in architecture.* New York: The Museum of Modern Art.

6 Venturi, R. and Scott Brown, D. (2004) *Architecture as signs and systems: For a mannerist time.* Cambridge, Massachusetts: Harvard University Press.

7 Bowley, M. (1966) *The British building industry: Four studies in response and resistance to change.* Cambridge: Cambridge University Press.

8 NJCC (1972) *Code of procedure for selective tendering.* RIBA; NJCC (1977) *Code of procedure for single stage selective tendering.* RIBA; and NJCC (1983) *Code of procedure for two stage selective tendering.* London: RIBA.

9 Emmerson Report (1962) *Survey of the problems before the construction industry.* London: HMSO.

10 Banwell Committee Report (1964) *The placing and management of contracts for building and civil engineering works.* London: HMSO.

11 Latham, M. (1994) *Constructing the team.* London: HMSO.

12 Ireland, V. (1984) Virtually meaningless distinctions between nominally different procurement forms. In: *Proceedings of the CIB W-65 4th international symposium on organisation and management of construction*, Ontario, Canada, 1, pp. 203–211.

13 NEDO (1983) *Faster building for industry.* London: HMSO.

14 Crichton, C. (ed.) (1966) *Interdepedence and uncertainty: A study of the building industry.* London: Tavistock Publications.

15 Higgin, G. and Jessop, N. (1965) *Communications in the building industry: The report of a pilot study.* London: Tavistock Publications.

16 NEDO (1974) *Before you build: What a client needs to know about the construction industry.* The Wilson report. London: HMSO.

17 Gameson, R.N. (1992) *An investigation into the interaction between potential building clients and construction professionals.* Unpublished PhD thesis, University of Reading.

18 Jacobs, J. (1992) *Systems of survival.* London: Hodder & Stoughton.

19 Gutman, R. (1988) *Architectural practice: A critical review.* Princeton: Princeton Architectural Press.

20 Allinson, K. (1993) *The wild card of design: A perspective on architecture in a project management environment.* London: Butterworth-Heinemann.

21 Wolfe, T. (1975) *The painted word.* London: Black Swan.

22 Kaye, B. (1960) *The development of the architectural profession in Britain: A sociological study.* London: George Allen & Unwin.

23 RIBA (1992–93) *Strategic study of the profession – Parts 1 & 2.* London: RIBA.

24 Norman Shaw, R. and Jackson, T.G. eds. (1892) *Architecture, a profession or an art: Thirteen short essays on the qualifications and training of architects.* John Murray.

25 Fraser, M. (1994) Educated, apolitical, anarchic satire. *Architects' Journal*, 11 August, p. 42.

26 Vitruvius, M. (c 30 BC) *The ten books of architecture.* New York: Dover (1960).

27 Cuff, D. (1991) *Architecture: The story of practice.* Cambridge, Massachusetts: MIT Press.

28 Van Deventer, R.C. (1993) *The law of construction contracts.* Chicester: Chancery Law.

29 Gutman, R. (1988) *Architectural practice: A critical review.* Princeton, New Jersey: Princeton Architectural Press.

30 Gutman, R. (1988) *Architectural practice: A critical review.* Princeton, New Jersey: Princeton Architectural Press.

31 Duffy, F. (1993) Designs on the detractors. *Financial Times*, 13 March, p. 34.

32 Cook, M. (1994) *The client and building procurement system selection*. Unpublished MSc thesis, University of Bath.

33 Gutman, R. (1988) *Architectural practice: A critical review*. Princeton, New Jersey: Princeton Architectural Press.

34 Latham, M. (1994) *Constructing the team*. London: HMSO.

35 Blau, J.R. (1987) *Architects and firms: A sociological perspective on architectural practice*. Cambridge, Massachusetts: MIT Press.

36 Gutman, R. (1988) *Architectural practice: A critical review*. Princeton, New Jersey: Princeton Architectural Press.

37 Smith, A. (1776) *The wealth of nations (Books I–III)*. Harmondsworth: Penguin (1986)

38 Blau, J.R. (1987) *Architects and firms: A sociological perspective on architectural practice*. Cambridge, Massachusetts: MIT Press.

39 RIBA (1962) *The architect and his office*. London: RIBA.

40 Porter, M.E. (1980) *Competitive Strategy*. New York: Free Press.

41 Winch, G. and Schneider, E. (1993) The strategic management of architectural practice. *Construction Management and Economics*, 11, pp. 467–473.

42 RIBA (1962) *The architect and his office*. London: RIBA.

43 Winch, G. (1989) The construction firm and the construction project: A transaction cost approach. *Construction Managment and Economics*, 7, pp. 331–345.

44 Andrews, J. (1983) The age of the client. *Architects' Journal*, 13 July, pp. 32–33.

45 Veblen, T. (1899) *The theory of the leisure class: An economic study of institutions*. London: George Allen & Unwin.

46 Greenberg, S. (1993) Architecture: A profession or commercial enterprise. *Architects' Journal*, 4 August, pp. 18–20.

47 Marriott, O. (1989) *The property boom*. London: Abingdon Publishing.

48 Rogers, R. (1991) *Architecture: A modern view*. London: Thames and Hudson.

Chapter 2

Building procurement

2.1 Evolution of the building industry and professionalism

The craft guilds of masons and carpenters formed in medieval times was the nascent phase of the emergent 'traditional' system of building procurement. Masters and journeymen comprised the embryonic building professions. Master craftsmen were latterday contractors, responsible to the client for organising labour and materials. Early designs were vernacular and oft repeated, possibly with embellishments by master craftsmen. This simple system prevailed, under socio-economic stability, until the sixteenth century, when master masons began to design. The title 'architect' was in use by this time, as the expansive aspirations of Elizabethan clients, and travel to the ancient world cultivated specialised design expertise.[1]

The forerunner of the traditional system, in which an architect supervised the work of individual trades was the prevalent procurement system in the eighteenth century (Figure 2.1). The industrial revolution began in Britain around 1760 and, as it was the first country to industrialise, Britain was transformed into the leading manufacturing power by about 1850. Larger and more complex building types emerged which required specialist expertise such as quantity surveyors, civil engineers, and service engineers.[2]

The strong flavour of social class distinctions that the system (relationships between building owners, professionals and builders) had acquired persisted until at least before World War I:

> *The architects were members of a profession concerned with a major art, they were confidants of gentlemen and to a considerable extent arbiters of taste. Successful architects at least were members of the upper middle-class élite. They were gentlemen or regarded themselves as such. Engineers on the other hand were closely associated with trade and industry; their training had no cultural significance; they were not artists; they might be industrialists. In the nineteenth-century social stratification they were not really regarded as gentlemen, although some aristocrats had made notable contributions to engineering. Certainly they seem to have been regarded by architects as their social inferiors. Indeed, according to some very distinguished engineers, this attitude still persisted after the Second*

World War and accentuated the difficulties of co-operation. Sur-
veyors of all sorts were even more definitely socially inferior.
Builders, however wealthy or successful, were in trade and small
builders were little more than glorified craftsmen, 'cap-in-hand
builders' as they are sometimes termed. In the architects' view
the system was hierarchical both socially and in terms of
working organisations. The builders and their workmen formed
the lowest ranks, the architects the highest; the other profes-
sions came in between . . . This was the only form of the system
that was really respectable, and which building owners con-
cerned with culture or social prestige would use.[3]

This 'social ranking' of construction professionals arguably remains largely
unaltered at the extremes; while considerable jockeying for position continues in-between. The project manager has recently entered the fray and
has rapidly become a threat to architects' ascendancy. The client was consistently left out of these surveys, until recently. The 1965 study maintained
that they did not ask for a rating of clients' social status, because they
thought it would vary too much for anyone to be able to make a general
statement about it (Figure 2.2).

The contradiction between architecture as an art or a profession led to
a lengthy debate, between the champions of architecture as an art; and
those who claimed it was a profession, at the end of the nineteenth century.
Some leaders of the profession expected that the architect's position would
become more powerful if the professionalisation movement, which began
during the 1850s, was successful. Their aims were to ground the knowledge of design in science and reason; an illusive goal when design quality
is so often intangible and sometimes intuitive. However, their efforts were
set against the inexorable rise of professions, based on the application of
scientific techniques to industry, in the mid-nineteenth century. Figure 2.3
shows the chronological separation between the two early professions of
law and medicine, and later professions.

This was the age of Benthamism, self-help, individualism and *laissez-faire*.
Public hostility to professional associations was probably based on experience of the physicians and barristers, and the 'exclusiveness, selfishness
and slothfulness of their fossilised corporations'.[4] The struggles associated
with the emancipation of architects from noble patronage contributed to
the slowness of their professional association, and the difficulty of distin-
guishing between artists and craftsmen led to several false starts. By the
end of the nineteenth century all the major professional occupations had
effective associations, and professionalism, as it is understood today, was
an accepted principle.

2.2 Modern building procurement systems

The term 'building procurement system' refers to the organisation structure used by the client to manage the design and construction of a building project – 'organisational structure encompasses those formal and
informal means that organisations use to divide and coordinate their work
in order to establish stable patterns of behaviour'.[5] Figure 2.4 illustrates the
main categories of building procurement system.

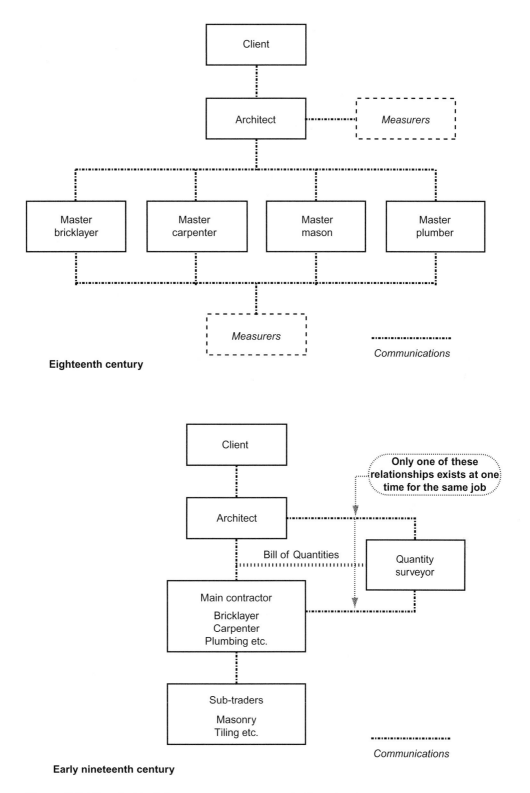

Eighteenth century

Early nineteenth century

Figure 2.1 Historical building procurement: organisation structures.

Rank	1914[i]	1965[ii]	1985[iii]	1990[iv]	1994[v]	2000[1]
1	Architect	Architect	Architect	Architect	Client	*Client*
2	Engineer	Engineer	Surveyor	Project mgr	Architect	*Project mgr*
3	Surveyor	Surveyor	Engineer	Surveyor	Project mgr	*Architect*
4	Builder	Contractor	Contractor	Engineer	Surveyor	*Contractor*
5				Contractor	Engineer	*Surveyor*
6					Contractor	*Engineer*

[i] Bowley, M. (1966) *The British building industry: Four studies in response and resistance to change.* Cambridge: Cambridge University Press.
[ii] Higgin, G. and Jessop, N. (1965) *Communications in the building industry: The report of a pilot study.* London: Tavistock Publications.
[iii] Faulkner, A.C. and Day, A.K. (1986) Images of status and performance in building team occupations. *Construction Management and Economics*, 4, pp. 245–260.
[iv] Stamatis, A.J.P. (1990) *Perspectives on project management: A survey of attitudes and perceptions of project management within the UK construction industry.* Unpublished MSc dissertation, University of Reading.
[v] Cook, M. (1994) *The client and building procurement system selection.* Unpublished MSc thesis, University of Bath.
[1] Predictive survey from the 1994 study.

Figure 2.2 Comparative social status rankings, 1914–2000.

Date	Profession	Institution
1400s	Barristers	Inns of Court
1518	Physicians	Royal College of Physicians
1617	Apothecaries	Society of Apothecaries
1739	Solicitors	Law Society
1745	Surgeons	Company of Surgeons
1791	Veterinary surgeons	Royal Veterinary College
1818	Civil engineers	Institute of Civil Engineers (Chartered in 1828)
1834	Architects	Institute of British Architects (Chartered in 1840)
1841	Pharmacists	Pharmaceutical Society
1841	Chemists	Chemical Society
1847	Mechanical engineers	Institution of Mechanical Engineers (Chartered in 1929)
1848	Actuaries	Institute of Actuaries
1853	Accountants	Association of Accountants
1855	Dentists	Ondontological Society
1868	Surveyors	Institute of Surveyors (Chartered in 1881)
1870	Teachers	National Association of Elementary Teachers
1871	Electrical engineers	Society of Telegraph Engineers (IEE) (Chartered in 1921)
1884	Builders	Institute of Builders (Chartered in 1980)
1908	Structural engineers	Concrete Institute
1922	Structural engineers	Institute of Structural Engineers (Chartered in 1934)
1938	Quantity surveyors	Institute of Quantity Surveyors (merged with RICS in 1983)

Figure 2.3 Chronological evolution of the professions.

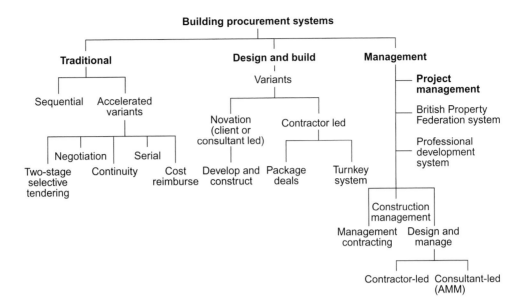

Figure 2.4 Categories of building procurement system.

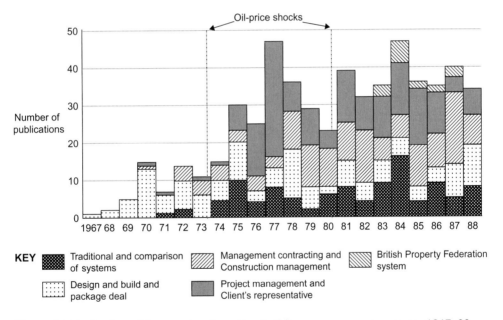

Figure 2.5 Indication of interest in alternative building procurement systems, 1967–88.

The 'oil shock' of the early 1970s skewed the clients' primary criteria of time, cost and quality. The burgeoning emergence of private sector clients and property developers as the industry's main clients, and the massive increases in interest and inflation rates caused by price increases in crude oil, meant that time was now of the essence for many projects. Projects have also become larger and more complex and their clients have encouraged the development of new management-based procurement systems (Figure 2.5).[6]

However, the recession of the early 1970s also prompted contractors, who could no longer rely on the professions as a source of work, to market package deals as a means of improving project performance (mainly time and cost); and their own position in the marketplace.[7] This has led to a proliferation of ostensibly different procurement systems, each being touted as the 'best' (seemingly regardless of the circumstances) by their various advocates. Some commentators argue that there are really very few generic systems, which should be discerned by the use of procurement variables such as price identification (competitive or negotiated); contractor selection (open or competitive); roles and responsibilities of specialists and so on.[8] In 1965 a Tavistock Institute report identified the area of communication with prospective clients as a major problem of the industry. They contended that many prospective customers did not know enough about the range of services, to make the first approach to the industry which was appropriate to their needs. The multiplication of 'nominally different' procurement systems in the intervening 40 years has not improved this situation.[9]

2.3 Traditional building procurement

The traditional building procurement system is the way in which UK clients have normally obtained their buildings for the last century and a half. The client separately appoints specialist consultants as his agents, on a fee basis, usually with an architect as the primary professional advisor. The role of the architect was traditionally that of independent designer and inspector of the construction process. This dual role was formalised in the RIBA Plan of Work for design team operation, which listed a separate design and management function for the architect at each work stage.[10] The RIBA updated the plan of work in 1998 to take account of changes in procurement systems. The new RIBA Plan of Work now distinguishes between situations where architects are the 'lead consultant and contract administrator' and where they are 'designer and designer leader'. Other changes to the Plan reflect changes in practice such as the omission of a 'bills of quantities' stage, due to the proliferation of performance and output specifications. Stage M – Feedback was also dropped from the Plan, which included 'studies of the building in use' to provide feedback for future designs. This latter omission was presumably because this stage was simply not happening in practice. However, there are rumours of the possible resurrection of Stage M – Feedback.[11]

The traditional system is a sequential process, and the design is usually largely completed before work commences on site. The independent consultants fully design the project and prepare tender documents upon which competitive bids, often on a lump sum basis, are obtained from main contractors. Theoretically, design is totally separated from construction in the traditional system; the successful construction tenderer carries out the work under the inspection of the original design consultants (Figure 2.6).

Due to changes in working practices, and the ever-increasing use of indirect labour by main contractors, subcontractors usually perform the majority of all work. This can result in organisational and programming problems, particularly if the subcontractors are nominated. As in all procurement

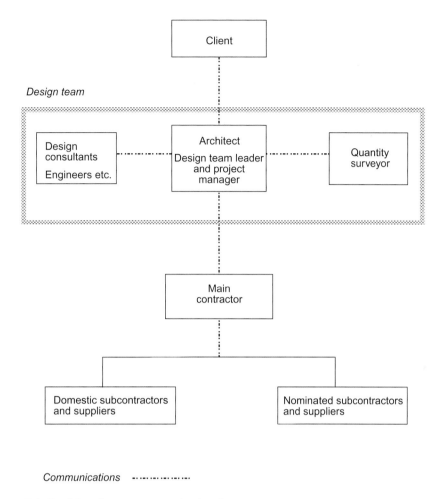

Communications ·· ·-·· ·-· ·-· ··

Figure 2.6 Traditional system: organisational structure.

systems the traditional system has its advantages and disadvantages, and its suitability should be objectively assessed. As ever, appropriately experienced people working harmoniously can often overcome theoretical disadvantages; while inappropriate people in conflict can lose potential advantages.

Advantages

- This system has stood the test of time; the well documented benefits are based on familiarity and the satisfaction found with a well established and well tried method.[12]
- The sequential nature and emphasis on design should add value to the quality of the eventual building for many years, compared to other procurement systems.[13]
- It is understood by experienced clients, who ideally should have a single knowledgeable design agent working for them.
- Lump sum tender and bills of quantities allows interim valuations and variations to be easily implemented.
- The international form of contract (FIDIC) is based on this system.[14]

Disadvantages

- The overall time of procurement under this system may be longer than other approaches. This can lead to escalating financing costs.
- Extremely low tenders may be submitted in order to win a contract, with the intention of profiting through claims.
- Clients have expressed dissatisfaction, especially in connection with large and complex buildings.
- Design and construction are separated; which can lead to problems of buildability, communication, and adversarial attitudes.

2.4 Variants of the traditional system

There are various accelerated forms of the traditional system, which differ from the parent system only in the way in which the contractor is appointed or reimbursed. These variants are attempts to speed up the traditional process by overlapping and integrating the design and construction stages to varying degrees. This usually means engaging a contractor earlier on the basis of partial information, by negotiation or in competition. These variants have not gained popularity mainly due to the fact that the certainty given by the lump sum and specified time are lost. This is because the variants usually rely on extending the principle of provisional sums, for work which has not yet been designed, in the traditional system – to the extent that pricing is based on approximate quantities or the reimbursement of actual cost, plus profit.

These variants are ubiquitously known as 'fast tracking'; where a system of overlapping the normally sequential stages in design, tendering and construction, involving the letting of subcontracts as the design proceeds, serves to reduce the overall building procurement time. The NEDO 1983 study, *Faster building for industry* sought to show that the British construction industry could deliver quickly and efficiently in the right circumstances; and concluded that fast building is possible without sacrificing either cost or quality. They also found that while the traditional system can give good results, an accelerated approach where stages overlapped tended to be quicker.[15]

2.4.1 Two-stage selective tendering

This allows for the early involvement of the main contractor before the scheme is fully designed. The system is suitable for large or complex buildings where buildability could be enhanced by collaboration with the contractor during the design stage. It may also expedite an early start on site, but this goal could be thwarted by prolonged negotiations at the second stage tender. A first stage selective competitive tender, based on approximate bills of quantities related to preliminary design information, decides the successful tenderer who will then negotiate a second stage tender figure.[16] Although a final tender figure is based on a total remeasurement of the project once detailed drawings are available; NEDO established that the effort required to prepare approximate bills was about half of that for a full measured bill.[17]

2.4.2 Negotiated contracts

This system restricts the negotiation to one contractor. Similar benefits as the preceding method can accrue, but usually at some cost premium. The system is useful where a business relationship, implying a degree of trust, already exists; such as a contractor already on site carrying out another contract, and where continuity is desired. Other appropriate circumstances include situations where sufficient tenders or realistic prices cannot be attracted; and where a special expertise is necessary.[18]

2.4.3 Continuity contracts

The successful tenderer on a single stage selective bid is advised that, subject to satisfactory performance, they will be awarded a similar project to follow on from the first; using the bills of quantity of the original project as a basis for negotiation. This system obviously requires two similar projects, although there is no guarantee that the contractor will perform consistently on the second project. The Wood Report grouped this system with serial contracts and found similar outstanding performance.[19]

2.4.4 Serial contracts

This system necessitates a number of similar projects (or a building 'programme') which are awarded to a single contractor on the basis of a competitive tender using a master bill of quantities. The Wood Report surveyed the performance of this system and found it to be outstanding in terms of all three of the usual criteria of time, cost and functionality/quality; when compared to the traditional procurement system. This approach allows continuity of experienced project teams, bulk buying of materials, and holds the potential for clients to form consortia to create sufficient demand. The ensuing economies of scale and cumulative experience gained by the contractor should result in financial benefits to the client.[20]

Many commentators have questioned the idea that every building project is unique and feel that serial building is the answer. This is the American phenomenon of 'serialised' or 'floorplate' buildings. This involves architects designing only the shell of a building, while the interior and environmental services and so on are separated into specialist sub-packages, provided by different consultants. American architects are used to working in a more standardised way, and these 'loft' buildings (as they are known in the US) provide tenant flexibility in uncertain and dynamic economic climates.

The American architect, Robert Venturi, recognised this phenomenon nearly 30 years ago, when he named this type of building the 'decorated shed'. Venturi Scott Brown Associates have designed several university laboratories on historic campuses – or rather they have designed the external envelope, common rooms and entrance halls. The cores, servicing and floorplates were designed by a firm of architects that specialises in laboratories. These 'loft' buildings are highly serviced floorplates, subject to frequent internal modifications.[21]

2.4.5 Cost-reimbursable contracts

The contractor receives all costs reasonably incurred in carrying out the work together with a fee. This system is suitable for emergency work or where, due to complexity or other factors, it is not possible to use even approximate bills. There are four common variations, cost plus percentage; cost plus fixed fee; cost plus fluctuating fee; and target-cost. This system can be advantageous to the client in times of high inflation or where other major risks are prevalent.[22]

2.5 Design and build

The essence of this system is that the contractor takes sole responsibility, normally on a lump sum fixed price basis, for both the design and construction of the client's project (Figure 2.7). The early 1970s 'oil shock', with its attendant dramatic increase in borrowing and inflation rates, provided the catalyst for the renewed evolution of design and build; with its promise of speedy building procurement. However, the principles of this system are nothing new, as architects such as Christopher Wren (1632–1723) were operating similar procurement methods centuries ago; before the rise of professionalism began to separate architecture from the construction process.[23] Nonetheless, some argue that the system was employed injudiciously, particularly on public buildings, bringing it into disrepute.[24] Others commented on the systematic attempts to downgrade the role of the architect.[25]

The introduction of a standard JCT form (JCT WCD 81) of contract in the early 1980s served to formalise this method; this recognition followed changes in British architects' codes of practice, which allowed architects to become directors of construction, or indeed, other limited companies. There is evidence that design and build standards improved as architects took up senior appointments in such construction companies, or founded design and build firms which are predominantly designer-led.[26]

Clients who prefer the design and build route emphasise the value of a single point of responsibility; buildability; and an early start on site. However, the principal shortcoming of the system relates to lack of control, particularly over quality, if the client has no independent advisor, or professional, safeguarding his interest. There are three different ways in which design and build contractors organised their activities:[27]

> (1) **Pure design and build**: specialist firms which endeavour to retain all the necessary resources and expertise in-house.

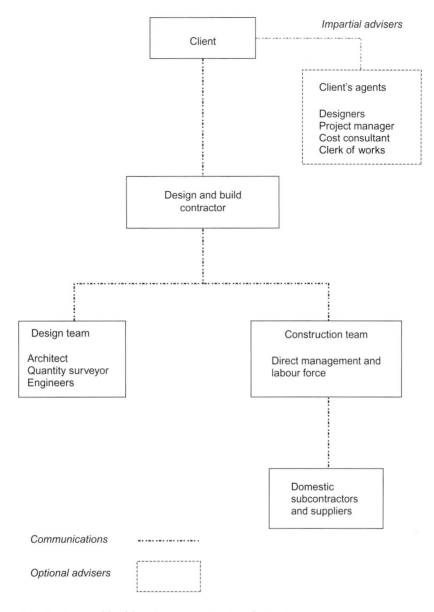

Figure 2.7 Design and build system: organisational structure.

(2) **Integrated design and build**: these firms have a core of designers and project managers, but buy in additional expertise.

(3) **Fragmented design and build**: external design consultants are
coordinated by in-house project managers. This permutation
manifests many of the communication and dissonance problems
of the traditional system.

The selection of a design and build contractor is by negotiation or selective tendering. If the latter option is chosen the number of contractors
should be limited to three at the most, because of the effort involved in
preparing a bid on the basis of the employer's requirements. There is also
a temptation to underspecify when a performance specification is trans-
lated into an operational version, with obvious repercussions in terms of
the quality, and even the functionality, of the completed building. The

system is most appropriate for standardised building types, such as industrial space and generic offices, where specialised details or specific quality are not too important.[28]

Advantages

- Single point responsibility.
- Virtually guaranteed fixed cost and completion date.
- Integration of design and construction; buildability and overlapping of stages.
- Functionality; the contractor undertakes that the finished building will be fit for its purpose (unless JCT WCD 81 is used – only dwellings).
- Simple communications.

Disadvantages

- Variations can be costly and difficult (no bills of quantities).
- The brief or employer's requirements need careful preparation (possibly by an independent consultant, such as an architect) to avoid ambiguity; if they are to be properly satisfied by the contractor's proposals.
- Design quality may suffer.
- Independent advice is recommended to prepare the brief and control quality. This will involve additional fees, despite the fact that contractor's design costs are not VAT rated.

2.6 Variants of design and build

2.6.1 Package deals

This refers to a design and build project which is chosen 'off the peg' from a catalogue; this affords the client the opportunity to visit similar completed buildings. While the idea of emulating the manufacturing industry (e.g. the automobile industry) for a building is attractive in theory, this system uses a proprietary building system, which rarely satisfies all the client's needs; in fact, it usually has to be adapted. A package deal may include the procurement of a suitable site and even arranging the financing and while package deals provide buildings rather than designs, there were some serious historic technical failures in systems buildings.

2.6.2 Turnkey system

In this system the contractor provides everything including furnishing and equipment from inception of the scheme to completion. All the client has to do is 'turn the key' at the end of the contract. The turnkey system shares many characteristics of the parent system, although the forms of contract used are drawn from the process engineering industry – as the system was pioneered in the US around the turn of the century, where it has been used for procuring process plants, oil refineries, power stations and such like.[29]

2.6.3 Develop and construct

The client retains a design consultant, such as an architect, to prepare a sketch design; which is then developed into detailed drawings by the contractor. This system has similar characteristics to the parent; but many of the advantages are lost and the responsibility for design becomes nebulous. This system is the most appropriate variant where novation is applied. Novation refers to the arrangement where a client insists that a successful contractor should engage one or more of his original consultants to complete the detailed design of the project.[30]

2.7 Management contracting

This procurement system has antecedents in the concept of fee contracting, which has a long history of specialist use in the UK; dating back to the 1920s and 1930s. Bovis Construction operated fee systems, notably with Marks & Spencer as a client, for more than 60 years with proven success. Management contracting increased in popularity in the 1970s when clients were striving for much shorter project times. Economic factors such as an increase in rental values for commercial property, caused by increased inflation rates as a result of the oil shocks, and the concomitant increase in interest on borrowed capital were the main driving forces behind this phenomenon. The management contractor is brought in virtually at the outset of the project, on a fee basis, to contribute construction expertise to the design and to manage, rather than carry out, the construction process. The appointment of the contractor on a percentage fee, professional basis, at the beginning of the project facilitates an early start on site by overlapping the design and construction phases. The work is divided into convenient packages which are put out to tender to works contractors, who execute the actual construction work (Figure 2.8). A competitive element is retained while allowing construction to commence on preliminary works.

Research has shown that reductions in project duration are due to this early start on site, rather than economies achieved during the construction stages. Further research also highlighted the need for appropriate procurement systems to be selected to suit the client's objectives and circumstances. This was illustrated by the fact that when management contracting was employed on large complex buildings time economies were recorded; whereas there was no evidence to suggest that management contracting performed better than the traditional approach on large simple buildings. Consequently, management contracting is most appropriate for large and complex projects when considerable coordination of specialists is required and early completion is vital.[31,32]

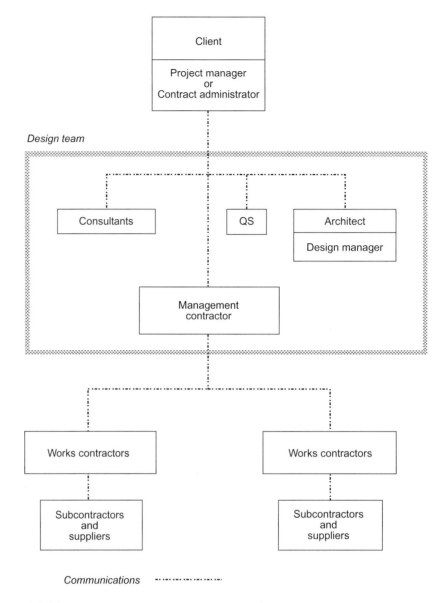

Figure 2.8 Management contracting: organisational structure.

This procurement system was formalised in 1987, with the launch of the JCT Standard Form of Management Contract (JCT 87) and supporting documentation. However, the popularity of this system waned towards the end of the 1980s, suggesting that it was losing out to construction management. Some influential clients publicly declared the difficulties they had experienced using the system. This culminated in Olympia and York switching over to construction management in mid-contract for the Canary Wharf development, ostensibly due to the intractable problems with the management contract they were using. However, it later transpired that they were experiencing financial difficulties, which could have been a contributory factor in their decision.

Advantages

- An early start on site is possible.
- Total project duration is reduced by overlapping design and construction stages.
- The contractor is integrated into the design team, which should improve communications and commitment.
- Price competition is retained as a result of the works package tenders.
- Reduction in the number of variations is possible.

Disadvantages

- The final price is not certain until the last works contract is let.
- The client carries most of the risk.
- The client has to make a critical early choice of management contractor.
- Less opportunity for design development.

2.8 Construction management

This procurement system closely resembles management contracting, with the critical difference that the construction manager becomes a true consultant to the client. Whereas the management contractor enters into sub-contracts with works contractors, the client enters into these contracts directly in construction management.[33] Many firms effectively offering the service of construction management erroneously call it management contracting.[34] The confusion over the differences between the two methods, particularly in the area of risk apportionment, led to the formation of the Construction Management Forum (CMF), which set out to analyse both systems and provide practical guidance. The Forum came down firmly in favour of construction management as the preferred option for clients wishing to pursue a management procurement system. The main advantages they cited for construction management are the clearer professional status accruing to the construction manager and his closer relationship with the client. Construction management is most appropriate when time is of the essence for clients who have large, complex and expensive buildings to procure. It gives the client a much greater degree of control and involvement in the project, at the expense of greater risks. In the UK the system was predominantly used by experienced clients, for the 'fast track' construction of multi-million pound prestige office complexes in high capital value areas such as central London.

The system originated in America in the 1960s under the guise of Construction Project Management (CPM), when architects and engineers began to offer construction management services to their clients. The system emerged coincident with high inflation resulting from the oil shocks of the 1970s; and the desire of inexperienced clients to augment their construction knowledge, by including a professional construction manager

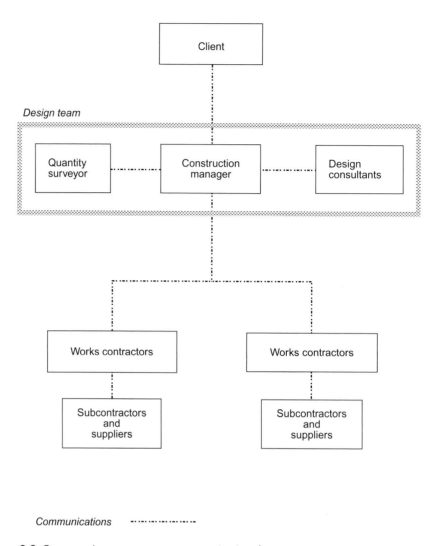

Figure 2.9 Construction management: organisational structure.

as part of their design team. Two different approaches developed to construction management: the pure and the quasi-general contractor approach. In the pure approach the construction manager remains the client's agent advisor throughout the process; while in the latter approach he changes roles to that of general contractor. This latter variant was been more prevalent in the UK (Figure 2.9).[35]

The Construction Round Table (CRT) submitted a paper to the Latham review, during the consultative period, which featured a construction management approach to procurement. There was also evidence of the original American concept of construction management being used in the UK. In this case an architect cum construction manager claims to have saved 37 per cent of costs by using construction management on projects worth a few million pounds. Other traditional consultants also embraced the role of construction manager; with quantity surveyors claiming that it overlaps with their conventional role.

Advantages

- Construction advice at the design stage.
- Client has complete control.
- Early start on site and shortened overall duration due to the overlap of design and construction stages.
- Enhanced client involvement leads to better communications.

Disadvantages

- The client takes all the risk.
- The final price is not certain until the last works contract has been let.
- The client is involved in additional administration and needs to take timely decisions.
- Less opportunity for design development.
- Quality may be jeopardised by emphasis on construction speed.

2.9 Design and manage

This system combines some of the attributes of design and build with those of generic management contracts. A single organisation is appointed to design the project, and manage the construction process using works contractors to execute the actual work. It is sometimes known as Design, Manage and Construct. The system is either contractor- or consultant-led, with the latter variant also referred to as the Alternative Method of Management (AMM). The AMM system was developed by an architect, and it attempts to improve communications and streamline management hierarchies (Figure 2.10). The main difference between the two variants is that in the consultant-led approach, the client enters into direct contracts with works contractors. The contractor-led variant is similar to the design and build system and tenderers are usually required to offer a guaranteed maximum price (GMP).[36]

The main advantage offered by design and management is an early start on site and the overlapping of design and construction. The system also provides for site presence of the designers, to liaise with works contractors, which facilitates improved communications and quicker decisions. In common with other management systems there is a need for close client involvement and timely decisions, all of which can place strain on some clients. Most management oriented procurement systems are usually appropriate on large, complex, fast moving projects, where the client has sufficient internal resources to become fully involved in the project.

Advantages

- Single-point responsibility.
- Suitable for all sizes and types of project.
- Improved communications and decision-making.
- Consultant-led to prioritise main criteria (e.g. architect for design quality).

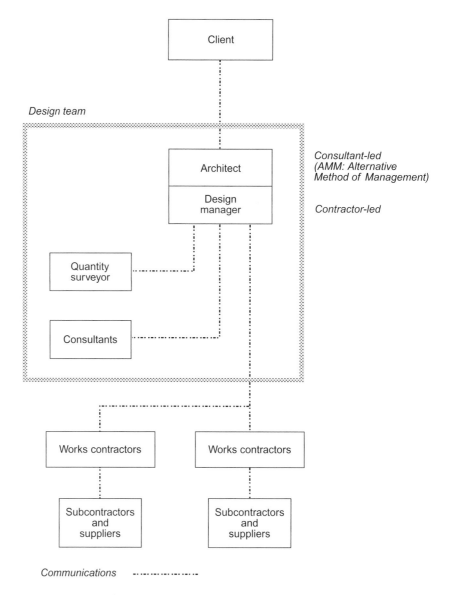

Design team

Consultant-led
(AMM: Alternative
Method of Management)

Contractor-led

Communications   — - — - — - — - — - —

Figure 2.10 Design and manage: organisational structure.

Disadvantages

- Client involvement and internal resources needed (i.e. experience).
- Designers on site can be costly.
- No guarantee of final cost, unless GMP used.
- Need for timely client decisions can pressurise some clients.

2.10 British Property Federation system

This system was developed by the British Property Federation, an organisation consisting of the main property developers and financial institutions, to 'unashamedly put the client's interests first'. Although the system was little used, it represents the emergence of the experienced client as a catalyst for change within the industry. Its conception was borne out of the BPF's members' frustration at the perceived antiquated structure and poor performance of the UK construction industry; particularly when compared to the USA. The system was described as 'a very detailed administrative framework' rather than a procurement system, and drew much from US practice of the early 1980s. In particular, the ability to pass the detailing of the design work to the builder, with the tender price based on scheme drawings and a very full specification. The BPF also claimed that many elements of the system were for other procurement systems, such as fast tracking, management contracting and construction management, but anecdotal evidence suggests that the method's use, or elements of it, remains limited to BPF members (Figure 2.11).[37]

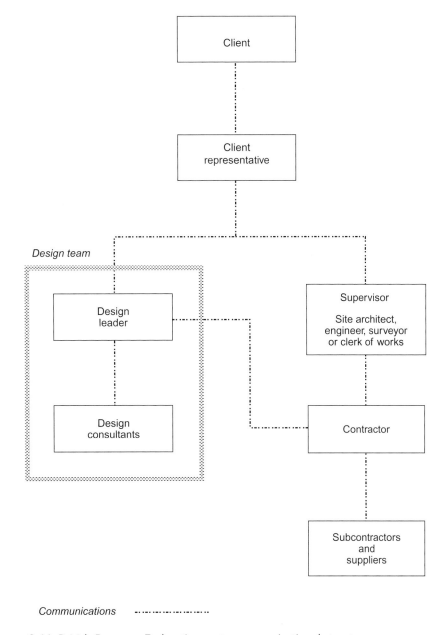

Figure 2.11 British Property Federation system: organisational structure.

The discouragement of a bill of quantities did not endear the system to many quantity surveyors, and other traditional roles were also challenged. Dr Martin Barnes, one of the main 'architects' of the system, describes his inspiration as follows:

> We looked at the US system, European and UK current practice and concluded that a forward system was necessary which was not reflected in any rivals. We started with a clean slate, wrote down what people should do and avoided using existing professional names. We tried to balance incentive with risk.

In an attempt to foster an attitude of shared commitment between members of the building team they are appointed on the basis of fixed lump sum, rather than percentages of the construction cost, fees – with bonuses and penalties for performance against set time and cost targets. The client appoints a client's representative, who project manages the process with no design or construction involvement. The BPF manual divides the building procurement process into five stages: (1) concept; (2) preparation of brief; (3) design development; (4) tender documentation and tendering; and (5) construction. At the beginning of the third stage a design leader is employed, usually an architect or engineer, who is responsible for the pre-tender design and approval of the contractor's design. The client further protects his interests during the construction phase by appointing a supervisor, who may be from any of the traditional roles, to ensure that the project is constructed in accordance with the contract documents.

Advantages

- The client's interests are paramount.
- Client's representative provides a single-point responsibility.
- Financial incentives encourage economic design.
- The client has the opportunity to 'name' subcontractors.

Disadvantages

- Limited usage resulting in unfamiliarity.
- The threat to traditional roles induced a hostile reaction from the industry, which is untempered by the BPF's unwillingness, or inability, to provide evidence that the system can achieve its idealised aims.
- The enlarged professional team and increased risk placed on the contractor by the absence of a bill of quantities could increase costs.

2.11 Project management

Project management has its roots in the American petrochemical, defence and aerospace industries of the late 1920s and 1930s, when a project co-ordinator function was created. This function of bringing projects of immense complexity, size and risk under single control was developed throughout World War II, mainly by the US Corps of Engineers in cases such as The Manhattan Project. However, the real development of modern project management concepts started with the US Atlas and Polaris missile programmes of the mid-1950s. NASA's Apollo programme spectacularly furthered the cause of project management in the 1960s. Some critics say that the discipline has failed to deliver on its promises of quality, cost and time control, and is obsessed with technique, resulting in a flow of forgettable acronyms, such as PERT, CPM, WBS, and so on. The origins of project management, such as in the defence industry, meant that there was a primary, possibly almost exclusive, concentration on the criterion of time. Nevertheless, Morris has been quoted in a more optimistic vein:

> We're beginning to know how to do it. There's now a professional body of knowledge, and we have pockets of expertise which the Association of Project Managers (APM) is doing a good job of propagating. But there is a constant problem of communicating the message from one generation to the next.[38]

2.11.1 Modern project management

Project management is achieving a more rounded profile with research attention focused on behavioural and organisational aspects, resulting in a growing body of knowledge to explain some of the human factors which affect project performance. The match of organisational structure to specific project circumstances plays a critical role. The increased emphasis on the human side of project management reflects a different attitude to the classical management functions of planning, organising, commanding, coordinating and controlling. The project manager needs to adapt to a matrix structure, where he frequently has responsibility for project success, while line managers have ultimate authority over staff resources – a potentially frustrating conundrum. Project managers are the persons in the middle, between line management and the technical specialist or professional expert: charged with effecting the potential efficiencies inherent in a matrix structure. This structure seeks to optimise the task-related (vertical structure) and functional (horizontal organisation) dimensions of the project, using the project manager as a catalyst. The most obvious possible disadvantage of the matrix is that at some level someone has two bosses.[39] To quote Gaddis' (1959) description of the matrix structure ideal created by project management; from his classic definition of the project manager:

> The obvious organisational goal is to seek the advantages of both – the vertical structure in which the control and performance associated with autonomous management are maintained for a given project, and the horizontal in which better continuity, flexibility, and use of scarce talents may be achieved in a technical group.[40]

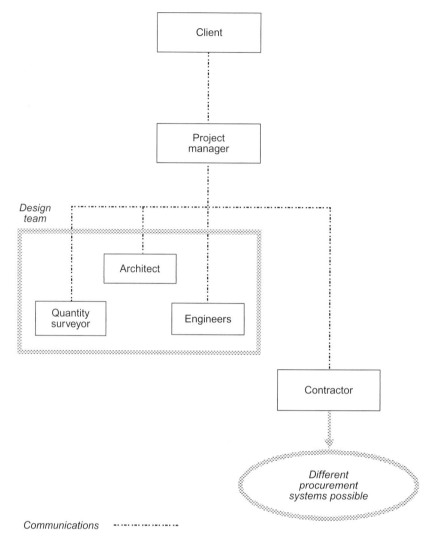

Figure 2.12 Project management: organisational structure.

2.11.2 Construction project management

The matrix arrangement is also the most common form of organisational structure for project management in the construction industry (Figure 2.12). The project manager has to deal with separate functions, such as the architect, quantity surveyor, engineers and contractors; and these functions are usually contained in separate autonomous firms. An attempt to enunciate a project management system for construction is represented by the CIOB's *Code of practice*, which defines project management as follows:

> *. . . the overall planning, control and co-ordination of a project from inception to completion aimed at meeting a client's requirements in order that the project will be completed on time within authorised costs and to the required quality standards.*[41]

Unfortunately such definitions focus on 'managing a project' and do not make specific reference to managing people to achieve a project; as another definition of construction project management does:

> *. . . the identification of the client's objectives in terms of utility, function, quality, time and cost, and the establishment of relationships between resources. The integration, monitoring and control of the contributors to the project and their output, and the evaluation and selection of alternatives in pursuit of the client's satisfaction with the project outcome are fundamental aspects of construction project management.*[42]

The CIOB Code goes on to define the client's objective as, 'obtaining a totally functional facility completed on time within the authorised cost and to the specified quality standard'. While this is a worthy objective it appears to pay scant attention to the human element and the fact that very few projects are completed within the original scope of the project. Human factors are particularly prevalent in the protagonists' different perceptions of project success, which can result in some projects being perceived as failures despite meeting all the objective standards of success, in terms of time, cost and quality. Project success defined in human terms is more along the lines of the following:

> *If the project meets the technical performance specifications . . . and if there is a high level of satisfaction concerning the project outcome among key people in the parent organisation, . . . project team, and key users or clientele of the project effort, the project is considered an overall success.*[43]

2.11.3 Project management – procurement system or management system?

Figure 2.12 suggests that it is possible to use project management with different building procurement systems. This treatment begs the question of whether project management is actually a building procurement system or a management system? This perplexity is further compounded by the fact that methods such as the BPF system advocate the appointment of a 'client's representative', but this is hardly surprising as a leading proponent of project management largely devised the system.

On balance, it seems that the commentators marginally favour the discrete procurement system. Although there is still confusion over this basic distinction and a lack of consensus over the nature of project management. Most architects feel that it is a procurement route, presumably in competition with other methods such as traditional architect-led procurement. This is hardly surprising when the RIBA Plan of Work delineates the separate functions of design and management as part of the architect's role – and project management largely assumes the latter role.

2.11.4 Role of the project manager

Project management became popular in the UK construction industry in the 1970s, as projects became larger and more complex. Rapidly increasing interest and inflation rates, caused primarily by the oil shocks, undoubtedly also played a part in stimulating experienced clients to seek quicker alternatives to the traditional system. However, the idea of a project manager is not new. Before the establishment of the architectural profession, clerks or masters-of-works were latter-day client's representatives or project managers. The CIOB's client's guide companion to their code describes the project manager's role as follows:

> . . . representing the client and providing on his behalf a cost effective and independent service, correlating, integrating and managing different disciplines to satisfy the objectives and provisions of the project brief from inception to completion. The service provided will ensure the client's satisfaction and safeguard his/her interests at all times, as well as giving consideration to the eventual user's needs, should these be known.[44]

NEDO identified the need for the inexperienced client to appoint a 'customer representative' with construction industry experience; a suggestion which was also mooted, although termed a 'principal advisor', in their earlier strategic client guide, *Thinking about building*. The 'Wood Report' of 1975 suggested that the public sector's 'client's representative' should act as a focal point of client requirements, create a clear brief for the designers, swiftly obtain client decisions, define the weighted objectives and monitor the performance of the project. The term 'client's representative' emerges as an alternative to 'project manager'. But, it is particularly unfortunate that confusion over nomenclature exists for a function whose primary objective is to coordinate and increase efficiency.

The primary role of the project manager is to make sure that the work of the functional specialists, such as designers and works contractors, is coordinated to reduce delays. The project manager becomes the manager of the whole procurement process for the client, who should integrate the design and construction phase into a relatively seamless whole. This system can combine the familiarity of traditional procurement with improvements to management and communications. Conversely, the appointment of a project manager can do little more than add an additional layer of bureaucracy, as they are duplicating a task that architects thought they already did. Consequently, it seems that the system is most suitable for large projects where the additional fees are eclipsed by the perceived benefits of employing a project manager.

Advantages

- Single-point responsibility, which should improve communications.
- There should be a reduction in time and cost, due to improved management and the overlapping of design and construction; particularly on large and complex projects.
- Consultants can concentrate on their own specialities.
- Flexibility of tendering arrangements.

Disadvantages

- Selection of a suitable person can be difficult.
- The client pays additional fee for a professional who may do no more than the design team would do anyway.

- The project manager could become a postbox, resulting in slow communication.
- Project manager often has no clearly defined role.
- Ideally the project manager should have construction industry experience, but this may cause disputes in the design team.

2.12 Professional development system

This system was formalised by Stanhope Properties, who saw their role as property developers encompassing the management of the entire building development process. They believed that by managing the process holistically each element was executed to maximum effect.[45] The professional development system represented a paradigm shift away from the traditional procurement system, as the developer is simply buying in a specialised design service from the architect; rather than entrusting architects with the whole process. Stuart Lipton and Peter Rogers of Stanhope perceived themselves as the coordinators of skilled professionals and consultants (e.g. architects, surveyors, engineers, construction manager, investors, agents, etc.), who constitute an 'information circle' to be utilised at the right time. Figure 2.13 illustrates the organisational structure of this system, with the experienced client acting as an interface between the client and the rest of the procurement 'team'.

The assertion is that clients are so bewildered by the complexities of procuring a building that they are reticent to approach a professional directly; preferring instead to deal with a professional or experienced client. The experienced client mediates between the needs of investors and the needs of users. Stanhope provided a selection of services to clients, tenants and investors; including a series of research and position papers on topics ranging from small power and structural loadings, to occupational densities and environmental health aspects for commercial offices. Generally, they contended that British buildings were over-specified, and consequently unnecessarily costly when compared to the USA and Europe. Lipton and Rogers were intent upon the challenge of bringing the construction industry, which they considered to be in the 1960s compared to the automotive industry, into the 1990s. They claimed that what was needed was:

> . . . one warranty, one PI cover, a complete set of drawings before you start, and a technical specification which reflects the need of the consumer rather than butt-covering and protectionism.

The model of a coordinating, experienced client buying in specialist services at the right time and to maximum effect is analogous to 'just-in-time' manufacturing processes. Although they admit that the variable nature of the building product necessitates building teams and running induction courses. Stanhope claimed that they established 'benchmarks' in eight key areas of construction: costs; times; specification; contracts; training; health

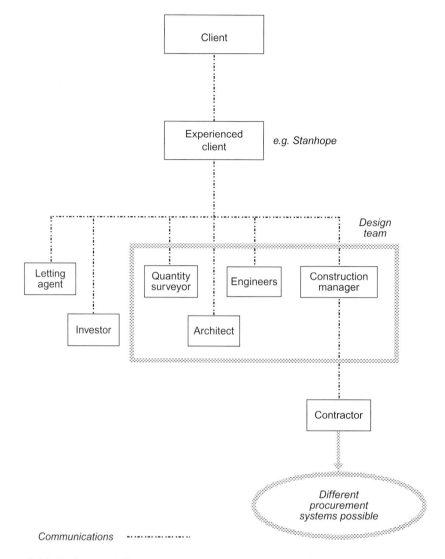

Figure 2.13 Professional development system: organisational structure.

and safety; environmental practice; and procurement. They claimed that by using their customised system of 'professional development', by their own admission a form of construction management (using a unique set of integrated contracts), they have regularly achieved construction savings of around 30 per cent between 1985 and 1991. Stanhope's experience showed them that poor briefing during the early stages of the procurement process results in problems during construction; and consequent cost and time over-runs. This emphasises the importance of setting achievable standards at the outset to ensure success. The implications of such procurement systems are profound for the professions, especially for architects who are placed on the supply side of the equation, as specialist subcontractors. Professional developers are becoming managers of the whole process, including parts previously controlled by the architect; making architecture a business rather than a profession.

2.13 New Engineering Contract

One of Latham's more controversial recommendations in 1994 was the desire to make a clean sweep of the existing JCT standard forms of building contract as 'endlessly refining existing conditions of contract will not solve adversarial problems'. He commended the New Engineering Contract (NEC) as fulfilling many of the principles on which a modern contract should be based. Although he admitted that there were some necessary alterations to form a hybrid contract, which he proposed to call the 'New Construction Contract'. Latham hailed the NEC as the 'model for all construction contracts'. It is purportedly based on three main objectives:

(1) Flexibility.
(2) Clarity and simplicity.
(3) Stimulus to good management.

It was designed for use on all construction works and consists of a series of main and secondary options, which means that the 'core' contract is tailored to suit a range of procurement systems: from a lump sum contract through to a management contract or even construction management. Each option allocates risk differently between the employer and the contractor, by using different arrangements for payment to the contractor. The main players in the NEC are the client's project manager, the client's supervisor (a sort of clerk of works); and a named adjudicator who is an independent dispute resolver. The emphasis in the NEC on the two parties to the contract (i.e. the employer and the contractor), and adjudicator would seem to further marginalise the architect. The contract was used on about 700 jobs worldwide, of which about 30 were in the UK, and about 600 in South Africa, with reasonably positive results. If an attitude of cooperation is adopted at the outset, and with sufficient contractor's management resources, it can reduce confrontation which improves staff efficiency. But, under those nearly ideal conditions virtually any contract should work.

Figure 2.14 illustrates the NEC organisation structure, which can be used for all of the six options. Options which include an 'activity schedule' or 'bill of quantities' generally prove most popular. It forces the client to ensure that the design is complete and the specification is well written. Although there is an increased volume of information, due to the necessarily quick decision-making, there is an emphasis on informal means of communication.[46]

2.14 Private Finance Initiative

In 2000, the government published *Public Private Partnerships – the Government's Approach* which defined public private partnerships (PPPs) into three categories:

(1) The introduction of private sector ownership into state-owned businesses, using the full range of possible structures, with sales of either a majority or a minority stake.
(2) The Private Finance Initiative (PFI) and other arrangements where the public sector contracts to purchase quality services on a long-

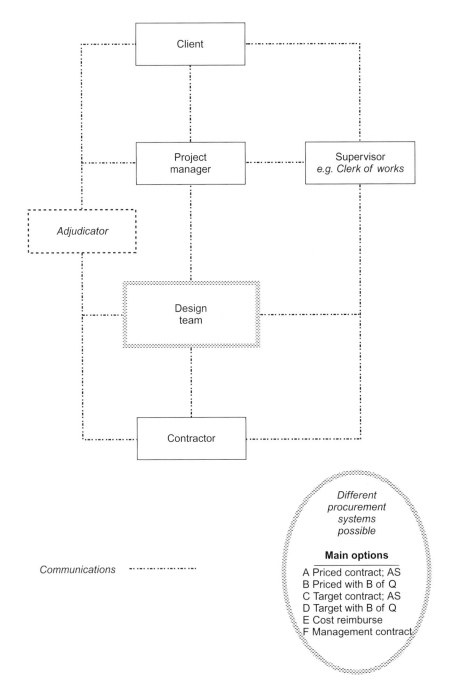

Figure 2.14 NEC: typical organisational structure. AS, activity schedule; B of Q, bill of quantities.

term basis so as to take advantage of private sector management skills incentivised by having private finance at risk. This includes concessions and franchises, where a private sector partner takes on the responsibility for providing a public service, including maintaining, enhancing or constructing the necessary infrastructure.

(3) Selling government services into wider markets and other partnership arrangements where private sector expertise and finance are used to exploit the commercial potential of government assets.

Source: HM Treasury, *PFI: meeting the investment challenge*, July 2003.

Architects were the traditional source of clients' guidance, and acted as agent or skilled intermediary between patron and builder. Increasing technical complexity and commercial pressures continue to threaten this role, and sophisticated clients will approach advisors who express compatibility with their primary objectives. Inexperienced clients are in a quandary and random selection of a seemingly appropriate, or well marketed, system can result in disastrous consequences. This fact was consistently noted in government reviews of the industry, such as the Latham review in 1994:

> Unnecessary disasters can be avoided by choosing the correct procurement route at the start of the project . . . choosing the most appropriate procurement route and contract will be essential . . .

Research has also consistently shown that the match of a project's organisation to its environment and objectives is crucial for success. This was particularly acute in the public sector, where rigid hierarchies were too cumbersome to flexibly and dynamically respond to external demands on the project.[47] Detailed analysis of potential clients' initial interviews, with building professionals, unsurprisingly shows that the character of such interactions were determined by the specific discipline of the professional involved. Inexperienced clients are dominated by the particular professional who sets the initial agenda. All disciplines give more priority to factors central to their own profession: whether they be programme, cost, type of contract, aesthetics, or structure. However, the only factor common to all professionals was that of procurement options or systems, suggesting that they all felt qualified to advise on this aspect, and undoubtedly give a parochial bias to that advice:

> Finally, it is clear that inexperienced clients need guidance when they are considering building. Although a number of guides have been produced there is a problem in disseminating such guides to clients, at the very early stages, before they have committed themselves to a particular option or professional.[48]

One of the earliest and presumably impartial, because it originated from a government source, was the 1974 NEDO guide *Before you build*. This publication distinguished between two generic procurement systems, consultant and contractor led. The guide was based on the results of a survey of commercial and industrial companies; which estimated that roughly half of the clients had no experience of the construction industry during the previous five years. While 20 per cent of the clients were dissatisfied with the service they had received, about a quarter of them had not clearly established their requirements before approaching the industry. The guide focused on the role of the client and suggested that this needed enhancement in the four areas of: unpreparedness; clearer requirements; explicit budget; and programme. The situation does not seem to have improved much almost ten years later, when the NEDO report *Faster building for industry* reported the following findings:

Customers lacked sources of information or impartial advice about the options and alternative courses of option open to them. They had no adequate means for assessing the suitability of any particular type of construction service for their circumstances. In consequence they did not make the best use of the services the industry had to offer, e.g. assistance with developing briefs and specifications, various management services, package deals etc.

Thinking about building was published in response to this report in 1985, and was preceded by a spate of guides into specific procurement systems emanating from organisations such as CIRIA. *Thinking about building* was accompanied by a publicity campaign, but its sole, ill-fated, dissemination route was through construction industry professionals. The guide was sold in packs of 100 copies to professionals, accompanied by a set of slides and marketing notes. The marketing notes encouraged consultants and contractors to offer their services as 'principal advisers', and suggested that the guide and slides could be used when communicating with clients. Christopher Groome, then secretary of the BEDC within NEDO and responsible for the guide, was quoted at the time of the launch of the guide in *Building* magazine:[49]

... potential customers will soon come to expect contractors and professional advisers to provide the guide as part of their advisory and support services ... and if Thinking about building *is universally adopted, no client will ever need to blunder into the building process again.*

Despite sales of around 30,000 the guide was not universally adopted, partly due to the method of dissemination and the inflexible 'job lots' of 100 copies – rather than smaller quantities available directly to prospective clients. The guide is a strategic overview of the building procurement process and contains a system selection matrix. It also lists the following 'seven steps to success':

(1) Selection of an in-house project executive.
(2) Appointment of a 'principal advisor', if required.
(3) Careful definition of your requirements for the project.
(4) Realistic determination of project timing.
(5) Selection of an appropriate 'procurement path'.
(6) Considered choice of organisations to be employed – 'choose the right people'.
(7) Commitment to a site held back until it is professionally appraised.

Faster building for commerce, published in 1988, was intended as a companion volume to the earlier study into industrial building, and identified the key influence of the client in certain areas. The degree of achieved project success was reflected in the client's skill in the following areas: expressing the client's objectives for the project in terms of building requirements, cost and time; defining the client's procurement strategy; bringing together a team of specialists; and determining the service the client expected from each member of that team. The report was accompanied by a plastic disk, which was intended as a decision aid for clients to 'dial' good and average construction times. Good practice for clients is explored in a chapter of the report, intended to be read alongside the *Thinking about building* publication, and synthesising both industrial and commercial 'best practice'. The following general conclusions were drawn as client advice for a successful project:

- Establish priorities.
- Assure the finance.
- Talk to other people.
- Decide on your own role.
- Establish a client contact point.
- Appoint an experienced client representative (if necessary).
- Set up a decision network.
- Use the industry properly.
- Choose your team carefully.
- Explain the project organisation.
- Get the brief right.
- Avoid variations (if possible).
- Monitor the project's progress.
- Ensure that the project is under control.

Recent guidance for clients from CABE echoes much of the sound historic advice, such as 'ten ways to be a successful client':

(1) Provide strong client leadership.
(2) Give enough time at the right time.
(3) Learn from your own and other successful projects.
(4) Develop and communicate a clear brief.
(5) Make a realistic commitment from the outset.
(6) Adopt integrated processes.
(7) Find the right people for the job.
(8) Respond and contribute to the process.
(9) Commit to sustainability.
(10) Sign off all key stages.[50]

2.16 Chapter summary

The choice of procurement route is influenced by many issues, not least the balance between the political and economic climate. In general, the chosen path is dependent on the client's priorities in respect of:

- Time.
- Cost.
- Quality.
- Control.
- Size/value.
- Complexity.
- Sustainability.

There are many variations on four general types of procurement:

- Traditional.
- Design and build.
- Management.
- PFI/PPP.

2.16.1 Traditional procurement

The traditional procurement method involves a complete separation between design and construction phases of the project. Full design documentation is produced by the design team prior to the contractors tendering for the work. The client commissions an architect to take a brief, produce designs and construction information, invite tenders and administer the project during the construction period and settle the final account. The architect will advise the client to appoint other consultants to deal with particular items such as quantities and costs generally, structural calculations and heating designs. The contractor, who has no design responsibility, will normally be selected by competitive tender.

Variations include: two-stage selective tendering; negotiated contracts; continuity contracts; serial contracts and cost-reimbursable contracts.

Advantages

- The specification is under the full control of the client.
- Higher level of design, delivers better build quality.
- Client's vision of sustainable building, if clearly set out within the production information, is more likely to be met.

Disadvantages

- Contractors have to price extensive production information documents.
- Contractual conflict.
- Split responsibility.
- 'Blame culture' can develop.
- Cost control.

Sustainability

As the contractor has no involvement in the design process, sustainability in the traditional procurement route is completely reliant on the client and the design team. Sustainability may be jeopardised during the construction phase if cost control becomes a significant factor.

2.16.2 Design and build

Design and build is an approach to procurement that grew in popularity in the late 1980s and 1990s. The contractor provides the client with a fixed fee to take responsibility of the design and construction of the project. The client's brief can range from a schedule of accommodation, to full scheme design, to which the contractor must adhere in the tender and design process. The employer may approach a design and build contractor as soon as they intend to build. The contractor then takes charge of the project until completion.

Variations include: package deals; turnkey system; develop and construct; design novation.

Advantages

- Quicker and cheaper tender period as less production information is required for tender.
- Speed of delivery.
- Low-cost process.
- Developers involved in the project at an earlier stage – able to gain a better appreciation of sustainability issues.
- Single responsibility.

Disadvantages

- The specification is limited and is usually in the hands of the contractor.
- Interpretation of specification.
- Design quality can suffer as the role of the original design team is reduced.
- Loss of sustainability through cost savings.

Sustainability

The key aim of the design and build contractor is to achieve the employer's requirements at minimum cost. Unless sustainability is adequately incorporated into the requirements, the contractor is unlikely to include any sustainable features within the project.

2.16.3 Management

Management contracting and *construction management* are known as 'fast track' procurement routes. In the former route the contractor is selected at an early stage and is responsible for a simple management function for which a fee is paid. The construction work is divided into a number of packages, with the contractor's advice and tenders for these individual packages invited as appropriate to the programme. The works contractors are in contract with the management contractor. In the case of construction management, trade contractors each have a contract directly with the client who also employs a construction manager to act as project manager. In both versions of management procurement work begins on site as soon as possible to enable the first contractors to start while the rest of the scheme is being designed.

Variations include: management contracting; construction management; BPF system; design and manage.

Advantages

- The client has greater flexibility and control over the specification.
- Speed of delivery: 'fast track'.
- Supply chain interaction.
- Single responsibility.

Disadvantages

- Pressured timescale.
- Coordination.
- Critical interdependence of subcontractor packages.
- Cost uncertainty.

Sustainability

As speed of delivery is of prime concern in management procurement, the time allowed for the employer to brief consultants or management contractors may be short. Consequently, many sustainable features may not be incorporated during the design process, or may be left out during the construction phase.

2.16.4 PFI/PPP

The PFI/PPP approach is a style of procurement aimed at determining the feasibility and cost effectiveness of allowing the private sector to provide the public sector with capabilities and services. The procedure involves a group/trust acting as a client body with the help of technical, financial and legal advisors to provide and manage a building that meets the client's requirements for a set period, normally between 10 and 50 years. During the contract period the client will pay the client body, the PFI provider, an agreed rent which usually includes running and maintenance costs. A critical consideration is the balance of risk between the client and PFI provider, to determine the optimum value for money of the service provision.

Advantages

- The specification concentrates on outcomes/outputs or services.
- Whole life cost is a fundamental consideration.
- All parties involved in decisions.
- Low-energy design encouraged.

Disadvantages

- Ownership at risk.
- Design quality.

- Fuel tariff fluctuations.
- Team breakdown over the long process.

Sustainability

Depending on the nature of the consortium's financial commitments to energy running costs over the life-cycle of a project, PFI should have the potential to provide a sustainable building. Energy savings may equate to more profit for the consortium. However, if this is not the case, there is far less of an incentive for the consortium to produce a sustainable building.

The type of procurement route has a significant impact on the outcome of a project. Design ideas may be compromised or, in the worse case, jeopardised by demands such as cost and the desire for ease of construction. Designs that start out with strong sustainability credentials may be realised as something quite different. The situation is worsened by conflicting approaches from consultants, contractors and subcontractors. The right people and good working relationships are necessary for a successful project. A good start is to involve all participants at the earliest stage possible in the project so they have a proper understanding of the key aims – this is especially true in the case of sustainable design.

2.17 References

1 Kaye, B. (1960) *The development of the architectural profession in Britain: A sociological study.* London: George Allen & Unwin.
2 Rubinstein, W.D. (1993) *Capitalism, culture and decline in Britain, 1750–1990.* London: Routledge.
3 Bowley, M. (1966) *The British building industry: Four studies in response and resistance to change.* Cambridge: Cambridge University Press.
4 Kaye, B. (1960) *The development of the architectural profession in Britain: A sociological study.* London: George Allen & Unwin.
5 Mintzberg, H. (1983) *Structure in fives: Designing effective organisations.* Englewood Cliffs, NJ: Prentice-Hall.
6 Franks, J. (1990) *Building procurement systems.* Ascot: CIOB.
7 Moore, R.F. (1984) *Response to change: The development of non-traditional forms of contracting.* Ascot: CIOB.
8 Ireland, V. (1984) Virtually meaningless distinctions between nominally different procurement forms. In: *Proceedings of the CIB W-65 4th international symposium on organisation and management of construction*, Ontario, Canada, 1, pp. 203–211.
9 Higgin, G. and Jessop, N. (1965) *Communications in the building industry: The report of a pilot study.* London: Tavistock Publications.
10 RIBA (1980) RIBA plan of work for design team operation. In: Powell, J. (ed.) *Handbook of architectural practice and management*, pp. 347–373. London: RIBA Publications.
11 RIBA (2000) *The architect's plan of work.* London: RIBA Publications.
12 Fellows, R. and Langford, D. (1993) *Marketing and the construction client.* Ascot: CIOB.

13 Birrell, G.S. (1989) *So you need a new building? A guide to clients on procurement approaches.* Gainesville, Florida: University of Florida. Technical publication number 60.

14 Greenhalgh, B. (1990) A general classification for the procurement of construction using the basis of functions and responsibilities, and investigating whether this can form the basis of a single form of contract. In: *International symposium on procurement systems: Proceedings of a CIB W-92 conference,* Zagreb, Yugoslavia.

15 Kwakye, A.A. (1991) *Fast track construction.* Ascot: CIOB Occasional Paper Number 46.

16 NJCC (1983) *Code of procedure for two stage selective tendering.* London: RIBA.

17 NEDO (1983) *Faster building for industry.* London: HMSO.

18 Chappell, D. (1991) *Which form of building contract?* London: Architecture Design and Technology Press.

19 Wood Report (1975) *The public client and the construction industries.* London: NEDO/HMSO.

20 Masterman, J.W.E. (1989) *The procurement systems used for the implementation of industrial and commercial building projects.* Unpublished MSc thesis, University of Manchester.

21 Venturi, R. *et al.* (1977) *Learning from Las Vegas: The forgotten symbollism of architectural form.* Cambridge, Massachusetts: MIT Press.

22 CIRIA (1985) *A client's guide to cost-reimbursable contracts in building.* London: CIRIA. Special publication 36.

23 Turner, A. (1990) *Building procurement.* Basingtoke: Macmillan.

24 Hillman, J. (1992) *Medicis and the millennium? Government patronage and architecture.* London: Royal Fine Art Commission/HMSO.

25 Warne, E.J.D. (1993) *Review of the architects (registration) acts 1931–1969.* London: HMSO.

26 Franks, J. (1990) *Building procurement systems.* Ascot: CIOB.

27 Rowlinson, S.M. (1988) *An analysis of factors affecting project performance in industrial buildings: with particular reference to design-build contracts.* Unpublished PhD thesis, Brunel University.

28 Birrell, G.S. (1989) *So you need a new building? A guide to clients on procurement approaches.* Gainesville, Florida: University of Florida. Technical publication number 60.

29 Greenfield, S.S. (1981) *Turnkey construction in the United States.* Paper to ASCE Annual Convention and Exposition, New York, May 11–15.

30 Janssens, D.E.L. (1991) *Design-build explained.* Basingtoke: Macmillan.

31 Naoum, S.G. (1989) *An investigation into the performance of management contracts and the traditional methods of building.* Unpublished PhD thesis, Brunel University.

32 Naoum, S.G. (1991) *Procurement and project performance: A comparison of management and traditional contracting.* Ascot. CIOB. Occasional paper number 45.

33 Construction Management Forum (1991) *Report and Guidance.* Reading: Centre for Strategic Studies in Construction.

34 NEDO (1985) *Thinking about building: A successful business customer's guide to using the construction industry.* London: HMSO.

35 Birrell, G.S. (1991) Choosing between building procurement approaches: concepts and decision factors. In: Bezelga, A. and Brandon, P. (eds) *Management, quality and economics in building,* pp. 24–33. London: E & FN Spon.

36 Moxley, R. (1993) *Building management by professionals.* Oxford: Butterworth-Heinemann.

37 BPF (1983) *Manual of the BPF system for building design and construction.* London: BPF.

38 Morris, P.W.G. (1994) *The management of projects.* London: Telford.

39 Galbraith, J. (1973) *Designing complex organisations.* Reading, Massachusetts: Addison-Wesley.

40 Gaddis, P.O. (1959) The project manager. In: *Harvard Business Review,* Project management. Boston, Massachusetts: Harvard Business School Publishing Division.

41 CIOB (1992) *Code of practice for project management for construction and development.* Ascot: CIOB.

42 Walker, A. (1989) *Project management in construction.* Oxford: BSP Professional Books.

43 Baker, B.N., Murphy, D.C. and Fisher, D. (1988) Factors affecting project success. In: Cleland, D.I. and King, W.R. (eds) *Project management handbook,* pp. 902–919. New York: Van Nostrand Reinhold.

44 CIOB (1992) *A client's guide to project management for construction and development.* Ascot: CIOB.

45 Stanhope (1993) *Setting standards in the construction industry: The Stanhope approach.* London: Stanhope Properties plc.

46 Broome, J. (1994) *The New Engineering Contract: Design principles, risk allocation and early use.* Unpublished PhD thesis, University of Birmingham.

47 Hughes, W.P. (1989) *Organisational analysis of building projects* Unpublished PhD thesis, Liverpool John Moores University.

48 Gameson, R.N. (1992) *An investigation into the interaction between potential building clients and construction professionals.* Unpublished PhD thesis, University of Reading.

49 Pieniazek, G. (1985) Educating the client. *Building,* 5 July, p. 31.

50 CABE (2003) *Creating excellent buildings: A guide for clients.* London: CABE.

Chapter 3

Schools

3.1 Historical evolution of schools

> *The school itself should be a lovely place, a feast for the eyes both within and without. Within there should be a bright, clean room adorned all round with pictures. Without, however, there should be an open space next to the school . . . but also a garden, where the children should be sent from time to time to feast their eyes on the sight of trees, flowers and herbs.*
>
> Jan Amos Comenius, Didacta magna, 1632

Schools were rarely purpose-built in the early middle ages in England, although many ecclesiastical buildings were turned into schools after the Reformation in the early sixteenth century. Many of these were actually former hospital buildings due to their appropriate size for school rooms for a hundred or so pupils. Surviving foundations such as Winchester and Eton, founded in 1382 and 1440 respectively, are two notable examples of early medieval educational buildings.[1] They followed typical collegiate models in the form of a courtyard or series of courtyards – along the lines of the respective quadrangles and courts of Oxford and Cambridge. Although there are no physical remains of earlier schools, it is likely that some cathedral cities such as York and Canterbury included grammar (i.e. Latin teaching) and choir schools several hundred years before the middle ages.[2] Most teaching was oral, with only the teacher possessing books, or manuscripts, before the invention of printing. Even in the mid-sixteenth century there are still reports of rote-learning in local grammar schools, such as one from Roger Ascham in Yorkshire:

> *. . . always learning, and little profiting; learning without book, everything; understanding within the book, little or nothing; their whole knowledge, by learning without the book, was tied only to their tongue and lips and never ascended up to the brain and head and therefore was soon spit out of the mouth again.*[3]

The Reformation started the reorganisation of school buildings and an increase in the building of new schools began in the Elizabethan era, with Westminster possibly being the most famous foundation. Individual benefactors gave way to groups who acted as founders for schools within their towns, with Shrewsbury being a good example. This set the scene for a renaissance of English grammar schools, and the beginnings of a national collection of schools in a county which included villages and hamlets as well as major towns by the late seventeenth century. Major grammar school foundations at this time included Charterhouse (1611), which met with some opposition from the philosopher, Roger Bacon. Bacon wrote to James I in 1612 to the effect that there were already too many grammar schools and that there was a danger of an oversupply of 'scholars'.[4] However, grammar schools continued to be founded and the original schoolhouse at Harrow was built in 1615 – originating from a royal charter obtained 40 years previously by a local yeoman, John Lyons, to provide a free education for local scholars.

The eighteenth century saw the decline of local grammar schools, with many only retaining a handful of free pupils. This spurred the development of fee-paying boarders into a common mechanism for grammar-school masters to make ends meet. Through this means some of the older grammar foundations expanded greatly and the term 'public school' was coined – in the sense of all comers, who could pay, were welcome, rather than just local, poor scholars. The early nineteenth century heralded a network of national schools to provide primary education throughout Britain and Ireland, and the foundation of many new 'public' and 'private schools', mainly providing fee-paying secondary education. Public schools reached their apogee in terms of numbers of foundations in the Victorian era, with nearly as many foundations, around a hundred, in that century as in the previous three. New foundations included Marlborough (1843), Radley (1847), and Clifton (1860). Church schools providing local elementary education were also widespread. Forster's Education Act of 1870 allowed the establishment of Education Boards to build Schools.*

The London School Board was established in 1870 as a result of the Education Act. Edward R. Robson FRIBA was appointed architect to the Board in 1871 and initiated the refurbishment of buildings, such as warehouses, to accommodate the first schools. He began to acquire confined, urban sites for new schools at the same time. Using the simple device of inviting six architects to compete for each of the first 30 sites meant that the Board acquired the ideas of over a hundred architects by late 1872, though not all the invited architects, leading figures such as Basil Champneys, wanted to submit schemes for such a modest building type. Evading the earlier ideas of the social reformer, Edwin Chadwick, who was a member of the Board, and wanted to experiment with prefabricated buildings to achieve the required output, '. . . on the Crystal Palace principle', Robson travelled

---

*Forster's Act was intended only to enhance the educational provision that existed. The two religious organisations that ran schools were given grants and the Act provided for the establishment of so-called 'Board Schools'. Education was neither free nor compulsory under this legislation. Sandton's 1876 Education Act encouraged school attendance and parents were made responsible for ensuring that their children received basic instruction. There was some financial help for poor parents to pay school fees, but this was not mandatory.

Figure 3.1 Typical London Board School – Harper Street School, 1873.

the continent to study school design. Although impressed by the Prussian model schools, he realised that a synthesis of the best educational and appropriate architectural ideas was necessary to achieve his vision of the Board schools ranking as public buildings, expressing dignity and civil character.

After the early trial and error stage Robson set about the large and intensive building programme, adopting a necessarily economic Queen Anne style, brick and sash, usually in London stock brick with accents of red 'rubbers' – the latter allowing for limited carved ornamentation (Figure 3.1), which Robson favoured over the ubiquitous terra cotta features of the time. Robson completed 174 London Board schools from 1872 to late 1876 with a small team of a dozen or so assistants, by standardising plans and detailing. Board school plans were invariably a variation on the idea of classrooms ranged around a central assembly hall. It was a monumental achievement, and consistent in quality. He also found time to write a book on school design entitled *School architecture: the planning, designing, building and furnishing of school-houses* in 1874 – his treatise on school design. His success lay in the integration of the latest educational theories, from home and abroad, with good architecture. Despite the sometimes stark appearance of the Board schools, largely in response to outcries of extravagance at this new burden on the public purse, there were also local complaints that some of the schools were so bland as to form blots on the landscape. The Queen Anne style certainly worked in terms of the dictates of light and ventilation, with the high ceilings and windows.[5]

Robson achieved his vision within a few decades, if the evidence of a fictional character is valid – Sherlock Holmes described the Board schools, in *The naval treaty* (1893), as:

> *. . . big, isolated clumps of buildings rising above the slates, like brick islands in a lead-coloured sea . . . out of which will spring the wiser, better England of the future . . .*

And there may have been some truth in these words, as by the 1886 general election only 38 000 votes were made by illiterates.[6] Robson

Figure 3.2 Norton Park Board School, Edinburgh, 1904.

continued as architect to the London School Board until 1889, and compounded his legacy as a great Victorian in a more visible fashion than the engineer, Joseph Bazalgette, whose sewers Londoners still depend on. Many of Robson's buildings are still used as schools today, although adapted and extended they have responded well to curriculum changes.[7] It is not surprising, given all the thorough research that went into Robson's school designs, that they were used as models, sometimes dressed in local materials, all over the country. Norton Park School in Edinburgh (Figure 3.2) is a good example of Robson's template exported north of the border, further showing the robust adaptability of these buildings with its recent transformation into offices for a collection of local charity organisations.

The Edinburgh School Board, like the English Boards, was an elected body set up in 1872 and supervised by the Scotch (sic) Education Department, then based in London. Although its permanent secretaries tended to be Scottish, its staff predominantly comprised Londoners, with the result that the type plans handed down to the Scottish Boards tended to reflect English, and in particular London, practice. However, the notable example of Charles Rennie Macintosh's Scotland Street School (1903–1906) followed a different course due to his disagreements with the Glasgow School Board's fixed ideas inherited from Robson's textbook. Macintosh succeeded in increasing the budget which allowed him to increase the architectural quality above the standard Board school design. This building is now, appropriately enough, the home of the Scottish Museum of Education, and another good example of the adaptive reuse of this building type, a century after it was built.[8]

The Board schools were, in many ways, good examples of sustainable development. They were always multi-storeyed, up to five storeys, with high ceiling heights for daylight penetration and cross-ventilation, in urban locations so that pupils could walk to school. Solid brick contruction, but uninsulated, gives them good thermal mass, while large areas of single glazing have led to attempts to reduce the volume of air to heat with suspended ceilings, which destroy the character of classrooms and compromise ventilation and daylighting. However, these buildings have served well for over a century, many of them are now listed buildings which convert readily into loft-style appartments, and health-inspired dictates of fresh air and sunlight are universal and timeless.[9]

3.2 The modern era of school building

I think of school as an environment of spaces where it is good to learn. Schools began with a man under a tree, who did not know he was a teacher, discussing his realization with a few who did not know they were students . . . the existence-will of school was there even before the circumstances of a man under a tree. That is why it is good for the mind to go back to the beginning, because the beginning of any established activity is its most wonderful moment.

Louis Kahn (1901–74)

Towards the end of the nineteenth century, the introduction of new local government setups allowed the raising of rates to fund education. The 1890 Secondary Education Act laid the foundations for state secondary education in the twentieth century. Local Education Authorities succeeded the School Boards and had a louder political voice. The dictates of hygiene and fresh air led to the extreme of the open-air school movement early in the twentieth centry, as an antidote to urban pollution, over-crowding and poverty. Open-air schools were built in the first decade of the twentieth century through to the 1930s and paralleled the sanatoria treating tuberculosis patients, but in this case while also educating children. However, the seemingly logical conclusion of the open-air school was a complete absence of architecture, and although it influenced school architects, who agreed with the provision of fresh air, it seemed diametrically opposed to the provision of better buildings, *per se*. One consequence of the ventilation imperative was the move away from the late-nineteenth century central-hall planned schools, and towards new 'pavilion' buildings in the early decades of the new century. Medical advances and the battle against insanitary living conditions, symbolised by Modern Movement architecture, ensured that school buildings were viewed in the light of social change, as well as purely educational terms – in much the same way as health buildings were seen.

There was also a continuation of the Board school architectural tradition which spilled over the *fin de siècle* and a number of new grammar schools were built in this idiom. One such example of this 'traditional' style was the King Edward VII School at King's Lynn, Norfolk (1906), designed by Basil Champneys. The design sought to give civic stature to an essentially domestic style of architecture, and a contemporary journalist remarked that it:

. . . realised an excellent type of school architecture, interesting and picturesque without being pretentious, preserving in fact the home-like character which school architecture ought to present.[10]

This was, and remains, a hybrid quality that architects strive to achieve in school design – melding a domestic scale with the presence of a public building. It is certainly a highly appropriate approach for primary schools, but difficult to achieve usually in secondary schools, because of their sheer size. Between the wars the LEAs consolidated their hold on educational provision at both levels, and educational reports advocated the age of eleven years as an appropriate junction between primary and secondary education. Stylistically, Modern Movement architecture, largely imperfectly imported from the Continent, continued to prevail – although compromise generally led to the selection of cheap features only. However, some model examples prevailed, such as Walter Gropius' and Maxwell Fry's series of village colleges in Cambridgeshire.

3.3 Twentieth century schools

English school-building . . . was the fullest expression of the movement for a social architecture in Britain which gathered pace in the 1930s and found its outlet in the service of the post-war welfare state. No more ambitious, disciplined, self-conscious or far-reaching application of the concept of archi-tecture as social service can be found in any western country.[11]

Andrew Saint, 1987

The post-war welfare state in Britain initiated a volume of school building to match the earlier impetutus created by the 1870 Act. Although resources were meagre after the war, over 10 000 primary and secondary schools were built in England and Wales from 1947–1970. The 1944 Education Act, the raising of the school-leaving age to 15, the post-war baby boom, and the predominantly Victorian, now bomb-damaged, legacy of school buildings all contributed to the need for a large programme of school building. The Act was followed by new building regulations prescribing generous space standards for new schools, but shortages in materials and skilled labour, as well as the need for economy, soon saw the standards reduced by as much as 10 per cent by 1954. Educationalists' imperatives and theories informed the school design renaissance and local authorities led the way. Towards the end of the 1950s nearly half of the architectural profession was working for government, and nearly a third were in local authorities.[12]

Experimental Modern Movement architecture was in the forefront of this mammoth national task to build a generation of new school buildings, and the dictat that 'form follows function' suited progressive educational organ-isation theories. Non-traditional forms of construction and pre-fabrication were used extensively to combat the lack of construction skills and dearth of materials – these included experimental aluminium frame systems emerging from the recently overloaded aircraft industry. A number of geographically adjacent local authorities created consortia to design and implement various pre-fabricated systems, such as CLASP, SCOLA and MACE.* Such collaboration and standardisation reduced design and construction times, and hence cost, which allowed such a huge logistical achievement in the post-war decades. But these lightweight 'kits of parts', which stressed flexibility with 'extruded' buildings and flat roofs were often sadly lacking in architectural and performance terms. Hertfordshire created a venerable legacy of modular, standardised, and prefabricated schools – some of which are now listed buildings. The 'Brutalist' Hunstanton School was a unique design, inspired by the sparse architecture of Mies van der Rohe, by Alison and Peter Smithson, but the vast majority of schools from this era were often the products of ubiquitous factory techniques of sometimes suspect quality.[13] However, Nikolas Pevsner considered Hunstanton 'the paramount example among the innumerable good post-war schools of England of a rigidly formal, symmetrical layout'. Alongside the infrastructural programme was the equally demanding task of recruiting and training sufficient teachers.

> More than any other modern programme of building, the English schools fulfilled Walter Gropius's ideals about an architecture which should be simple, practical, universal and imaginative . . . practically none was built to a uniform pattern, and most enjoyed space, facilities and a quality of environment unimagined before the war.[14]

The design diktats of providing well daylit, ventilated, and heated learning environments were timeless, and similar to the previous century – but twentieth century scientific methods were now applied to the problem. Dogmatic guidance on levels of daylighting necessary throughout classrooms, such as the requirement for a minimum 2 per cent daylight factor, inevitably led to some mistakes.[†] Ironically, research at the Building Research Station showed that visual performance in classrooms could be improved through other means, such as increasing the size and contrast of the writing or illustration being viewed, rather than simply raising lighting levels. Simply moving children a few feet nearer the blackboard improved visual performance to the same degree as increasing the lighting level by 30 times! Quality of daylight is generally more important than quantity to produce visual comfort among building users.[15] Additionally, an acoustically

---

*CLASP: Consortium of Local Authorities Special Programme; SCOLA: Second Consortium of Local Authorities; MACE: Metropolitan Architectural Consortium for Education.

†The crudest rule-of-thumb for side lighting is to multiply the minimum daylight factor by 10, and to take the result as a measure of the amount of glazing required in terms of percentage of floor area. To provide a minimum 2 per cent daylight factor for a 50 sq. metre classroom would require one external wall (say 7 m × 2.4 m) to be at least 60 per cent glazed. Excessive glare from such arrangements will often significantly decrease visual improvements from higher lighting levels. Classroom walls were often almost fully glazed in the 1960s and 1970s in pursuit of 2 per cent daylight factors throughout the room – with attendant overheating in summer and cold down-draughts in winter, and their implications for educational efficiency.

controlled automatic window was developed by BRS, and used in a school near Heathrow airport where intermittent and high-level aircraft noise was succesfully isolated.[16]

'Finger-plan' school layouts with sprawled classroom wings fell out of favour due to their expense and educationalists' theories involving biological metaphors that invoked the assembly hall as the 'heart' of the school, with the classrooms as 'limbs'. The effect was a return, in some respects, to centralised layouts around the timeless academic typology of open or closed courtyards. The oil shocks of the 1970s encouraged compact designs and environmental imperatives such as passive solar inspired schemes. St George's School, Wallasey, near Liverpool was a notable pioneer in this respect, from the early 1960s, where the whole of the south-facing wall is double-glazed, and a thermally heavyweight fabric avoids overheating. Wallasey relied on metabolic and lighting heat, somewhat counter-intuitively, and the back-up boiler system was never used – but there were some complaints concerning air quality due to the energy-conscious low air-change rate.[17]

School building reduced to a minimum after the mid-1970s, when the post-war baby-boomers had passed through the system. However, Hampshire County Council, under the stewardship of Sir Colin Stansfield Smith in the 1970s and 1980s, was synonomous with a high level of design quality in schools, and other building types. A legacy which appears to have continued. School building in Hampshire, in the latter decades of the last century, was a backlash against the systems-building approach of previous decades. They largely rejected universal solutions as simplistic and inappropriate responses to unique sites and users – presaging later research into the correlation between infrastructural capital investment and educational peformance and outcomes. These included schools such as Stoke Park with its 'big roof' concept, the organic Woodlea, and Queens Inclosure with its fluid planning. The head of the latter school is quoted as saying '. . . this is the best primary school in Britain. When I walk in every morning my heart lifts because of the way it works for children'.[18]

3.4 Twenty-first century schools

The best designed schools encourage children to learn . . . I am determined that this additional money should be well spent, leaving behind a legacy of high quality buildings that can match the best of what we inherited from the Victorians and other past generations.[19]

Tony Blair, 2000

While some other notable examples of well-designed, child-focused primary schools were developed throughout the 1990s – most pioneering projects required a funding premium. The age of school buildings stock in the new century (Figure 3.3) pointed to the need for a new generation of inspirational school buildings. Although some good historic examples remained, much of the stock had suffered from chronic under-maintenance,

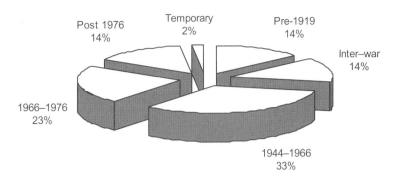

Figure 3.3 Age of school building stock – England, 2003.

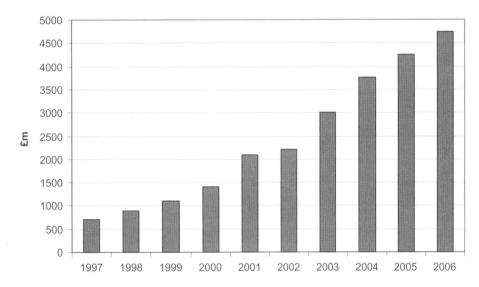

Figure 3.4 Capital spending on school buildings.

and the vast majority of educational infrastructure needed upgrading to respond to the computer age. The post-war public sector building boom accounted for most of the stock, while the sizeable rump of temporary school buildings was an embarrassment. In the late 1990s, the socio-economic commentator, Will Hutton, claimed that '... underfunding, competitive contracting, and a bugeoning private sector – are undermining the notion of a universal education system ... school buildings, equipment and playing fields are inadequate.[20] The scale of proposed investment in new school building is enormous, with 600 schools currently in the pipeline (Figure 3.4).

The sheer scale of secondary schools makes design quality more challenging to achieve than in primary schools. Secondary schools invariably house several hundred pupils, over an area of 10 000 square metres, and have elements such as sports halls that are 9 metres in height. The Department for Education and Skills (DfES) recommends three plan strategies for secondary schools: street plan; campus plan; and linked pavilions.[21] The street plan is probably the most ubiquitous recent form, for reasons of compactness and economy. The street or mall plan allows for a two-storey atrium, which usually serves as a central circulation spine, providing a sociable space that can also be used for other community purposes.

The Private Finance Initiative (PFI) has rapidly become the procurement method for new schools. Early results from this system suggest that design time is limited, compared to traditional design-led methods, and client involvement is not always adequate. A recent Commission for Architecture and the Built Environment (CABE) survey concluded that:

- Efficient and functional schools with architectural merit can be achieved given the right partnership ingredients. However, many examples of poor design and inferior detailing will live on as a legacy of PFI.
- Head teachers and staff were generally satisfied with new schools.
- Many challenges were experienced in the PFI process.
- Internal environments in terms of natural light, solar gain and ventilation are inadequately addressed. None of the schools visited were totally successful in this area.

Fears that design quality was marginalised in the early PFI schemes led CABE to publish a list of 10 key principles of good school design:

(1) Good clear organisation, an easily legible plan, full accessibility.
(2) Spaces that are well-proportioned, efficient, and fit for purpose.
(3) Circulation that is well organised, and sufficiently generous.
(4) Good environmental conditions throughout, including appropriate levels of natural light and ventilation. Environmentally-friendly materials.
(5) Attractiveness in design, comparable to that found in other quality public buildings, to inspire pupils, staff and parents.
(6) Good use of the site, public presence as a civic building, wherever possible, to engender local pride.
(7) Attractive external spaces offering appropriate security and a variety of different settings.
(8) A layout that encourages broad community access and use out-of-hours.
(9) Robust non-institutional materials, that will look good and weather and wear well.
(10) Scope for change in both the physical and ICT environment, possibility of extension where appropriate.

3.5 PFI schools in England and Wales – Introduction

American research has found that primary school children in classrooms with high daylight levels learn faster than those in classrooms with poor daylighting.

BRE, Building for people, 2004

The Audit Commission wished to ascertain the design quality of new schools in England and Wales, and particularly to quantitatively and qualitatively analyse schools procured by PFI contracts compared to traditional means. This small study of 18 primary and secondary schools procured by both routes is part of a wider investigation into the design quality of PFI projects.* The Audit Commission wanted to find out whether:

- *Construction materials and components used for PFI schools are significantly different to those used for traditionally financed schools, due to life-cycle considerations for key components?*
- General trends revealed that PFI schools used metal and plastic sheet roofs and cladding systems. Traditionally procured schools tended to favour traditional materials such as facing brickwork and concrete roofing tiles. Aluminium window and doorframe systems were ubiquitous throughout the sample. The only 'lightweight' framed building was a PFI school. There was, in general, a sparsity of finishes throughout the PFI schools, extending to the complete omission of ceiling finishes. The generally poor detailed design on PFI schools will probably impact upon expected life-cycles of key components.
- *Whole life costs for PFI schemes are adequate in the context of the workmanship and materials used in initial construction?*
- Observations from the sample of 18 schools visited suggest that the PFI schools would need larger maintenance budgets. PFI schools were generally of a lower design quality than traditionally procured ones. The latter seemed to benefit from the prescriptive nature of a conventional route as well as the tried and tested detailing of traditional materials. The PFI schools were significantly lower in the areas of architectural design, cost of ownership, and detail design. However, the areas of building service design quality and user productivity indicators showed little difference between PFI and traditionally procured schools.
- *Decisions relating to whole life costs have considered the period beyond the PFI contract period?*
- These decisions varied considerably across the sample, but the use of traditional materials with conventional detailing tends to ensure a higher quality of detailed design, which in turn helps to ensure longer life for components and materials. Residual value and ultimate life of the schools will depend on adequate maintenance, repair and replacement of key components. The conundrum of higher maintenance costs as a percentage of lower capital costs could ultimately compare well to higher capital costs with resultant lower maintenance costs. In the case of the PFI schools the respective consortiums will, presumably, eventually foot the bill for the former strategy, at least for the concession period.
- *PFI schools provide material DBO synergies beyond the PFI contract period?*
- This evidence tends to suggest that the promised DBO synergies are not being achieved in PFI school designs. While it was assumed that all schools were constructed close to DfES

---

*Audit Commission (2003) *PFI in schools: The quality and cost of buildings and services provided by early Private Finance Initiative schemes.*

budgetary and space standards, better examples occurred where the 'right people' were assembled into design teams, including a full-time in-house client representative. Such informed clients, or independent advisors, are able to interrogate design proposals in a sophisticated manner and obtain higher standards of design quality.

The Audit Commission needed to assess the overall design quality of new schools, and to compare any differences between procurement routes in the following key areas:

- Quality of materials used for key building components.
- Energy efficiency.
- Disabled access.
- Compliance with other legislation, such as building and fire regulations.

3.6 PFI schools in England and Wales – Design Quality Matrices

Clients are the key to the whole construction process. Since ultimately they fund it, their wants and needs should be paramount. They want, and have the right to expect, buildings or projects which meet their needs and aspirations fully.

Michael Latham, Trust and money, *1993*

The main means to achieve the objectives set out in the project brief centred on visual surveys of the sample of 18 schools by a small team of expert consulting architects and engineers. The surveys were non-intrusive to the building fabric, but included roof and plant room inspections. All principal spaces and typical classrooms were examined. Scientific instrumentation was used to measure light, sound and temperature levels. In all but a few cases, where they were unavailable, head teachers were informally interviewed. Other teaching and maintenance staff were also interviewed during the course of a walk around the building and grounds. Whether this sample is representative of all new school buildings is not known and appropriate levels of confidence should be attached to the data:

- Ten traditional and eight PFI schools.
- Ten primary and eight secondary schools.
- Six traditional primary; four PFI primary; four traditional secondary; four PFI secondary.
- Wide geographical spread throughout England and Wales.
- Variety of PFI contracts – early; one-off; and serial or package.
- Traditional procurement includes design and build.
- Size of school varies from 50 to 1800 pupils.
- Only one 'lightweight' frame building, which was PFI.

The BRE team focused on the key elements of roof; wall; cladding; windows/doors; lavatories; finishes; electrical; and mechanical services – and used a series of matrices to assess the design quality of the sample of schools. The design quality matrices are suitable for completion by professional experts with relevant experience, and can be adapted for any building type. They can be robust and powerful tools in the hands of experts. Although the matrix scoring levels are set objectively using published standards, such as British Standards and consensual good practice, there is obviously an element of inherent subjectivity in this system.* Extreme views are ameliorated by group consensus, even among a small group of expert construction professionals. The results must be viewed as the expert opinion of a few consulting architects and engineers – for this reason we have defined levels of significance for the results, below.

The limitations of the sample size must also be considered, as well as the visual and non-intrusive nature of the surveys. The surveys were as thorough as time allowed and included roof and plant room inspections. They were non-intrusive and did not include reference to any further project-specific documentation, apart from a few instances where detailed architectural drawings were available. No capital cost data were made available. The informal interviews with head teachers, teaching staff, and maintenance staff were often revealing, but they must also be treated with caution as anecdotal evidence can be subject to personal bias. Despite that, they contributed to the research and helped to shape BRE recommendations. The BRE team saw the physical evidence of successful strategies, such as seconding a member of staff to the construction of a new school for a number of months, and unfortunately also saw the results of less successful approaches.

BRE's set of five matrices measures all aspects of the design quality of schools, from the architectural strategy of site planning through to the detailed design of junctions of different materials. Each matrix has six sub-factors in columns and scoring levels in rows. The matrices were developed by objectively establishing a fully competent level of performance at the top level of Level 4. Although it is theoretically possible to register a score of 4.5, this would be an exceptional example of the very best practice. This ideal score was not recorded for any sub-factor in the present study, and there was only a handful of scores at Level 4. Once a top level is established it is a simple matter to cascade lower levels of performance, descending to Level 0. Each descent in performance usually implies a failure to achieve best practice in at least one significant area, or several minor shortcomings. A set of matrices was completed for each school, and highlights problems and successes. Matrix averages (medians) revealed quality trends between procurement routes – comparative differences in the median matrices are probably more revealing than 'league tables' of ranked schools for each factor.

Due to the uncertainties in the matrix scoring process, median results of less than one level apart in small sample groups of matrices should be given limited significance.

---

*The basis of the definitions is always linked at the highest level (Level 4) to widely accepted definitions of competence acceptable to appropriately skilled professionals and artisans.

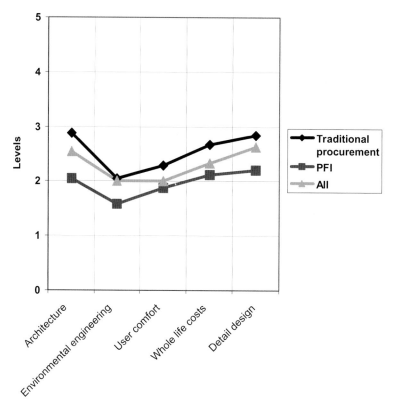

Figure 3.5 Overall summary matrix – median scores of all five matrices (Level 3 is good practice).

3.7 PFI schools in England and Wales – Overall summary matrix

For better results the potential client will have to do a good deal of homework.

Courtney Blackmore, The client's tale, *1990*

Matrix 0 – Summary

The overall summary matrix collects the results of the six matrices below: architecture; environmental engineering; user comfort; whole life costing; detail design; and user satisfaction. The summary matrix shows any major trends and any major differences between design quality achieved between building procurement routes (Figure 3.5).

Matrix 1 – Architecture

Probably the most subjective matrix in the areas of internal and external architectural merit, but more robust in areas such as site and space planning. The historic terms of firmness, commodity and delight are used to convey the concepts of structural integrity, functionality and uplifting of the spirits. Views of building users were considered, particularly for the often intangible and ephemeral areas of 'spiritual uplift'!

Matrix 2 – Environmental engineering

Far more objective in nature, and scientifically measurable (e.g. lighting levels in lux and noise levels in dBA). The integration of services and architectural fabric was obviously, if symbolically, evident in two traditional schools, which used the conceit of housing boiler flues in brick chimneys. This helps to give primary schools an appropriate domestic scale. Maintainability and sourcing of replacement components are critical to continuous quality. Environmental sustainability is necessary for LAs to achieve Local Agenda 21 objectives.

Matrix 3 – User comfort

Comfort conditions are scientifically measurable (e.g. lux, dBA and ambient and radiant temperature) and links between such conditions and user productivity are increasingly empirically evident – excessive noise, sunlight and poor ventilation degrade internal environments. However, ideal environments are more subtly created by the integration of art and science rather than crudely engineered by actions such as increasing lighting levels. Psychological aspects also play a crucial part in individual comfort and productivity.

Matrix 4 – Whole life costs

This matrix concentrates on the potential whole life performance of the building's fabric and environmental services also considering ease of facilities management and the adaptability of the building for future alteration or extension. This matrix helps to expose the trade-offs between capital and running costs, which affect future performance.

Matrix 5 – Detail design

Anomalies in building performance are often caused by errors or inconsistencies in detailing, such as architectural junctions of different materials at abutments or incorrectly sized components, furnishings and fittings. The former can lead to leaks or even flooding, while the latter often causes loss of functionality or even serious accidents. Such failures can often be attributed to poor detailed design or bad workmanship – or a combination of both (Figure 3.6).

3.7.1 Summary matrix – commentary

Matrix 1 – Quality of architectural design

There is one point between the traditionally procured and PFI schools, indicating a significant difference in architectural quality. The possibility of achieving such quality appears enhanced in the traditionally procured schools. Architectural quality is often a precursor to subsequent indicators (Figure 3.7).

Figure 3.6 Traditional materials and detailing on a traditionally procured school.

Figure 3.7 Unclear entrance to a PFI secondary school.

Matrix 2 – Quality of services design

There is only a difference of 0.5 between traditional procurement and PFI, which cannot be viewed as significant due to the variability of the matrix scoring process. Services were ostensibly similar in the two procurement routes and with many departures from good practice across the entire sample.

Matrix 3 – User productivity indicators

There is only a difference of 0.5 between traditional and PFI, which cannot be viewed as significant. However, the median score for all schools is comparatively low – suggesting that there is significant opportunity for improvement.

Matrix 4 – Building cost of ownership

There is a difference of 0.65 between traditional procurement and PFI which, although of limited significance, suggests that capital costs are driving PFI designs more than traditional solutions.

Matrix 5 – Detail design

The difference of 0.75 between traditional procurement and PFI, and the comparatively reasonable score of the traditional schools, suggests that PFI solutions are not receiving as much attention to detail as traditional ones.

3.7.2 Summary matrix – conclusions

A matrix analysis can highlight potential problems and prioritise them. The areas of service design; user productivity; and cost of ownership appear to need improvement to achieve a level line score. But they are also inextricably linked to architectural design and detailed design.

3.8 PFI schools in England and Wales – Architecture

Schools are incredibly complex and unique organisations. Some of the problems have come about because the people that are building schools have no real understanding of how they work. The designs have often been bland, and there is too little opportunity for some of our talented designers to bring forward their ideas because they are not linked to the big consortia.

Sharon Wright, MD of Schoolworks, 2004

3.8.1 Architecture (Matrix 1) – Level 4 definitions

Architectural, exterior. Design has obvious firmness, commodity and delight. No features that are obvious architectural excesses. Users like and respect the building. Excellent materials selection and placement. Adequate weathering and maintenance (Figure 3.8 to Figure 3.11).

Site planning. Functional separation and integration optimises use of site. Good site displacement of built elements and layout. Good solar orientation. Good vehicle access/parking/pedestrian access. Adequate parking provision. Adequate space for future building extension.

Interior design. Design has obvious beauty and clarity of purpose. Internal aspects of good scale and ergonomics. Daylight quality and acoustics excellent. Excellent use of colour, finishes and furniture. Interior allows flexibility and potential refurbishment.

SCHOOL	Architectural exterior	Site planning	Interior design	Space planning	Specification	Sustainability	TOTAL
School B	4	3.5	3.5	3	3	2.5	**19.5**
School C	3	4	3	2.5	3.5	2.5	**18.5**
School D	3	3.5	3	3	3.5	2	**18**
School E	3	3.5	3.5	3.5	2.5	2	**18**
School F	3.5	4	3	3	2.5	2	**18**
School H	2	4	3	3	2.5	2	**16.5**
School M	3	3.5	2.5	2.5	3	2	**16.5**
School A	3	3	3	3	3	1	**16**
School G	2	3.5	2.5	3	2.5	2	**15.5**
School R	2.5	3	2.5	3	2.5	1.5	**15**
School J	2	4	2	2.5	2.5	1.5	**14.5**
School K	1.5	3	2	2.5	2.5	2	**13.5**
School S	3	1	2.5	2.5	2	2	**13**
School T	3	2.5	2	2	2	1.5	**13**
School L	2	2	2	2	1.5	1.5	**11**
School N	1.5	2	2	2	1.5	1.5	**10.5**
School P	1	2	1	2	1.5	1	**8.5**
School Q	1	2.5	0	3	0	1	**7.5**

Figure 3.8 Architecture (Matrix 1) scoring table – PFI schools are shaded.

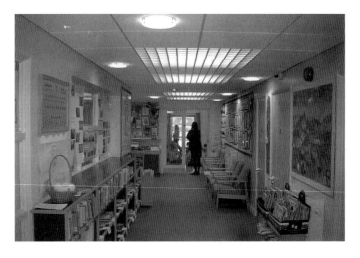

Figure 3.9 Flexible spaces within circulation areas in a traditionally procured school.

Space planning. Excellent use of space with good juxtaposition of key spaces. Support spaces, storage and circulation all adequate. Imaginative use of servant to served space.* Good social space. Compliance with guidance in *Building Bulletin 98*.[22]

---

*This phrase is used in the sense intended by the American architect, Louis Kahn (1901–74). Served space represents the essential purpose of the building, such as wards, consulting rooms and laboratories in a hospital – places where people are. Servant space represents areas such as circulation space, environmental engineering voids and risers, and storage spaces.

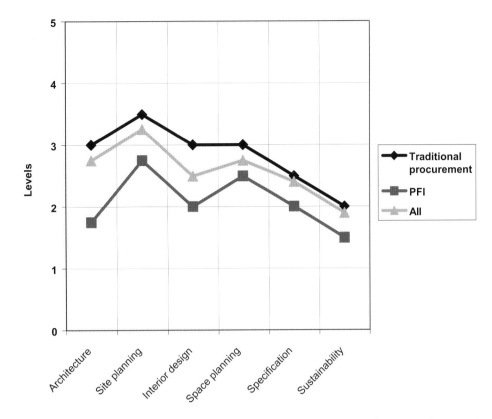

Figure 3.10 Architecture (Matrix 1) – median scores of sample (Level 3 is good practice).

Figure 3.11 Dramatic and symbolic architecture of a traditionally procured primary school.

Specification. Excellent component selection and placement, with adequate input from experienced users and maintenance staff. Excellent detailing and provision for maintenance. No obvious potential design defects at materials' junctions.

Sustainability. Environmental impact minimised by proper consideration of environmental, economic and social factors. Heating, lighting and ventilation systems and components robust, reliable and competently optimised and integrated with passive counterparts. Potential for an excellent BREEAM rating.

3.8.2 Matrix 1: Architecture – commentary

Architectural exterior.   There is a difference of 1.25, combined with the all-mean score much nearer the traditional mean, suggesting a far more consistent quality is being achieved under traditional procurement. The PFI score suggests that this route is resulting in mundane architecture with significant potential maintenance difficulties.

Site planning.   There is a difference of 0.75 between the traditionally procured and PFI schools. But the median of all schools score (the all-median) suggests that PFIs are let down by a few examples in this sample, as one PFI scored Level 4 and one traditional school scored Level 1.

Interior design.   Difference of one level between traditional procurement and PFI, which is again significant. The traditional score indicates only minor failures to achieve Level 4. The PFI score indicates significant single, or many minor failures to achieve this level. Such architectural failures affect the fitness for purpose of interior spaces.

Space planning.   There is a limited difference between traditional procurement and PFI, suggesting that space planning, on average, is only suffering from minor failures.

Specification.   Limited difference, but overall there are worrying specification failures.

Sustainability.   Limited difference, but overall sustainability failures.

3.8.3 Matrix 1 – conclusions

The real purpose and value of a matrix analysis is to highlight potential problems and to prioritise them for attention. The areas of specification and sustainability are most in need of attention. PFI falls significantly short of the traditionally procured on architectural quality.

3.9 PFI schools in England and Wales – Environmental engineering

Development which meets the needs of the present without compromising the ability of future generations to meet their own needs.

Brundtland definition of sustainability 1987

3.9.1 Environmental engineering (Matrix 2) – Level 4 definitions

Integration.   Services design sympathetic to and optimises all aspects of the architecture. Well-informed consideration of thermal and lighting issues. No intrusion of services into occupied space. No compromise on user access to windows (Figures 3.12–3.15).

Mechanical systems design.   Robust good practice utilising the most appropriate components integrated into efficient reliable systems. Covers heating, ventilation, cooling and plumbing. Nil acoustic intrusion from services into the use of the building.

SCHOOL	Integration	Mechanical systems	Electrical systems	Maintainability	Sourcing	Sustainability	TOTAL
School K	3	2	1.5	3	3	1.5	14
School B	3	2	2	2	3	1.5	13.5
School A	2.5	2	2	2	2.5	2	13
School E	2.5	1.5	2	2.5	2.5	2	13
School F	2.5	2	2	2	2.5	2	13
School J	2.5	2	2	2	2.5	1.5	12.5
School H	2.5	2	2	2	2.5	1.5	12.5
School M	2.5	2	2	2	2.5	1.5	12.5
School C	2.5	2	2	2	2.5	1	12
School D	2.5	1.5	2	2	3	1	12
School R	2.5	1	1.5	2	3	1	11
School S	2.5	1.5	1	2	3	1	11
School G	1.5	1.5	2	1	3	1	10
School P	1	1	1	2	2.5	1.5	9
School L	1	1.5	1	1	3	1	8.5
School N	1	1.5	1	1	3	1	8.5
School Q	0.5	1	1.5	1.5	3	1	8.5
School T	1	1.5	1	1	3	1	8.5

Figure 3.12 Environmental engineering (Matrix 2) scoring table – PFI schools are shaded.

Figure 3.13 All too typical 'blinds down – lights on' situation in a classroom.

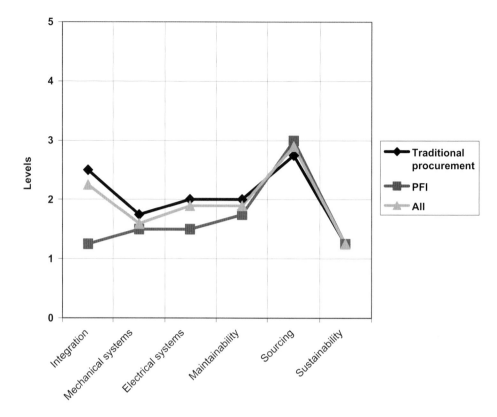

Figure 3.14 Environmental engineering (Matrix 2) – median scores of sample (Level 3 is good practice).

Figure 3.15 Boiler flues integrated into chimneys in a traditionally procured primary school.

Electrical systems design. Robust good practice utilising the most appropriate components integrated into efficient reliable system(s). Covers internal and external lighting, communications. Cables, conduits and ducts not intrusive. Well selected components.

Maintainability. Maintenance facilities and access designed to minimise loss of beneficial use, minimise time to clean and repair, and avoid need for specialised access for revenue replacement. All components and service data widely available.

Sourcing. All capital and revenue repairable/replaceable items selected for wide availability and compliance with well-known standards. Design has avoided use of specially manufactured items that could incur long lead times/high replacement costs.

Sustainability. Services components, system arrangement and controls selected and commissioned to minimise environmental impact. Comprehensive and easily useable data available for maintenance. Minimal use of materials deleterious to the environment.

3.9.2 Matrix 2: Environmental engineering – commentary

Integration. Difference of 1.25 is significant and confirmed by the median of all schools score, suggesting that there are frequent and obvious clashes between services and architecture in the PFI schools.

Mechanical. Significance of difference is limited, but the median of all schools is low at 1.5, suggesting that the minimal design approach to comply with codes is prevalent.

Electrical. Difference is of limited significance, and the median of all schools suggests one or two departures from the ideal defined in Level 4.

Maintainability. Limited difference, but the median suggests some significant cost and availability impacts across the board.

Sourcing. Limited difference, but PFI marginally ahead suggesting slightly more standardisation of components in this route. The median of all schools score (the all-median) indicates only one or two minor departures from Level 4.

Sustainability. No difference, but widespread minor non-compliance with published Local Agenda 21 policy objectives.

3.9.3 Matrix 2 – conclusions

The areas of mechanical, electrical, maintenance and sustainability are most in need of attention. PFI falls significantly short of traditional procurement on the integration of environmental services with architecture.

3.10 PFI schools in England and Wales – User comfort

British studies (Heriot-Watt University) have shown that the majority of classrooms in the UK suffer from poor acoustics which often reduces children's ability to learn.

BRE, Building for people, *2004*

3.10.1 User comfort (Matrix 3) – Level 4 definitions

Summertime overheat. Building interior unlikely to experience more than 30 hours per year above environmental temperature greater than 27 °C, and occupants have very limited beam radiation from the sun (Figures 3.16 to 3.19).

SCHOOL	Summer overheating	Visual environment	Heating comfort	Audible and visual intrusion	Acoustics	Air quality	TOTAL
School B	2.5	2	2	3	2	3	**14.5**
School H	2	2.5	2	3.5	2.5	2	**14.5**
School A	2	2.5	2	3	2	2.5	**14**
School C	2.5	2	2	3	2	2.5	**14**
School D	2	2.5	2.5	2	2.5	2.5	**14**
School M	2.5	2	2	3	2	2.5	**14**
School E	1.5	1.5	2	3	3	2.5	**13.5**
School F	2	2	2	3	2	2.5	**13.5**
School G	2	3	2	2	1.5	1.5	**12**
School J	2	2	2	2	2	2	**12**
School K	1.5	1.5	2	3	1.5	2.5	**12**
School N	2.5	1	2	2	1	2	**10.5**
School S	2.5	1	2.5	2	1	1.5	**10.5**
School T	2	1	2	2	1.5	2	**10.5**
School R	1.5	1	2	1.5	1.5	1.5	**9**
School L	1	1.5	1.5	2	2	0.5	**8.5**
School P	1	1	1.5	2.5	1	1	**8**
School Q	1	1.5	1	2	1	1	**7.5**

Figure 3.16 User comfort (Matrix 3) scoring table – PFI schools are shaded.

Figure 3.17 Clerestory windows provide a comfortable visual environment in a primary school classroom.

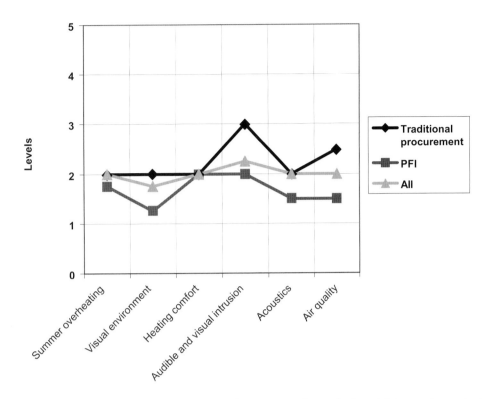

Figure 3.18 User comfort (Matrix 3) – median scores of sample (Level 3 is good practice).

Figure 3.19 South-facing computer room in a PFI secondary school provides a harsh visual environment for users.

Visual environment.   Daylight and artificial lighting sources entirely appropriate for task and promote a cheerful but non-distracting atmosphere. Full compliance with workplace regulations. Compliance with guidance in *Building Bulletin 90*.[23]

Heating comfort. Internal air temperatures within −1.5 °C to +2.0 °C of target temperature. No reason for occupant discomfort from asymmetric thermal radiation. No 'Monday morning' discomfort.

Audible and visual intrusion. No interference to work or leisure from continuous, intermittent or impulsive background noise within interior or exterior occupied spaces. No unwanted or noticeable visual intrusion.

Acoustics quality. All occupied areas free of acoustic features that act to the detriment of efficient working and enjoyment of the building. Covers reverberation time, intelligibility of speech, and music. Compliance with guidance in *Building Bulletin 93*.[24]

Air quality, internal. No noticeable odour or dust, or noticeable allergic or health symptoms from any contaminants such as micro-organisms, organic or non-organic compounds. Humidity satisfactory in all spaces. Carbon dioxide levels below 1500 parts per million.

3.10.2 Matrix 3: User comfort – commentary

Summertime overheat. Limited difference. All-median at Level 2 – summertime overheating is an occasional problem. Three PFI schools were Level 1, where summertime overheating is a frequent problem and ventilation was inadequate.

Visual environment. Limited difference. All median just below Level 2, suggesting significant departures from Level 4 standards in a few spaces.

Heating comfort. No difference. All median at Level 2, indicating occasional discomfort from uneven heating and cold Monday mornings.

Audible and visual intrusion. Significant difference between traditional procurement and PFI. Level 2 for PFIs means that occupants notice noise and visual intrusion.

Acoustics quality. All-median and traditional procurement at Level 2, indicating less than ideal acoustics, but PFI at Level 1.5 indicates that many spaces are acoustically impaired, to the extent that speech levels have to be raised and words repeated occasionally.

Air quality, internal. Traditional procurement 0.75 higher than PFI. Three PFIs at Level 1 or below suggests obvious problems, with one school complaining of potential 'sick building syndrome' in the assembly hall.

3.10.3 Matrix 3 – conclusions

The median of all schools is at Level 2, which indicates significant departures from the ideal of Level 4. The areas of summertime overheating, visual environment, acoustics, and air quality are most in need of attention – particularly in PFI schools.

3.11 PFI schools in England and Wales – Whole life costs

There has not been enough involvement in the past, and this can be a particular problem with PFI because it is such a cost-driven model.

Sharon Wright, MD of Schoolworks, 2004

3.11.1 Whole life costs (Matrix 4) – Level 4 definitions

External materials. All components selected and installed to achieve lowest cost of ownership. All have good resistance to vandalism, sun, wind, rain. Graceful degradation of appearance with wear. Detailing to best practice (Figures 3.20 to 3.23).

Internal fabric and finishes. Fabric and finishes chosen for lowest cost of ownership. Properties include ease of routine and special cleaning, graceful degradation of appearance with wear, easy repair/replacement.

SCHOOL	External materials	Internal fabric and finishes	Building services capital	Building services maintenance	Facilities management fitness	Flexibility	TOTAL
School B	3.5	3.5	2.5	2.5	3	3	18
School C	3.5	3	2	3	2.5	2.5	16.5
School E	3	3	3	2	3	2.5	16.5
School F	3.5	3	2	2	2.5	3	16
School M	3	3	2.5	2	2.5	3	16
School R	3	3	3	2.5	2.5	2	16
School D	3.5	3	2	3	2.5	1.5	15.5
School S	3.5	3	2.5	2.5	2	1	14.5
School J	2	2.5	2	2	2.5	3	14
School P	2.5	2	2.5	2.5	2.5	2	14
School H	2.5	3	2	2	2	2.5	14
School T	2.5	2.5	2	2.5	2	2	13.5
School G	2.5	2.5	2	2	2	2	13
School K	1.5	2.5	2	2.5	2.5	2	13
School N	2	2	2	2.5	2	2	12.5
School L	2.5	2	2	2	2	1.5	12
School A	1	1.5	2	2	1.5	2	10
School Q	1	0.5	1.5	2.5	0.5	3	9

Figure 3.20 Whole life costs (Matrix 4) scoring table – PFI schools are shaded.

Figure 3.21 Typical metal roof covering of a PFI school.

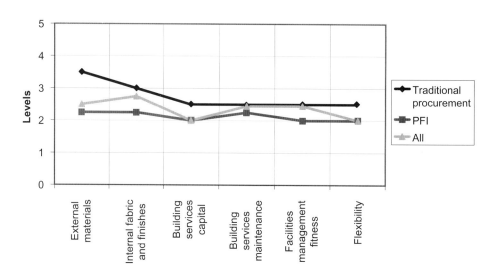

Figure 3.22 Whole life costs (Matrix 4) – median scores of sample (Level 3 is good practice).

Building services capital items. All components selected for minimum cost of ownership. Adequate space for minor and major maintenance. Design enables most service activities to be undertaken during occupation.

Building services revenue maintenance. All components selected for minimum cost of ownership. Component arrangement/availability good. Easy maintenance access. Most service activities possible during occupation.

Figure 3.23 Typical concrete tile roof of a traditionally procured school.

Facilities management: fitness for function. All architectural fittings, fitments, furniture and furnishings selected for minimum cost of ownership and support to organisational objectives. All items eminently suitable for purpose. Mean time to repair is short.

Flexibility for layout change and extension. Building plan, positioning within site, construction and materials facilitate easy future adaptation and extension without excessive cost/disturbance to occupiers.

3.11.2 Matrix 4: Whole life costs – commentary

External materials. Significant difference of 1.25 between traditional procurement and PFI, with traditional approaching Level 4. PFI schools at a median of Level 2 suggests that optimum whole life costing is not being achieved for all major external materials (two PFIs at Level 1).

Internal fabric and finishes. One point difference indicates significance. The PFI median at Level 2 indicates that not all major internal fabric and finishes are being chosen for the lowest cost of ownership (two PFIs at Level 1).

Building services capital items. Little difference. Level 2 indicates some failures to specify and properly install components with the highest appropriate efficiency.

Building services revenue maintenance. Little difference. Median Level 2 suggests Level 4 requirements satisfied for most of the important items.

Facilities management: fitness for function. Limited difference. Level 2 suggests that Level 4 requirements satisfied for most but not all important components.

Flexibility for layout change and extension. Limited difference. Level 2 suggests that Level 4 requirements satisfied for most but not all major aspects.

3.11.3 Matrix 4 – conclusions

The median of PFI schools is at Level 2, which suggests that Level 4 requirements are being satisfied for many but not all of the major components and factors.

3.12 PFI schools in England and Wales – Detail design

The devil is in the details.

Popular aphorism

3.12.1 Detail design (Matrix 5) – Level 4 definitions

External detail. Good resistance to vandalism, sun, wind, rain. Graceful degradation of appearance with wear. Detailing to best practice. Good functional and aesthetic detailing to all roofs, walls, plinths, e.g. damp-proof courses at least 150 mm from the ground (Figures 3.24 to 3.27).

SCHOOL	External detail	Internal detail	Junction detail	Furniture and furnishings	Fittings	Safety and security	TOTAL
School B	4	3.5	3.5	2.5	2.5	3	19
School C	3.5	3.5	3	3	2.5	3	18.5
School D	3.5	3	3	3	2.5	3	18
School E	3.5	2.5	3.5	2.5	2.5	2.5	17
School S	3	3	3	2	3	3	17
School T	3	3	3	2.5	2.5	3	17
School G	2.5	2.5	2.5	3	3	3	16.5
School F	3.5	2.5	3	2.5	2.5	2.5	16.5
School H	3	3	2.5	2.5	2.5	2.5	16
School M	3	2.5	2.5	2.5	2.5	2.5	15.5
School A	2	2.5	2.5	2.5	2.5	2.5	14.5
School R	2.5	2	2.5	2	2.5	3	14.5
School K	1.5	2.5	1	3	2.5	3	13.5
School L	2	2	1.5	3	2	3	13.5
School J	2	2.5	1	2.5	2	3	13
School P	2	2	2	2	2	3	13
School N	1.5	2	1.5	2	2	3	12
School Q	1	1	0.5	2	2	3	9.5

Figure 3.24 Detail design (Matrix 5) scoring table – PFI schools are shaded.

Figure 3.25 Traditional materials and detailing of a traditionally procured school. This figure is also reproduced in colour in the colour plate section.

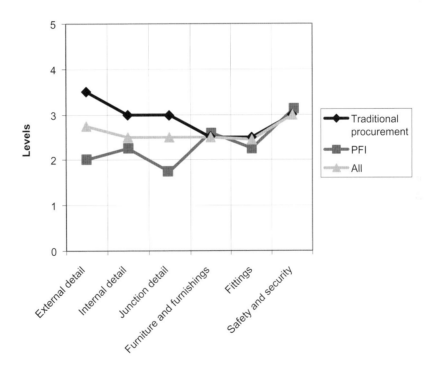

Figure 3.26 Detail design (Matrix 5) – median scores of sample (Level 3 is good practice).

Internal detail. Ease of routine and special cleaning, graceful degradation of appearance with wear, easy repair/replacement. Good functional and aesthetic detailing to all floors, walls, ceilings, e.g. shadow gaps to suspended ceilings.

Junction details. Architectural junctions of different materials, such as roof/wall abutments, detailed to good practice with good workmanship.

Figure 3.27 Lightweight materials and acoustically 'hard' surfaces in the restaurant of a PFI school.

Good functional and aesthetic detailing to all door and window openings and thresholds, e.g. crafted flashings rather than mastic excretions.

Furnishings. All furnishings selected for ability to retain good appearance and for minimum cost of ownership. All seating comfortable for expected occupancy – anthropomorphically suitable to BS 5873. Correctly sized, robust and solid.

Fittings. All architectural fittings eminently suitable for purpose. Anthropomorphically suitable to BS 5873. Correctly sized, robust and solid. Suitable provision for disabled persons' use/access.

Safety and security. Detailed architectural disposition to good practice and avoiding potential hazards. External and internal hazards controlled by design, such as minimum entrances, which are capable of observation and/or CCTV and/or fencing.

3.12.2 Matrix 5: Detail design – commentary

External detail. Significant difference. PFI median at Level 2 indicates that not all major external components are being detailed satisfactorily.

Internal detail. Difference is of limited significance.

Junction details. Significant difference. PFI median at Level 1 suggests a few obvious failures.

Furnishings.   No difference.

Fittings.   Little difference.

Safety and security.   No difference. All schools have implemented robust security strategies involving fencing or CCTV, or both. Minimum, effectively controlled entrances. Some minor safety hazards, such as ground floor, perimeter, opening windows without sufficient detail of plinth obstruction to reduce risk.

3.12.3 Matrix 5 – conclusions

Detailed design problems mainly prevalent in PFI schools. Security appears to have been adequately addressed across the board.

3.13 PFI schools in England and Wales – Conclusions

3.13.1 General

- Overall design quality has significant room for improvement.
- PFI schools are of lower design quality, in general.
- Cost of ownership appears higher in PFI schools.
- Schools that sought to be informed clients achieved better buildings.
- Poor internal environments were widespread and are likely to impact on educational achievement.
- There has been a major loss of schools design experience since 1985.
- Solutions to some of the problems will have cost implications.
- Major shortfalls from Local Agenda 21 objectives were identified.
- Major opportunities exist to improve energy efficiency.

3.13.2 Top ten problems

- Banal and mundane architecture – mainly PFI.
- Poor specification – lack of attention to detail.
- Lack of environmental sustainability.
- Little integration of environmental services with architecture – PFI.
- Poor acoustics, ventilation, and visual environments.
- Lack of flexibility for change and extension.
- Poor detailing, particularly at junctions – PFI.
- Circulation space often at a premium.
- Inadequate car parking for staff.
- Lack of storage for pupils' clothes and bags, and for school materials.

3.13.3 Top ten successes

- Good architecture – mainly traditional procurement approaches.
- Good site planning.
- Good space planning.
- Good sourcing of standard components.
- Good furniture specification, especially for younger pupils.
- Good security during school hours.
- Notable reduction of vandalism.
- A few examples of good daylighting strategies.
- Good acoustics existed in a few isolated instances.
- Good examples of detail design – mainly traditional approaches.

3.14 PFI schools in England and Wales – Recommendations

An informed client is needed to ensure design quality. This client representative, or in-house project executive, can come from the LEA or school staff, or both, and must have knowledge of good practice in all areas that relate to school management and pupil productivity. The best examples from the present sample had invariably benefited from a sophisticated client, for the LEA (e.g. Hampshire schools) or the school's staff. Independent advice for clients is recommended by the recent Egan review of the construction industry* and, in fact, most reviews of the industry since the 1960s.[†]

Informed client training. Changing naïve clients into sophisticated ones requires training courses and visits to learn from excellent existing buildings.

Informed client funding. Additional funding is required to enable members of staff to become sophisticated clients. This will include training costs and necessitates release time from school duties for up to 2 years (6 months for small schools; 18 months for larger schools).

Improve space standards and/or budgets. Perhaps unsurprisingly, most head teachers complained of insufficient and out-of-date space standards and budgets. In many cases this has led to the sacrifice of adequate circulation space (particularly in entrance halls and corridors) to make classrooms larger, and even to extensions being sought for relatively new schools.

---

*'The need for independent, expert advice for clients has been identified as being vital to providing wider solutions to clients' needs'. Sir John Egan, *Rethinking construction: accelerating change*, p. 12, 2002.
[†]G. Higgin and N. Jessop, *Communications in the building industry*, 1965. And successive NEDO reports throughout the 1970s and 1980s, such as *Before you build* (1974) through to *Faster building for commerce* (1988).

Design appraisal tools.* In order to aid the in-house project executive there should be a set of publicly available design appraisal tools that will help schools assess the extent of best practice in the designs they are being asked to consider.

Ofsted inspections of design. A simple 'building quality' assessment could be included in periodic Ofsted inspections. These results could be collated nationally and related to premises' costs and educational performance.

Improve daylight design. Despite some skilful and effective daylighting strategies in the present sample, artificial lighting was defaulted to in every school visited – all the electric lights were on! In many cases this was necessary due to the great variability of light levels across the classroom. But in some cases there was adequate and consistent daylight available (e.g. 300 lux), due to skilful disposition of devices such as clerestory northlights, but all of the lights were on.[†] Recent research into the daylighting of schools in America has shown that educational progress was significantly increased (up to 25 per cent faster progress) with improved daylighting.[‡] But the quality and consistency of the daylight is more important than crudely increasing window areas and setting simplistic standards (e.g. 2 per cent daylight factor throughout the classroom).[§]

Improve acoustic design. Poor acoustic environments were ubiquitous across the sample, and very often caused by less than ideal space planning

---

*For example, the School Works Tool Kit developed by the CITB (Construction Industry Training Board) and others, published in 2001. A practical handbook to initiate and develop the project briefing process, suitable for any procurement route. Free to schools from School Works Ltd.

[†]Ironically, research at the Building Research Station, decades ago, showed that visual performance in classrooms could be improved through other means, such as contrast, rather than simply raising lighting levels – sometimes by a factor as great as 30! Quality of daylight is generally more important than quantity to produce visual comfort among building users. R. G. Hopkinson and J. D. Kay, The lighting of buildings, pp. 170–73, 1972.

[‡]The study just looked at daylight and controlled all other influences. Changes in student test scores were monitored over a full year at the Capistrano school district in California. Similar studies in Seattle and elsewhere, based on year-end scores only, showed that 'students in classrooms with the most daylight were found to have 7–18 per cent higher scores than those in rooms with the least'. Heschong Mahone Group, Daylighting and productivity study: daylighting in schools, USA, August 1999. Cited in Michael Benedikt, Environmental stoicism and place machismo, Harvard Design Magazine, Harvard University Graduate School of Design, pp. 21–27, Winter/Spring 2002.

[§]The crudest rule-of-thumb for side lighting is to multiply the minimum daylight factor by 10, and to take the result as a measure of the amount of glazing required in terms of percentage of floor area. To provide a 2 per cent daylight factor for a 50 square metre classroom would require one external wall (say 7 m × 2.4 m) to be at least 60 per cent glazed. Classroom walls were often almost fully glazed in the 1960s and 1970s in pursuit of 2 per cent daylight factors throughout the room – with attendant overheating in summer and cold down-draughts in winter, and their implications for educational efficiency. R. G. Hopkinson and J. D. Kay, The lighting of buildings, p. 108, 1972.

(e.g. kitchens adjacent to libraries or halls). But more often than not caused by the absence of ceiling finishes in PFI projects (this practice results in external noise disturbance from rain and hail disrupting lessons, as well as poor internal acoustics) – many of these were already retrofitted with acoustic ceiling tiles at the school's expense. Retrofitting halls with soft furnishings to dampen 'lively acoustics' was commonplace across the sample. Well-documented, good design practice was flaunted, presumably for reasons of false economy.*

Building use manuals. For occupiers. Despite the best of design intentions, buildings are rarely used exactly as envisaged. Producing guidance as to the intended use of schools' spaces would also focus designers' minds on end-users, and help to enhance the design development process. Building use manuals could also form part of the design appraisal process and highlight potential problems.

Prescriptive detailed specifications. Many schools were failed by performance specifications, which were not followed through into detail design and ideal functionality. Detailed, and often prescriptive specifications may be necessary to improve design performance – tested by informed clients at successive design stages, and empirically challenged before practical completion certificates are signed (e.g. daylight levels and acoustics).

3.15 PFI schools in England and Wales – Summary

The Audit Commission wished to ascertain the design quality of new schools procured by PFI routes. They selected a sample of 18 schools, built in the past few years, from Local Authorities across England and Wales. The sample contained a balance of primary and secondary PFI schools; traditionally procured schools were included as a control group. A small BRE team visited each school and conducted a visual survey, non-intrusive to the building fabric, focusing on the following key elements and components:

- Roof.
- Walls.
- Cladding.
- Windows.
- Doors.
- Toilets.
- Finishes.
- Building services.

---

* 'To avoid the spread of noise through the school all corridors and circulation spaces should have highly sound-absorbing ceilings, as should dining-rooms and rooms rated as high-level noise sources'. P. H. Parkin and H. R. Humphreys, *Acoustics, noise and buildings*, p. 197, 1969.

BRE also conducted informal interviews with head teachers, teachers, and maintenance staff. A series of five matrices were used to score the schools. The matrices contain several sub-factors and scoring levels are objectively set for completion by construction or property professionals. They cover the following main areas:

- **Architectural design quality**. This covers the relatively subjective area of aesthetic merit, and also the more prosaic qualities of specification, site and space planning.
- **Building services design quality**. A more objective area and supported by scientifically measurable lighting, noise and temperature levels. Sympathetic integration with architecture is crucial, not to mention maintainability and replacement sourcing.
- **User productivity indicators**. Internal comfort conditions are also scientifically measurable and links between them and productivity are increasingly empirically evident. Integrating art and science creates ideal environments, e.g. the quality of daylight is just as important as the measurable quantity. Optimum environments are critical to successful school design and often reflected in the enhanced educational performance of pupils.*
- **Building cost of ownership**. This covers the occupancy costs of schools and the potential whole-life performance of building fabric and services. It provides an analysis of the trade-offs between capital and running costs that affect future building performance.
- **Detail design**. Failures in building performance are often caused by poor detailed design or bad workmanship. Rectifying and coping with such failures will increase maintenance and occupancy costs.

The BRE team encountered variable design quality throughout the sample. There was design inconsistency across the board, with single schools containing examples of good and bad design practice. All schools visited left significant room for design improvements, particularly at a detailed level, but PFI schools were generally of a lower design quality than traditionally procured ones. The latter seemed to benefit from the prescriptive nature of a conventional route. The PFI schools' mean score for the five main categories was below that of traditionally procured schools, and significantly less in the areas of architectural design quality, cost of ownership, and detail design. However, the areas of building service design quality and user productivity indicators showed little difference between PFI and traditionally procured schools.

Trends emerged regarding the materials used for different procurement routes, with PFI schools generally using metal roofs and cladding systems. Traditionally procured schools tended to favour traditional materials such

---

*Heschong Mahone Group, *Daylighting and productivity study: daylighting in schools*, USA, August 1999. Cited in Michael Benedikt, Environmental stoicism and place machismo, *Harvard Design Magazine*, Harvard University Graduate School of Design, pp. 21–27, Winter/Spring 2002.

as facing brickwork and concrete roofing tiles. Aluminium window and doorframe systems were ubiquitous throughout the sample. The only 'lightweight' framed building was a PFI school.* There was, in general, a sparsity of finishes throughout the PFI schools, extending to the complete omission of ceiling finishes. Apart from the utilitarian aesthetic this gave to most PFI schools, potential acoustic and lighting problems accruing from this policy were scientifically measured. These choices of materials, or lack of them, may go some way to explain the perceived differences in costs of ownership between PFI and traditionally procured schools. However, there was also variety in the specification of some traditional schools, which gave rise to doubts over their ideal functionality. Despite some successful attempts to provide uniform daylight throughout classrooms, and indeed other areas, no school was visited which did not have the vast majority of its artificial lighting switched on.

Recent industry standards suggest that about 1.5 to 4 per cent of the capital cost of a school should be spent on annual maintenance costs, averaged over the first two decades of the building's life.[†] This includes decoration, fabric and services maintenance, cleaning, utilities, and administrative costs. Our review suggests that many of the PFI schools would need maintenance budgets towards the top of the recommended range, and this may have implications for the residual value of the building at the end of the concession period.

Ranked tables were produced from the five scored matrices, which show that PFI schools tend to rank lower than traditional schools. However, there are sub-areas of success and failure in both traditional and PFI schools, which are shown by the median scores plotted in the resultant graphs. The following five matrices were scored within defined levels of significance:

- **Architectural design quality**. External and internal architectural merit was generally superior in traditionally procured schools. Specification quality, sustainability, and site and space planning were similar in both procurement routes.
- **Building services design quality**. There was little difference between procurement routes, but the crucial area of architectural integration was considered better in traditionally procured schools.
- **User productivity indicators**. Similar, but audible and visual intrusion, acoustics and air quality were generally inferior in PFI schools.

---

*While there is no reason why a lightweight school building cannot perform well with appropriate heating and maintenance strategies etc., it is likely to need a higher maintenance budget than a more structurally robust building. It may also be more susceptible to vandalism, particularly in a secondary school.
[†]Various BMI (Building Maintenance Information) and SCALA (Society of Chief Architects of Local Authorities) sources. This range represents estimated typical LA approved expenditure to recommended expenditure. It varies according to the type of school, i.e. nursery; primary; secondary; special school, and may well be considerably above this range in the advent of major defects.

- **Building cost of ownership**. Similar, but exterior materials and internal fabric and finishes with lower costs of ownership were generally chosen for traditionally procured schools.
- **Detail design**. Areas of external, internal and junction details were superior in traditionally procured schools.

This evidence tends to suggest that the promised DBO (design, build and operate) synergies are not being achieved in PFI school designs.* While it was assumed that all schools were constructed close to DfES budgetary and space standards, better examples occurred where the 'right people' were assembled into design teams, including a full-time in-house client representative. Such informed clients, or independent advisors, are able to interrogate design proposals in a sophisticated manner and obtain higher standards of design quality. Good practice methods such as those listed below need to be extended to the design and refurbishment of all schools, whatever the procurement route:

- **Informed client or independent advisor to ensure design quality**. This client representative, or in-house project executive, can come from the LEA or school staff, or both, and must have knowledge of good practice in all areas that relate to school management and pupil productivity.
- **Improved space standards and budgets**. Guidance in BB82 was being updated at the time of the surveys. The then current DfES proviso that 60 per cent of the area has to be teaching space caused circulation and ancillary spaces to be tight or skimped. Increased capital budgets were felt by teachers to be the answer to space problems and materials choices for optimum whole-life costing.
- **Design appraisal tool to monitor quality from the briefing stage onwards**. This could take the form of a checklist with which to interrogate design proposals at successive stages. This will become increasingly necessary as the government's proposals for PFI expenditure threaten to outstrip competent supply in the construction industry.
- **Prescriptive specifications in areas such as daylighting and acoustics**. Daylighting prescriptions will have to be subtle to capture the quality of light needed rather than producing quantity alone. Acoustics may be as simple as 'To avoid the spread of noise through the school all corridors and circulation spaces should have highly sound-absorbing ceilings, as should dining-rooms and rooms rated as high-level noise sources'.
- **Building use manuals for occupiers to complete the loop of design intentions**. Even with the very best of design intentions,

---

*The concept of continuity from design through to building and operation is much vaunted for PFI schemes. Letting tranches of schools for development and subsequent long-term operation contracts should create economies of scale.

buildings are rarely used exactly as envisaged. Producing guidance as to the intended use of schools' spaces would also focus designers' minds on end-users, and help to enhance the design development process. Building use manuals could also form part of the design appraisal process and highlight potential problems. For example, guidance to close blinds in the afternoon to west-facing, high-level windows to classrooms suggests the need for vertical blinds, or a different orientation for the building.

3.16 PFI schools in Northern Ireland – Introduction

The Northern Ireland Audit Office (NIAO) wished to review the use of the Private Finance Initiative (PFI) to provide educational facilities. They wished to engage technical support to analyse the design and construction of PFI facilities compared with traditionally procured schools and colleges. This study of 14 post-primary schools and four colleges of higher and further education, procured by both routes, is part of a wider investigation into the design quality of PFI projects in Northern Ireland.* An assessment of the overall design quality of new facilities should establish whether:

- *Construction materials and components used for PFI schools are significantly different to those used for traditionally financed schools, due to life-cycle considerations for key components?*
- General trends revealed that PFI schools used metal sheet roofs. Traditionally procured schools tended to favour traditional materials such as facing brickwork and concrete roofing tiles – but there was a notable exception in the further and higher education sector. Aluminium window and doorframe systems were ubiquitous throughout the sample. The generally poor detailed design on PFI schools will probably impact upon expected life-cycles of key components.
- *Whole life costs for PFI schemes are adequate in the context of the workmanship and materials used in initial construction?*
- Observations from the sample of 18 facilities visited suggests that the PFI schools, and particularly FHE colleges, would need larger maintenance budgets. PFI schools were generally of a lower design quality than traditionally procured ones. The latter seemed to benefit from the prescriptive nature of a conventional route as well as the tried and tested detailing of traditional materials. We noted the 'diocesan architect' effect, first observed in Church of England schools in England and Wales, to a more marked degree in Northern Ireland – perhaps unsurprisingly. Such architects are generally trusted confidantes, with a lengthy relationship with the school, displaying high degrees of professionalism and attention to detail for their clients – in anticipation of a continued

---

*NIAO (2004) *Building for the future: A review of the PFI education pathfinder projects.*

relationship. Good design quality, including innovation and flexibility, invariably ensues. This is often augmented by additional funding from church sources to provide both additional facilities, and possibly a higher than normal specification. Site inspections from such an ideal adviser could also result in better workmanship. The PFI schools scored significantly lower in the often crucial areas of architectural design and detail design. However, the areas of building service design quality, user productivity, and user productivity indicators showed little difference between PFI and traditionally procured schools in general.

- *Decisions relating to whole life costs have considered the period beyond the PFI contract period?*
- These decisions varied considerably across the sample, but the use of traditional materials with conventional detailing tends to ensure a higher quality of detailed design, which in turn helps to ensure longer life for components and materials. Residual value and ultimate life of the schools and colleges will depend on adequate maintenance, repair and replacement of key components. The conundrum of higher maintenance costs as a percentage of a lower capital costs could ultimately compare well to higher capital costs with possible resultant lower maintenance costs. In the case of the PFI schools the respective consortiums will presumably eventually foot the bill, at least for the concession period.
- *PFI schools provide material design, build and operate (DBO) synergies beyond the PFI contract period?*
- The evidence tends to suggest that the promised DBO synergies are not being achieved in PFI school and FHE college designs in Northern Ireland, as in England and Wales. In Northern Ireland only six PFI 'pathfinder' projects are completed (four post-primary schools and two FHE colleges). These were usually new buildings on new sites, where this procurement route may have more chance of success. The often complex and constrained school sites, involving a combination of refurbishment and extension were invariably traditionally procured. If this is by chance, it is fortunate that an appropriate traditional route was employed to cope with the complexity of site and phased construction, if by design, exemplary judgement was exercised to identify the potential pathfinder PFI sites. An appropriate procurement route for the circumstances is far more important to achieve success in construction projects, than the current dogma of particular trends.

The NIAO needed to assess the overall design quality of new schools and FHE colleges, comparing any differences between procurement routes in the following key areas:

- Quality of materials used for key building components.
- Energy efficiency.
- Disabled access.
- Compliance with other legislation, such as building and fire regulations.

3.17 PFI schools in Northern Ireland – Description of the project

The main means to achieve the objectives set out in the project brief centred on visual surveys of the sample of 14 post-primary schools and four colleges of higher and further education, by a small team of expert consulting architects and engineers. The surveys were non-intrusive to the building fabric, but included roof and plant room inspections. All principal spaces and typical classrooms were examined. Scientific instrumentation was used to measure light, sound, temperature, and air quality (carbon dioxide levels). In all cases the education facilities' principals and/or their deputies were informally interviewed.

These initial interviews were structured by six questions which asked the principals to rank aspects of the building in terms of their satisfaction, on a scale of one to five (five representing maximum satisfaction). The six questions were a pilot study for developing a 'sixth matrix' to add a user satisfaction dimension to the BRE Design Quality Matrix (DQM). Although the questions proved very useful in structuring the interviews, the building's architects and other consultants were often present; probably causing principals to give a more generous score than they may have done otherwise. A self-completion matrix will be developed for future studies to eliminate this bias.

The sample of 18 facilities was selected by the NIAO, to represent new educational facilities in Northern Ireland. The sample contains the six 'pathfinder' PFI projects completed in Northern Ireland at that time, and major traditionally procured post-primary schools completed in the same period. The sample comprised:

- 14 post-primary schools and 4 colleges of FHE.
- 10 traditional and 4 PFI post-primary schools, and 2 traditional and 2 PFI colleges of FHE.
- 10 educational facilities in or around Belfast; 4 in Londonderry; and 4 in other areas of Northern Ireland.
- The six 'pathfinder' PFI projects completed in Northern Ireland.
- Some of the traditionally procured facilities were extensions to existing buildings, but the study concerned only the new-build elements. Refurbishment was not included.
- The size of post-primary schools ranges from 500 to 1000 pupils. One post-primary school accommodated only half of its potential capacity – 300 pupils rather than 600.
- The size of colleges of FHE averages a few thousand full-time equivalent students.

3.18 PFI schools in Northern Ireland – Design Quality Matrices

BRE's team used a set of five matrices, which were used in the similar study in England and Wales for the Audit Commission, to score individual facilities on all aspects of design quality. An additional sixth matrix, covering user satisfaction, was also used in Northern Ireland. The matrices were:

- Architectural design.
- Environmental services design.
- User productivity indicators.
- Building cost of ownership.
- Detail design.
- User satisfaction (pilot version).

The design quality matrices are suitable for completion by professional experts with relevant experience, and can be adapted for any building type. They can be robust and powerful tools in the hands of experts. Although the matrix scoring levels are set objectively using published standards, such as British Standards and consensual good practice, there is obviously an element of inherent subjectivity in this system.* Extreme views are ameliorated by group consensus, even among a small group of expert construction professionals. The results must be viewed as the expert opinion of a few consulting architects and engineers – for this reason we have defined levels of significance for the results.

The sample of facilities was selected by the NIAO, and they understand that it fully represents the population of new educational facilities in Northern Ireland. The sample contains the six 'pathfinder' PFI projects completed in Northern Ireland to date, and all major traditionally procured post-primary schools completed in the same period. However, the limitations of the visual and surface nature of the surveys should be borne in mind. The visual surveys were as thorough as time allowed and included roof and plant room inspections, where possible. One particular plant room, adjacent to the sports hall, appeared to have a large over-specification of mechanical ventilation equipment contained within an over-sized plant room. The surveys were non-intrusive and did not include reference to any further project-specific documentation, apart from a few instances where detailed architectural drawings were available. The informal interviews with principals and staff were often revealing. But they must also be treated with caution as anecdotal evidence subject to personal bias. Despite that, they contributed to the research and helped to shape our conclusions. We saw the physical evidence of successful strategies, such as supplementing budgets with church funds to provide additional facilities (e.g. a sports hall at school five), and unfortunately also saw the results of less successful approaches (e.g. inadequate sound insulation).

BRE's set of five matrices measures all aspects of the design quality of schools, from the architectural strategy of site planning through to the detailed design of junctions of different materials. Each matrix has six sub-factors in columns and scoring levels in rows. The matrices were developed by objectively establishing a fully competent level of performance at the top level of Level 4. Although it is theoretically possible to register a score of 5, this would be an exceptional example of the very best practice. This ideal score was recorded in one instance, for a sub-factor, in the present

---

*The basis of the definitions is always linked at the highest level (Level 4) to widely accepted definitions of competence acceptable to appropriately skilled professionals and artisans. Level 3 is considered a minimum acceptable standard.

study. There was a handful of scores at Level 4. Once a top level is established it is a simple matter to cascade lower levels of performance, descending to Level 0. Each descending step in performance usually implies a failure to achieve best practice in at least one significant area, or several minor shortcomings. A set of matrices was completed for each school, which highlight problems and successes. Matrix averages (medians) revealed quality trends between procurement routes – comparative differences in the median matrices are probably more revealing than 'league tables' of ranked schools for each factor.

Due to the uncertainties in the matrix scoring process, median results of less than one level apart in small sample groups of matrices should be given limited significance.

3.19 PFI schools in Northern Ireland – Overall summary matrix

Matrix 0 – Summary

The overall summary matrix collects the results of the five matrices below: architecture; environmental engineering; user comfort; whole life costing; and detail design. The summary matrix shows any major trends and any major differences between design quality achieved between building procurement routes (Figures 3.28 and 3.29).

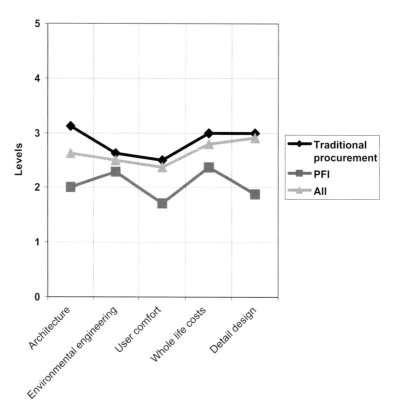

Figure 3.28 Overall summary matrix (NI) – median scores of all five matrices (Level 3 is good practice).

Figure 3.29 Traditionally procured school, which houses a flexible atrium space.

Matrix 1 – Quality of architectural design

Probably the most subjective matrix in the areas of internal and external architectural merit, but more robust in areas such as site and space planning. The historic terms of firmness, commodity and delight are used to convey the concepts of structural integrity, functionality and uplifting of the spirits. Views of building users were considered, particularly for the often intangible and ephemeral areas of 'spiritual uplift'!

Matrix 2 – Quality of services design

Far more objective in nature, and scientifically measurable (e.g. lighting levels in lux and noise levels in dBA). The integration of services and architectural fabric can be symbolically evident in conceits such as housing boiler flues in architectural-feature chimneys. Maintainability and sourcing of replacement components are critical to continuous quality. Environmental sustainability is necessary for LAs to achieve Local Agenda 21 objectives.

Matrix 3 – User productivity indicators

Comfort conditions are scientifically measurable (e.g. lux, dBA and ambient and radiant temperature) and links between such conditions and user productivity are increasingly empirically evident – excessive noise, sunlight and poor ventilation degrade internal environments. However, ideal environments are more subtlety created by the integration of art and science rather than crudely engineered by actions such as increasing lighting levels. Psychological aspects also play a crucial part in individual comfort and productivity.

Matrix 4 – Building cost of ownership

This matrix concentrates on the potential whole life performance of the building's fabric and environmental services also considering ease of facilities management and the adaptability of the building for future alteration or extension. This matrix helps to expose the trade-offs between capital and running costs, which affect future performance.

Matrix 5 – Detail design

Anomalies in building performance are often caused by errors or inconsistencies in detailing, such as architectural junctions of different materials at abutments or incorrectly sized components, furnishings and fittings. The former can lead to leaks or even flooding, while the latter often causes loss of functionality or even serious accidents. Such failures can often be attributed to poor detailed design or bad workmanship – or a combination of both.

Matrix 6 – User satisfaction (pilot matrix)

Initial interviews with principals and directors of educational facilities were structured with six questions which they were asked to rank in terms of their satisfaction, on a scale of one to five (five representing maximum satisfaction). The six questions were a pilot study for developing a 'sixth matrix' to add a user satisfaction dimension to the BRE design quality matrix (DQM). A self-completion matrix will be developed for future studies to eliminate any confidentiality bias.

3.19.1 Summary matrix – commentary

Matrix 1 – Quality of architectural design

There is one point between the traditionally procured and PFI schools, indicating a significant difference in architectural quality. The possibility of achieving such quality appears enhanced in the traditionally procured schools – confirmed by the all-median scores close to Level 3. Architectural quality is often a precursor to subsequent indicators. The Northern Ireland sample was similar to that of the England and Wales study.

Matrix 2 – Quality of services design

There is only a difference of 0.5 between traditional procurement and PFI, which cannot be viewed as significant due to the variability of the matrix scoring process. Services were ostensibly similar in the two procurement routes and with departures from good practice across the entire sample. The Northern Ireland sample was marginally better than that of England and Wales.

Matrix 3 – User productivity indicators

There is only a difference of 0.5 between traditional procurement and PFI, which cannot be viewed as significant. However, the median score for all schools is comparatively low suggesting that there is significant opportunity for improvement. The Northern Ireland sample was similar to that of England and Wales.

Matrix 4 – Building cost of ownership

There is a difference of just over half-a-level between traditional procurement and PFI which, although of limited significance, suggests that capital costs are driving PFI designs more than traditional solutions. The Northern Ireland sample was slightly better than that of England and Wales.

Matrix 5 – Detail design

The difference of one level between traditional procurement and PFI, and the comparatively reasonable score of the traditional schools, suggests that PFI solutions, in general, are not receiving as much attention to detail as traditional ones. The Northern Ireland sample was similar to that of England and Wales.

Matrix 6 – User satisfaction

Suggests that users are slightly more satisfied with traditionally procured facilities, subject to the fact that the interviews were not in confidence, the building's consultants were often present.

3.19.2 Summary matrix – conclusions

A matrix analysis can highlight potential problems and prioritise them. The areas of service design and user productivity appear to need improvement to achieve a level line score. But they are also inextricably linked to architectural design and detailed design. The Northern Ireland sample, overall, was of a similar design quality to that of the England and Wales sample, apart from the quality of services and cost of ownership, which appear slightly better in Northern Ireland.

3.20 PFI schools in Northern Ireland – Architecture

3.20.1 Architecture (Matrix 1) – Level 4 definitions

Architectural exterior. Design has obvious firmness, commodity and delight. No features that are obvious architectural excesses. Users like and respect the building. Excellent materials selection and placement. Adequate shelter from rain and sun (Figures 3.30 to 3.33).

Site planning. Functional separation/integration optimises use of site. Good solar orientation. Good vehicle access/parking/pedestrian access. Parking level. Adequate playing ground(s) and field. Adequate space for future building extension.

Interior design. Design has obvious beauty and clarity of purpose. Internal aspects of good scale and respect user's size. Daylight quality and acoustics excellent. Excellent use of colour, finishes and furniture. Interior allows furniture layout flexibility.

SCHOOL	Architectural exterior	Site planning	Interior design	Space planning	Specification	Sustainability	TOTAL
School EE	4	4.5	4.5	5	4	2.5	**24.5**
School RR	4	3.5	4	4	3.5	3.5	**22.5**
School FF	3	3.5	3.5	3	3	3.5	**19.5**
School JJ	3	3.5	3.5	3.5	3	3	**19.5**
School AA	3	3	4	3.5	3	2.5	**19**
School NN	3	4	3	4	3	2	**19**
School LL	3.5	3	3	3	3.5	2.5	**18.5**
School DD	2.5	3	2.5	3	3	2.5	**16.5**
School KK	2.5	2.5	2.5	3	3	2.5	**16**
School TT	2.5	3	2.5	2.5	3	2	**15.5**
School MM	2.5	3	2.5	3	2	2	**15**
School GG	2	3	2	2.5	3	2	**14.5**
School BB	3	2.5	2.5	2.5	2	2	**14.5**
School HH	2	2.5	2	2.5	1.5	1.5	**12**
School QQ	1.5	2.5	2	2.5	1.5	2	**12**
School CC	1.5	2	2	2.5	1.5	2	**11.5**
School SS	1.5	2	2	2.5	1.5	1.5	**11**
School PP	1	3	1	2	2	1.5	**10.5**

Figure 3.30 Architecture (Matrix 1 NI) scoring table – PFI schools are shaded.

Figure 3.31 Flexible atrium, which converts into a dining hall for lunch-hour in a traditionally procured school.

Space planning. Excellent utilisation of space, meeting business need with good juxtaposition of key spaces. Support spaces, storage and circulation all adequate. No congested areas at any time. Good social space.

Specification. Component selection and placement obviously very carefully considered with adequate input from experienced users and maintenance staff. Good provision for maintenance. No obvious potential design defects at materials' junctions.

Sustainability. Environmental impact minimised by proper consideration of environmental, economic and social factors. Heating and lighting systems and components robust, reliable and competently optimised.

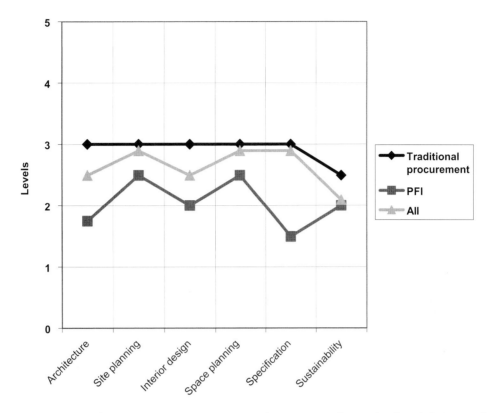

Figure 3.32 Architecture (Matrix 1 NI) – median scores of sample (Level 3 is good practice).

Figure 3.33 Lift shaft colloquially known as 'the lipstick' in a traditionally procured school. This figure is also reproduced in colour in the colour plate section.

3.20.2 Matrix 1: Architecture – commentary

Architectural exterior. There is a difference of 1.25, combined with the all-mean score nearer to the traditional mean, suggesting a far more consistent quality is being achieved under traditional procurement. The PFI score suggests that this route is resulting in mundane architecture with significant potential maintenance difficulties.

Site planning. There is a difference of 0.5 between the traditionally procured and PFI facilities, and the all-median score is at the same level as traditional procurement. The Northern Ireland sample is slightly below the overall median of the England and Wales sample (all-median), possibly because there were more constrained sites in Northern Ireland.

Interior design. Difference of one level between traditional procurement and PFI, which is again significant. Such architectural failures affect the fitness for purpose of interior spaces. The all-median is at the same level as the England and Wales all-median.

Space planning. There is a limited difference between traditional procurement and PFI, suggesting that space planning, on average, is only suffering from minor failures.

Specification. There is a difference of 1.5 between traditional procurement and PFI, and the all-median is at the same level as the traditional. This suggests a worrying amount of specification failure in PFI. The all-median is slightly better than in the England and Wales sample.

Sustainability. Limited difference, but overall sustainability failures.

3.20.3 Matrix 1 – conclusions

The real purpose and value of a matrix analysis is to highlight potential problems and to prioritise them for attention. The areas of specification and sustainability are most in need of attention. PFI falls significantly short of the traditionally procured on architectural quality.

3.21 PFI schools in Northern Ireland – Environmental engineering

3.21.1 Environmental engineering (Matrix 2) – Level 4 definitions

Integration. Services design sympathetic to and optimises all aspects of the architecture. Well-informed consideration of thermal and lighting issues. No intrusion of services into occupied space. No compromise on user access to windows (Figures 3.34 to 3.37).

SCHOOL	Integration	Mechanical systems	Electrical systems	Maintainability	Sourcing	Sustainability	TOTAL
School RR	3	2.5	3	3.5	4	2.5	18.5
School TT	2.5	3	3.5	3.5	3.5	2	18
School EE	3	3	3	3	3	3	18
School JJ	3	3	3	3	3	3	18
School LL	3	2.5	3	3	3.5	2.5	17.5
School GG	2.5	2.5	3	3	3	2.5	16.5
School DD	2.5	2.5	3	3	3	2.5	16.5
School KK	2.5	2.5	2.5	3	3	2.5	16
School FF	3	2.5	3	2.5	2.5	2	15.5
School AA	2.5	2.5	2.5	3	3	2	15.5
School NN	2.5	2.5	2.5	2.5	3	2.5	15.5
School BB	2	2.5	3	2.5	3	2.5	15.5
School MM	2	2	2.5	3	3	2	14.5
School PP	2	2.5	2.5	2.5	3	2	14.5
School SS	2	2	2.5	2.5	3	2	14
School CC	1.5	2	2.5	2.5	3	2	13.5
School HH	2	2	2.5	2	3	2	13.5
School QQ	1.5	2	2.5	2.5	3	2	13.5

Figure 3.34 Environmental engineering (Matrix 2 NI) scoring table – PFI schools are shaded.

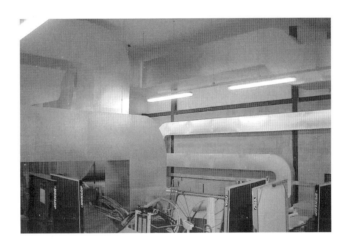

Figure 3.35 Oversized plant room in a traditionally procured school.

Mechanical systems design. Robust good practice utilising the most appropriate components integrated into efficient reliable systems. Covers heating, ventilation, cooling and plumbing. Nil acoustic intrusion from services into the use of the building.

Electrical systems design. Robust good practice utilising the most appropriate components integrated into efficient reliable system(s). Covers internal and external lighting, communications. Cables, conduits and ducts not intrusive. Well selected components.

Maintainability. Maintenance facilities and access designed to minimise loss of beneficial use, minimise time to clean and repair, and avoid the need

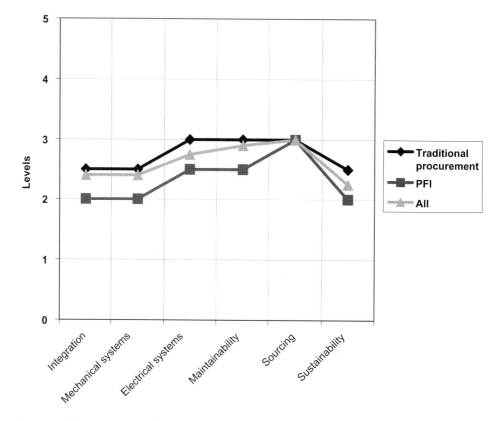

Figure 3.36 Environmental engineering (Matrix 2 NI) – median scores of sample (Level 3 is good practice).

Figure 3.37 Poor electrical specification in a PFI school.

for specialised access for revenue replacement. All components and service data widely available.

Sourcing.   All capital and revenue repairable/replaceable items selected for wide availability and compliance with well-known standards. Design has avoided use of specially manufactured items that could incur long lead times/high replacement costs.

Sustainability. Services components, system arrangement and controls selected and commissioned to minimise environmental impact. Comprehensive and easily useable data available for maintenance. Minimal use of materials deleterious to the environment.

3.21.2 Matrix 2: Environmental engineering – commentary

Integration. Difference of only 0.5, and the median of all schools score is at the upper level – the same as the all-median of the England and Wales sample. Building services integration with architecture in Northern Ireland is similar to England and Wales.

Mechanical. Difference between traditional procurement and PFI is only 0.5, and the median of all schools is at the upper level. This aspect is significantly better in Northern Ireland than England and Wales.

Electrical. Difference is again of limited significance, but better than England and Wales.

Maintainability. Limited difference, but the median of all schools is significantly better than England and Wales.

Sourcing. No difference, and almost identical level and profile to England and Wales.

Sustainability. Little difference, but significantly better than England and Wales.

3.21.3 Matrix 2 – conclusions

The areas of mechanical, electrical, maintenance and sustainability are most in need of attention. No significant differences between procurement routes overall.

3.22 PFI schools in Northern Ireland – User comfort

3.22.1 User comfort (Matrix 3) – Level 4 definitions

Summertime overheat. Building interior unlikely to experience more than 30 hours per year above environmental temperature greater than 27 °C, and occupants have very limited beam radiation from the sun (Figures 3.38 to 3.41).

Visual environment. Daylight and artificial lighting sources entirely appropriate for task and promote a cheerful but non-distracting atmosphere. Full compliance with workplace regulations.

SCHOOL	Summer overheating	Visual environment	Heating comfort	Audible and visual intrusion	Acoustics	Air quality	TOTAL
School FF	3.5	3.5	3	3	3	3	**19**
School RR	2.5	2.5	2.5	3	3	3	**16.5**
School JJ	2.5	3	2.5	3	2.5	3	**16.5**
School EE	2.5	3	3	2.5	2.5	2.5	**16**
School DD	3	2.5	2.5	2.5	2.5	2.5	**15.5**
School LL	2	2.5	3	2.5	3	2	**15**
School AA	1.5	2.5	3	3	3	2	**15**
School BB	2	2	2.5	3	2.5	3	**15**
School TT	2.5	2.5	3	2.5	2	2	**14.5**
School KK	2	2.5	2.5	2.5	2	2.5	**14**
School GG	2	2.5	3	2.5	2	2	**14**
School NN	2	2.5	2.5	2.5	2	2	**13.5**
School MM	1.5	2	1.5	2	3	3	**13**
School PP	2	1.5	2.5	1.5	3	2.5	**13**
School CC	1.5	2	2	1.5	2	1.5	**10.5**
School HH	1	1	2	1.5	2.5	2	**10**
School SS	1.5	2	2	2	0.5	2	**10**
School QQ	1.5	2	2	0.5	1	1	**8**

Figure 3.38 User comfort (Matrix 3 NI) scoring table – PFI schools are shaded.

Figure 3.39 Clerestory windows provide daylighting to the back of a traditionally procured secondary classroom.

Heating comfort.   Internal air temperatures within –1.5 °C to +2.0 °C of target temperature. No reason for occupant discomfort from asymmetric thermal radiation. No 'Monday morning' discomfort.

Audible and visual intrusion.   No interference to work or leisure from continuous, intermittent or impulsive background noise within interior or exterior occupied spaces. No unwanted or noticeable visual intrusion.

Acoustics quality.   All occupied areas free of acoustic features that act to the detriment of efficient working and enjoyment of the building. Covers reverberation time, intelligibility of speech, and music.

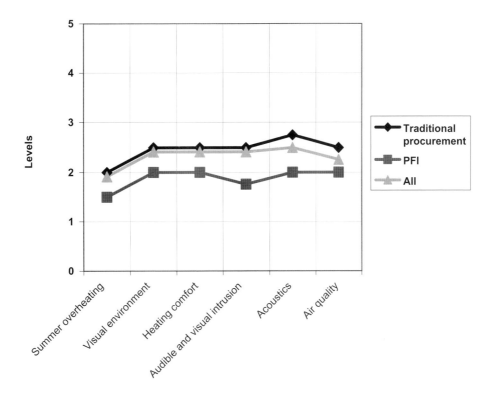

Figure 3.40 User comfort (Matrix 3 NI) – median scores of sample (Level 3 is good practice).

Figure 3.41 High-level opening lights to a stairwell with no easy means of opening.

Air quality, internal. No noticeable odour or dust, or noticeable allergic or health symptoms from any contaminants such as micro-organisms, organic or non-organic compounds. Humidity satisfactory in all spaces.

3.22.2 Matrix 3: User comfort – commentary

Summertime overheat. Limited difference. All-median at Level 2 – summertime overheating is an occasional problem. Several facilities were Level 1.5 or below, where summertime overheating is a frequent problem and ventilation was inadequate.

Visual environment. Limited difference. All-median at Level 2.5, and somewhat better than England and Wales.

Heating comfort. A difference of only 0.5. All-median at Level 2.5, indicating occasional discomfort from uneven heating and cold Monday mornings.

Audible and visual intrusion. Difference of 0.75 between traditional procurement and PFI. Below Level 2 for PFIs means that occupants notice noise and visual intrusion.

Acoustics quality. Traditional procurement at Level 2.75, indicating less than ideal acoustics, but PFI at Level 2 indicates that many spaces are acoustically impaired, to the extent that speech levels have to be raised and words repeated occasionally.

Air quality, internal. Difference of only 0.5. But high levels of carbon dioxide were recorded in many full classrooms – largely a management issue, needing strategies for window and trickle-vent opening.

3.22.3 Matrix 3 – conclusions

The median of all schools is around Level 2.5, indicating departures from the ideal of Level 4. All areas are in need of attention, particularly in PFI schools.

3.23 PFI schools in Northern Ireland – Whole life costs

3.23.1 Whole life costs (Matrix 4) – Level 4 definitions

External materials. All components selected and installed to achieve lowest cost of ownership. All have good resistance to vandalism, sun, wind, rain. Graceful degradation of appearance with wear. Detailing to best practice (Figures 3.42 to 3.45).

Internal fabric and finishes. Fabric and finishes chosen for lowest cost of ownership. Properties include ease of routine and special cleaning, graceful degradation of appearance with wear, easy repair/replacement.

Building services capital items. All components selected for minimum cost of ownership. Adequate space for minor and major maintenance. Design enables most service activities to be undertaken during occupation.

Building services revenue maintenance. All components selected for minimum cost of ownership. Component arrangement/availability good. Easy maintenance access. Most service activities possible during occupation.

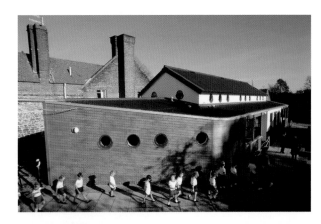

Figure 1.3 Imaginative buildings for young children – 'ducks'. The boat and waves are primary schools. Copyright Joe Low/Architectural Association.

Figure 3.25 Traditional materials and detailing of a traditionally procured school.

Figure 3.33 Lift shaft colloquially known as 'the lipstick' in a traditionally procured school.

Figure 4.1 Hôtel-Dieu, Beaune, France, *circa* 1443 – used as a hospital until 1948. Reproduced with permission from Emmanuel Thirard/RIBA Library Photographs Collection.

Figure 4.7 St Mary's Hospital, Isle of Wight (1990) – a low energy hospital.

Figure 4.14 Causeway Hospital, Coleraine, Northern Ireland – atrium, rooflight gantries and water feature.

Figure 5.6 Ronan Point, London: after building collapse in May 1968. Reproduced with permission from RIBA Library Photographs Collection.

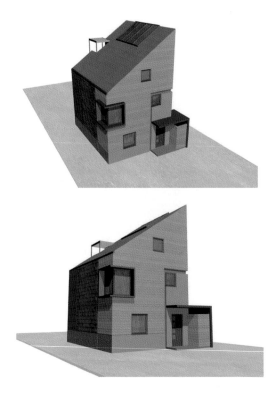

Figure 5.7 Concept proposals for an MMC house on the BRE Innovation Park, using SIPs.

SCHOOL	External materials	Internal fabric and finishes	Building services capital	Building services maintenance	Facilities management fitness	Flexibility	TOTAL
School RR	3.5	4	3.5	3	3.5	3	**20.5**
School EE	3	3	3	3	3.5	5	**20.5**
School LL	4	4	3	3	3	3.5	**20.5**
School TT	3.5	3.5	3	3	3.5	3	**19.5**
School FF	3	3	3	3	3	3.5	**18.5**
School AA	3.5	2.5	3	3	3	3	**18**
School NN	3.5	3.5	2.5	2.5	2.5	3.5	**18**
School MM	3	3	3	3	3	3	**18**
School KK	3	2.5	3	3	2.5	3	**17**
School JJ	3	3	2.5	2.5	2.5	3	**16.5**
School DD	3	3	2.5	2.5	2.5	3	**16.5**
School BB	3.5	3.5	2	2.5	3	2	**16.5**
School GG	2.5	2.5	3	3	3	2	**16**
School CC	3	2.5	2	3	1.5	2.5	**14.5**
School QQ	3	2.5	2	3	1	2.5	**14**
School PP	1	2.5	2.5	2.5	2	3	**13.5**
School HH	2.5	2	2.5	3	2	1.5	**13.5**
School SS	2.5	2.5	2	2	1.5	2	**12.5**

Figure 3.42 Whole life costs (Matrix 4 NI) scoring table – PFI schools are shaded.

Figure 3.43 Vegetation growing at the top of a downpipe of a recently opened PFI school.

Facilities management: fitness for function. All architectural fittings, fitments, furniture and furnishings selected for minimum cost of ownership and support to organisational objectives. All items eminently suitable for purpose. Mean time to repair is short.

Flexibility for layout change and extension. Building plan, positioning within site, construction and materials facilitate easy future adaptation and extension without excessive cost/disturbance to occupiers.

3.23.2 Matrix 4: Whole life costs – commentary

External materials. Little difference between procurement routes, and slightly better than England and Wales. PFI facilities at a median of Level

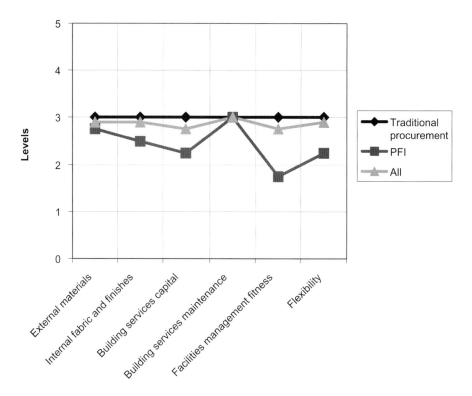

Figure 3.44 Whole life costs (Matrix 4 NI) – median scores of sample (Level 3 is good practice).

Figure 3.45 Plastic flat roof covering in a severe climatic exposure zone, by the coast.

2.5 suggests that optimum whole life costing is not being achieved for all external materials. One traditional procured FHE college displayed poor specification of external materials for its micro-climate and scored Level 1.

Internal fabric and finishes.   Little difference all round.

Building services capital items.   Little difference. Level 2 indicates some failures to specify and properly install components with the highest appropriate efficiency.

Building services revenue maintenance.   Little difference. Median Level 2.5 suggests Level 4 requirements satisfied for most of the important items.

Facilities management: fitness for function.   Significant difference of 1.25, with the overall median close to the traditional procurement Level 3, suggesting that this aspect is a problem in PFI – particularly the colleges of FHE.

Flexibility for layout change and extension.   Limited difference. Level 3 suggests that Level 4 requirements satisfied for most major aspects. PFI less flexible, and one traditionally procured school scored Level 5.

3.23.3 Matrix 4 – conclusions

The overall median of around 3, suggests that Level 4 requirements are being satisfied for many of the major components and factors. Traditional procurement more or less follows the overall median, while PFI is adrift on many aspects, particularly facilities management fitness for function in FHE colleges. Overall slightly better than England and Wales.

3.24 PFI schools in Northern Ireland – Detail design

3.24.1 Detail design (Matrix 5) – Level 4 definitions

External detail.   Good resistance to vandalism, sun, wind, rain. Graceful degradation of appearance with wear. Detailing to best practice. Good functional and aesthetic detailing to all roofs, walls, plinths, e.g. damp-proof courses at least 150 mm from ground (Figures 3.46 to 3.49).

SCHOOL	External detail	Internal detail	Junction detail	Furniture and furnishings	Fittings	Safety and security	TOTAL
School RR	3.5	3.5	3.5	3.5	3.5	3.5	21
School EE	3.5	3.5	3.5	3	3	3.5	20
School LL	4	3.5	3.5	2.5	3	3	19.5
School TT	3	3	3	3.5	3.5	3.5	19.5
School JJ	3	3	3	3	3	3	18
School NN	3	3	3	2.5	3	3.5	18
School KK	3	3	3	3	3	3	18
School MM	3.5	2.5	3	3.5	3	2.5	18
School AA	3	2.5	3	3	3	3	17.5
School DD	3	3	3	3	2.5	3	17.5
School BB	3	3	3	3	3	2.5	17.5
School FF	3	3	3	2.5	2.5	3	17
School GG	2.5	2.5	2.5	3	3	2.5	16
School PP	2	2.5	2	2.5	2.5	2.5	14
School SS	2	2	2	2.5	1.5	1.5	11.5
School CC	2	2	2	2.5	1	1.5	11
School HH	2	1.5	2	2	1.5	2	11
School QQ	2	2	2	2.5	1	1.5	11

Figure 3.46 Detail design (Matrix 5 NI) scoring table – PFI schools are shaded.

Figure 3.47 Poor detailed specification in a PFI school.

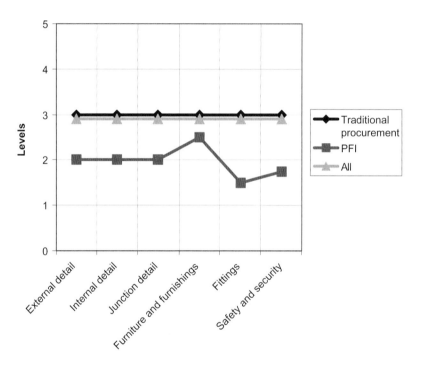

Figure 3.48 Detail design (Matrix 5 NI) – median scores of sample (Level 3 is good practice).

Internal detail.   Ease of routine and special cleaning, graceful degradation of appearance with wear, easy repair/replacement. Good functional and aesthetic detailing to all floors, walls, ceilings, e.g. shadow gaps to suspended ceilings.

Junction details.   Architectural junctions of different materials, such as roof/wall abutments, detailed to good practice with good workmanship. Good functional and aesthetic detailing to all door and window openings and thresholds, e.g. crafted flashings rather than mastic excretions.

Figure 3.49 Gutter failure due to excessive snow loading in a traditionally procured school.

Furnishings. All furnishings selected for ability to retain good appearance and for minimum cost of ownership. All seating comfortable for expected occupancy – anthropomorphically suitable to BS 5873. Correctly sized, robust and solid.

Fittings. All architectural fittings eminently suitable for purpose. Anthropomorphically suitable to BS 5873. Correctly sized, robust and solid. Suitable provision for disabled persons' use/access. Correctly sized, robust and solid.

Safety and security. Detailed architectural disposition to good practice and avoiding potential hazards. External and internal hazards controlled by design, such as minimum entrances, which are capable of observation and/or CCTV and/or fencing.

3.24.2 Matrix 5: Detail design – commentary

External detail. Significant difference. PFI median at Level 2 indicates that not all major external components are being detailed satisfactorily.

Internal detail. Significant difference. PFI median at Level 2 indicates that not all major internal components are being detailed satisfactorily.

Junction details. Significant difference. PFI median at Level 2 suggests that not all major junctions are being detailed satisfactorily.

Furnishings. Little difference.

Fittings. Significant difference. PFI at Level 1.5 suggests a few obvious failures.

Safety and security.   Significant difference. Some major failures among the PFIs.

3.24.3 Matrix 5 – conclusions

Detailed design problems mainly prevalent in PFI schools. Fittings and security are major issues in PFI. Northern Ireland is slightly better, overall, than England and Wales.

3.25 PFI schools in Northern Ireland – User satisfaction

3.25.1 User satisfaction (Matrix 6) – questions asked

Initial interviews with principals and directors of educational facilities were structured with six questions, which they were asked to rank in terms of their satisfaction, on a scale of 1 to 5 (five representing maximum satisfaction). The six questions were a pilot study for developing a 'sixth matrix' to add a user satisfaction dimension to the BRE Design Quality Matrix (DQM). Although the questions proved very useful in structuring the interviews, the building's architects and other consultants were often present, probably causing principals to give a more generous score than they may have done otherwise. A self-completion matrix will be developed for future studies to eliminate this bias. The six questions were (Figures 3.50 to 3.53):

(1) Does the building work well?
(2) Does the building lift the spirits?
(3) Will the building weather well, withstand wear and tear, and be easily maintained?

SCHOOL	Bldg works?	Uplift spirits?	Wear and tear?	Flexibility?	Security?	Fitness?	TOTAL
School LL	5	5	5	5	5	5	30
School NN	5	5	5	5	5	5	30
School EE	5	5	4	4.5	4	4	26.5
School MM	4	5	5	4	3	4	25
School RR	4	5	4	4	4	4	25
School DD	4	5	4	4	3	4	24
School SS	3.5	4	3.5	4	4	4	23
School TT	4	5	4	3.5	2.5	4	23
School JJ	4	4	4	3	3	5	23
School PP	4	4	3	4	4	4	23
School GG	3.5	4	4	3	4	4	22.5
School FF	4	4	3	3.5	4	4	22.5
School CC	3	5	2	4.5	4	3	21.5
School KK	4	4	3	1	4	5	21
School AA	4	5	2	4	1	2.5	18.5
School QQ	2.5	4	3	3	2	3	17.5
School BB	2.5	4.5	3.5	2	2	3	17.5
School HH	2	3.5	4.5	1	3	3	17

Figure 3.50 User satisfaction (Matrix 6 NI) scoring table – PFI schools are shaded.

Figure 3.51 Entrance portico to a traditionally procured school.

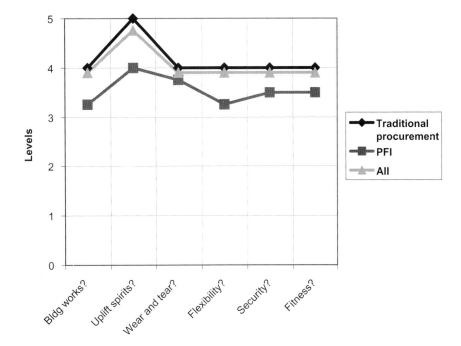

Figure 3.52 User satisfaction (Matrix 6 NI) – median scores of sample (Level 3 is good practice).

Figure 3.53 Entrance to one of two virtually identical PFI schools.

(4) Is the building flexible?

(5) Is the building secure?

(6) Is the indoor environment of the building fit for purpose, in terms of daylighting, heating, ventilation and acoustics?

3.25.2 Matrix 6: User satisfaction – commentary

There is no specific commentary on any of the six questions/aspects.

3.25.3 Matrix 6 – conclusions

The main difference between the two procurement routes occurs in the 'lifting of spirits', where traditional procurement is assessed as significantly better than PFI. The other two areas where traditional procurement is felt to be ahead of PFI are the functioning and flexibility of the buildings.

3.26 PFI schools in Northern Ireland – Conclusions

3.26.1 General

- Overall design quality of schools and FHE colleges in Northern Ireland has significant room for improvement.
- In general, PFI schools are of lower design quality – with the exception of one PFI school. There was no discernable difference in the design quality of FHE colleges, in general.
- Cost of ownership appears higher in PFI schools, and similar in FHE colleges.
- Poor internal environments were widespread and are likely to impact on educational achievement – this is a management issue to some extent.
- Solutions to some of the problems will have cost implications.
- Major opportunities exist to improve energy efficiency.

3.26.2 Top five problems

- Token architecture predominant in PFI – two schools were virtually identical, showing little respect for identity, let alone *genius loci*.
- Poor specification – lack of attention to detail – mainly PFI.
- Lack of environmental sustainability.
- Poor acoustics, ventilation, visual environments, and indoor air quality.
- Poor detailing, particularly at junctions – PFI.

3.26.3 Top five successes

- Good architecture – mainly traditional procurement approaches, which included two outstanding examples – both 'diocesan architect'.
- Good site planning.
- Good space planning and flexibility.
- Notable reduction of vandalism.
- A few examples of good daylighting strategies.

3.27 PFI schools in Northern Ireland – Recommendations

Acoustics.   Intelligibility of speech was below the standard that would be reasonable to expect in a number of areas, especially assembly halls, sports halls and dining halls. The main cause was reverberation time (the time for sound to decay by 60 dB) being too long. This also makes the rooms noisier than necessary which makes conversation difficult. Measured noise levels in some dining and assembly halls were above 74 dBA – getting close to the 80 dBA level where occupants in an industrial workplace would be required to wear ear-muffs to avoid hearing damage.

Ventilation.   Measurements of carbon dioxide levels were made in all premises. As a guide to good practice, a level of 1000 parts per million (ppm) corresponds to the optimum ventilation rate in teaching spaces of 8 litres per person per second. The general limit of acceptability is 1500 ppm, corresponding to 4.5 litres per person per second. Higher ppm figures are associated with stuffy rooms and reductions in alertness of occupants. Danger to health starts at 3000 ppm with significant risk to health above 5000 ppm. Frequently, the ppm figures were above 1500, with figures in the range of 1800 to 2500 ppm being common. Where high ppm figures were measured, both inadequate window opening area and poorly positioned window openings were commonplace. Also, single-sided ventilation was used for rooms up to 10 m deep, beyond the generally accepted limit of 7 m. Ventilation problems were observed in most assembly and sports halls, the main problem being that while provision was made for exhaust air by means such as high-level windows, there was no source of inlet air, and therefore inadequate ventilation for occupants.

Daylight.   The great majority of teaching spaces had inadequate daylighting. Typical daylighting levels were 0.2 to 0.6 per cent, which compares badly with the 4 per cent threshold needed to achieve the educational building design objective of 'daylight being the main source of lighting energy'. In addition, the quality of daylight was poor in most teaching spaces, with uniformity ratios (a measure of how uneven the lighting level is) being well below guidance figures. A frequent cause was entirely inadequate floor to ceiling height for the depth of room away from the window wall, and/or lack of daylighting provision to the rear of rooms. The lack of daylighting was compounded by the tops of windows being well below ceiling level. Building structure costs increase with floor-to-ceiling height, and attempts to minimise capital costs are likely to be the main driver. Observations of visual comfort issues identified frequent problems related to glare from windows, veiling reflections on ICT screens, glare from work-tops, and unsatisfactory selection of furniture, fabric and VDU screen sur-round colours. Recent published papers show strong correlations between ample daylight and good educational productivity. Statistically robust find-ings show improvements of 14–23 per cent in end of year assessment scores with good daylighting.*

Sustainability and energy efficiency. Widespread evidence of unneces-sarily high heating levels, often associated with poor thermal comfort were observed. Room temperatures of 23 °C or above were frequently observed. Differences of more than the good practice 3 °C between floor and ceiling temperatures were commonplace, leading to problems of hot heads and cold feet. In most instances, this is a heating design issue where a revision to the standard approach to heating systems is warranted. These high heating levels can impact adversely on educational productivity, and on heating costs.

Many opportunities to install efficient boilers together with matching heat emitters (radiators etc.) had been lost at the design stage, especially where natural gas was available. Heating energy cost reductions of 12 per cent are possible by using condensing boilers, with payback periods less than four years. The use of whole life costing approaches, such as ISO 2000: 15686 Constructed assets, would provide a rational basis for decisions.

3.28 PFI schools in Northern Ireland – Summary

The Northern Ireland Audit Office wished to ascertain the design quality of new educational facilities procured by PFI routes. They selected a sample of 14 post-primary schools and 4 FHE colleges, built in the past few years, from across Northern Ireland. The sample contained 4 PFI post-primary schools and 2 PFI colleges of FHE; traditionally procured schools and colleges were included as a control group. The sample of facilities was selected by the NIAO, and they understand that it fully represents the population of new educational facilities in Northern Ireland. The sample contains the 6 'pathfinder' PFI projects completed in Northern Ireland to date, and all major traditionally procured post-primary schools completed in the same period. Appropriate levels of confidence should be attached to the data. A small BRE team visited each school and conducted a visual survey, non-intrusive to the building fabric.

---

*Heschong Mahone Group, *Daylighting and productivity study: daylighting in schools*, USA, August 1999.

BRE also conducted informal interviews with principals and directors, during which six structured questions were asked – as a pilot for the development of a 'user satisfaction' matrix (the sixth matrix). A series of six matrices were used to score the schools. The matrices contain several sub-factors and scoring levels are objectively set for completion by construction or property professionals. They cover the following main areas:

- **Architectural design quality**. This covers the relatively subjective area of aesthetic merit, and also the more prosaic qualities of specification, site and space planning.
- **Building services design quality**. A more objective area and supported by scientifically measurable lighting, noise and temperature levels. Sympathetic integration with architecture is crucial, not to mention maintainability and replacement sourcing.
- **User productivity indicators**. Internal comfort conditions are also scientifically measurable and links between them and productivity are increasingly empirically evident. Integrating art and science creates ideal environments, e.g. the quality of daylight is just as important as the measurable quantity. Optimum environments are critical to successful school design and often reflected in the enhanced educational performance of pupils.*
- **Building cost of ownership**. This covers the occupancy costs of schools and the potential whole-life performance of building fabric and services. It provides an analysis of the trade-offs between capital and running costs that affect future building performance.
- **Detail design**. Failures in building performance are often caused by poor detailed design or bad workmanship. Rectifying and coping with such failures will increase maintenance and occupancy costs.
- **User satisfaction**. Six structured questions were put to the heads of the facilities to assess their satisfaction with the building. They were asked to score each aspect on a scale of one to five (five representing the highest level of satisfaction). The results are necessarily subjective and possibly biased as the interviews were not in confidence.

The team encountered variable design quality throughout the sample. There was design inconsistency across the board, with single facilities containing examples of good and bad design practice. All facilities visited left significant room for design improvements, particularly at a detailed level, but PFI schools were generally of a lower design quality than traditionally procured ones. The latter seemed to benefit from the prescriptive nature of a conventional route, as well as the tried and tested detailing of traditional materials. We noted the 'diocesan architect' effect to a marked degree in Northern Ireland – perhaps unsurprisingly. Such architects are

---

*Heschong Mahone Group, *Daylighting and productivity study: daylighting in schools*, USA, August 1999.

generally trusted confidantes, with a lengthy relationship with the school, displaying high degrees of professionalism and attention to detail for their clients – in anticipation of a continued relationship. Good design quality, including innovation and flexibility, invariably ensues. This is often augmented by additional funding from church sources to provide both additional facilities, and possibly a higher than normal specification. Site inspections from such an ideal adviser could also result in better workmanship. Such procurement circumstances often provided both better aesthetic and physical environments, such as architectural, daylighting and ventilation strategies, which can positively impact on pupils' educational attainment. The PFI schools' mean score for the six main categories was below that of traditionally procured schools, and significantly less in the areas of architectural design quality and detail design.

Trends emerged regarding the materials used for different procurement routes, with PFI schools generally using metal roofs, but this was not as marked as in England and Wales. Traditionally procured schools tended to favour traditional materials such as facing brickwork, render and concrete roofing tiles. Aluminium window and doorframe systems were ubiquitous throughout the sample. Despite some successful attempts to provide uniform daylight throughout classrooms, and indeed other areas, no school was visited which did not have the vast majority of its artificial lighting switched on. Indoor air quality was a problem in the majority of the facilities visited, and was measured with a carbon dioxide meter. In most cases this was a management issue, involving strategies for opening windows and using trickle vents. The latter were often unfamiliar to occupants, revealing a need for a user manual, or at least staff briefing.

Ranked tables were produced from the first five scored matrices which show that PFI facilities tend to rank lower than traditional ones. However, there are sub-areas of success and failure in both traditional and PFI facilities, which are shown by the median scores plotted in the resultant graphs. The following five matrices were scored within defined levels of significance:

- **Architectural design quality**. External and internal architectural merit was generally superior in traditionally procured schools, as was specification. Sustainability, site and space planning were similar in both procurement routes. Northern Ireland seemed slightly better overall when compared to the England and Wales sample.
- **Building services design quality**. There was little difference between procurement routes. But this seemed better overall in Northern Ireland compared to the England and Wales sample.
- **User productivity indicators**. Similar, but with traditional procurement having a slight edge over PFI, in general terms. Again, slightly better than the England and Wales sample.
- **Building cost of ownership**. Similar, but facilities management fitness for purpose shows PFI to be significantly lower than traditional. Flexibility slightly better in traditional procurement.

- **Detail design**. Traditional procurement was significantly superior in all but the furnishings aspect.
- **User satisfaction**. The pilot 'sixth matrix' where ranked tables are not included. The matrix shows that user satisfaction appears slightly better for traditionally procured buildings.

Supplementary research was also conducted, which involved collecting broad initial price and specification data from schools' design teams. A whole-life-costing model was applied to the data to estimate the initial costs and capital replacement costs of components over 60 years. The maintenance costs were omitted because of lack of information concerning maintenance strategies between schools and, indeed, between procurement routes. The results of this supplementary research suggest that the PFI route, generally, has higher initial costs than traditional procurement. But whether this is the price paid for shifting risk to a PFI consortium for a typical concession period of 25 years, or due to more fundamental discrepancies cannot be ascertained from this exercise.

These data may also contain discrepancies over definitions, such as the capital costs of PFI facilities including site acquisition, while most of the traditionally procured facilities were on existing sites. Definitive value for money conclusions are not drawn from this financial analysis due to the fact that the costing data were self-reported and not audited by BRE. However, the additional study does suggest that further investigation, possibly by specialist financiers, is probably warranted. The results of this exercise are contained in a supplementary report to this main report.

3.29 International case studies

3.29.1 Whiteley Primary School, Hampshire, UK

Rural site, sustainability, building as educational resource, traditional procurement, 1997

This school is a shallow curve in plan, sensitively sited to retain the best woodland on the location, with a watercourse and playing fields to the south. Built on a limited budget to contain several hundred pupils, the main materials are stock bricks and cedar shingle roof tiles, with double-glazed, aluminium patent glazing at high level to provide northlight and stack-effect ventilation. The school also includes community facilities serving the nearby village of Whiteley. The majority of pupils cycle to the school as a result of heightened awareness of environmental sustainability taught by using the school building as an educational resource. Classrooms run from east to west, with large eave overhangs to shade the southern façade and clerestory northlights. The southern orientation also allows low winter sun angles to provide passive solar gain. High levels of building fabric insulation, natural light, and occupant awareness (e.g. switching off lights when not necessary) reduce energy bills.

3.29.2 Diamond Ranch High School, Pomona, California, USA

Public sector, dynamic architecture, subterranean, daylighting, 2000

The site for this American, public-sector high school was so steep that it was considered impossible to build on, so it was donated to the local education authority for the nominal sum of $1. However, the steeply sloping site presented the opportunity to embed the clusters of buildings into the hillside, reducing the building envelope's exposure to the harsh Californian sun, significantly reducing heat gain. Despite extensive terracing of the site, existing vegetation such as oak trees were replanted. Playing fields were placed at the top and bottom of the site, with campus-style groupings of buildings in between, along a pedestrian street. Groups of buildings each house a manageable cohort of a hundred-odd students. However, value for money was demonstrated for this public sector project by using a limited range of economic materials, combined with dynamic forms which echo the nearby mountains. Natural lighting is also a prerogative.

3.29.3 Druk White Lotus School, Ladakh, India

Appropriate sustainable technology, local materials, cultural symbolism, 2001

A generous courtyard template is essential in the high mountains of the Himalaya, to provide shelter from winds and allow solar ingress. The plan of this infants' school also draws upon Tibetan Buddist symbolism as it follows the nine-square *mandala*, which represents the cosmos. European funding allowed the use of appropriate sustainable technology, including a melding of local vernacular traditions with modern technology. The walls are made of mud bricks encased in granite and the roof is timber. Western steel and concrete construction is impractical due to the remote site in an earthquake zone. However, Trombe walls and solar panels are used to exploit the solar exposure at high altitude, with the thermal mass of the construction acting as a heat store to ameliorate cold nights. Water is a scarce resource in an area of low rainfall, relying on glacial-melt water. Consequently, pit latrines are the norm, although in this case ventilation is improved by solar-driven flues which dry human waste into an odourless fertiliser.

3.29.4 Cummins Engine Child Development Centre, Columbus, Indiana, USA

Corporate patronage, internal playground, natural light, underfloor heating, 2001

Corporate social responsibility is demonstrated in this American child-care centre which provides employees' children of the Cummins Engine

Company with pre-school education. The focus of the plan is an internal playground, which makes sense in terms of security and supervision, which is surrounded by a single-loaded corridor serving classrooms for different age groups. Although probably conforming to Robert Venturi's idea of the 'decorated shed' in its relative 'ordinariness', the architecture works well on fundamental levels – such as the clearly symbolised entrance. As young children spend most of their time on the floor, the design includes an under-floor heating system.

3.29.5 Hampton Gurney School, London, UK

Urban site, open-air school, access ramps, vertical school, 2002

This Church of England school replaces a two-storey building on a former Blitz bombsite in the centre of London. The tight urban site close to Edgware Road tube station dictates the concept of a vertical school, with six levels of teaching and ancillary spaces, including terraced 'playdecks' (and open-air classrooms on warm days). Fortunately, the corner of the urban block it is sited on faces south-west to give good insulation. Ancillary spaces, such as the kitchen and hall, are placed in the basement, with a reception, offices and nursery school on the ground floor. Ramps give access to the school entrances for small children and prams. Three levels of teaching spaces rise from the first floor to a tensile membrane structure on the roof, which shelters a 'technology garden'. The school accommodates 240 primary school children and provides a template for urban schools which is reminiscent of open-air schools from the twentieth century (Figure 3.54).

Figure 3.54 Hampden Gurney School, London.

3.30 Further international case studies

- **Strawberry Vale School, BC, Canada** – ecological materials, passive solar, 1995.
- **Little Village Academy, USA** – compact urban site, cultural symbolism, public, 1996.
- **Ecological Middle School, Austria** – compact design, multistorey, 1998.
- **Haute Vallee School, Jersey** – energy efficient, competition, campus plan, 2000.
- **Freie Waldorfschule, Germany** – user consultation, extended 1950s school, 2002.

3.31 References

1 Seaborne, M. (1971) *The English school: Its architecture and organisation, 1370–1870.* London: Routledge & Kegan Paul.

2 Gardner, B. (1973) *The public schools: An historical survey.* London: Hamish Hamilton.

3 Ascham, R. (1570) *The Scholemaster.*

4 Seaborne, M. (1971) *The English school: Its architecture and organisation, 1370–1870.* London: Routledge & Kegan Paul.

5 Service, A. (1975) *Edwardian architecture and its origins.* London: Architectural Press.

6 Gardner, B. (1973) *The public schools: An historical survey.* London: Hamish Hamilton.

7 Dudek, M. (2000) *Architecture of schools: The new learning environments.* Oxford: Architectural Press.

8 Dudek, M. (2000) *Architecture of schools: The new learning environments.* Oxford: Architectural Press.

9 Dudek, M. (2005) *Children's spaces.* Oxford: Architectural Press.

10 Seaborne, M. and Lowe, R. (1977) *The English school: Its architecture and organisation, 1870–1970.* Volume II. London: Routledge & Kegan Paul.

11 Saint, A. (1987) *Towards a social architecture: The role of school building in post-war England.* New Haven: Yale University Press.

12 Bullock, N. (2002) *Building the post-war world: Modern architecture and reconstruction in Britain.* New York: Routledge.

13 Macmillan, S. (ed.) (2004) *Designing better buildings: Quality and value in the built environment.* London: Spon.

14 Saint, A. (1987) *Towards a social architecture: The role of school building in post-war England.* New Haven: Yale University Press.

15 Hopkinson, R.G. and Kay, J.D. (1972) *The lighting of buildings.* London: Faber & Faber.

16 Parkin, P.H. and Humphreys, H.R. (1958) *Acoustics, noise and buildings.* London: Faber & Faber.

17 Littler, J. and Thomas, R. (1984) *Design with energy: The conservation and use of energy in buildings.* Cambridge: Cambridge University Press.

18 Macmillan, S. (ed.) (2004) *Designing better buildings: Quality and value in the built environment.* London: Spon.

19 DCMS (2000) *Better public buildings.* (Foreword.) London: TSO.

20 Hutton, W. (1997) *The state to come*. London: Vantage.
21 DfES (2002) *Schools for the future*. BB 95. London: TSO.
22 DfES (2004) *Briefing framework for secondary school projects*. BB 98. London: TSO.
23 DfES (1999) *Lighting design for schools*. BB 90. London: TSO.
24 DfES (2003) *Acoustic design of schools*. BB 93. London: TSO.

Chapter 4

Hospitals

4.1 Historical evolution of hospitals

It may seem a strange principle to enunciate as the very first requirement in a hospital that it should do the sick no harm. It is quite necessary nevertheless to lay down such a principle, because the actual mortality in hospitals, especially those of large crowded cities, is very much higher than any calculation founded upon the mortality of the same class of patient treated out of hospital would make one expect.*

Florence Nightingale, Notes on hospitals, *1859*

Hospitals were a medieval building type, usually attached to an ecclesiastical building, and the name derives from the Latin root (*hospes*, the guest or the host) for 'hospitality'. Medieval church foundations provided alms for the poor and shelter for travellers in remote terrain – the Abbot's kitchen and infirmary symbolised these functions in religious foundations such as monasteries and priories. The church extended spiritual care of the soul into physical care for the ailing and infirm. The Christian rule of St Benedict dictates that 'every arriving guest must be welcomed as if he were Christ'. However, they were not necessarily treated as such if they stayed for too long! The medieval hospital performed a multitude of functions: hospital; almshouse; asylum; orphanage; foundling home; guest house for travellers and pilgrims; and poorhouse.

During the twelfth and thirteenth centuries a number of institutions were founded to cater for the poor, the old, and the sick – and called hospitals. An early example is the Hospital of St Cross in Winchester, which was founded in the 1130s by Bishop Henry of Blois for 'thirteen poor men, feeble and so reduced in strength that they can scarcely or not at all support themselves without other aid'. This hospital was placed under the care of the Knights of St John whose successors still wear black gowns emblazoned with the Jerusalem Cross. St Mary's Hospital in Chichester is

---

*Florence Nightingale's statement was actually pre-dated by a century. Sir John Pringle wrote that 'Hospitals are the chief cause of mortality in the army' in his 1752 work, *Observations on the diseases of the army.*

another later medieval hospital, founded in about 1300, which displays a typical plan for such institutions. Medieval hospitals were generally modelled on churches and contained a long hall, subdivided into a central space with spaces to either side, which were further divided into patients' compartments by wooden screens. The hospital chapel was usually at the east end of this long hall, all of which was covered with a large roof. They housed anything from a dozen to over a hundred inmates, but more usually around a few dozen.

Medieval hospitals were usually located on the edges of towns, outside the walls, due to their late development in relation to the rest of the town and the need to isolate the sick. Leprosy, or other skin diseases mistaken for it, was rife across early medieval Europe which led to the development of separate leper houses, until the Black Death (*circa* 1350) culled most of the sick and over a third of the population of England overall. Later hospitals resembled almshouses for the poor and elderly while some of the earlier leper houses also became hospitals. The Hôtel-Dieu in Beaune (Figure 4.1) was founded in 1443 and comprises a main hall, the *Grande Salle de Malades*, with beds lining each side, separated from the chapel by a wooden screen. The colonnades around the courtyard form outdoor

Figure 4.1 Hôtel-Dieu, Beaune, France, *circa* 1443 – used as a hospital until 1948. Reproduced with permission from Emmanuel Thirard/RIBA Library Photographs. This figure is also reproduced in colour in the colour plate section.

treatment areas and precedents for twentieth century tuberculosis sanatoriums. It continued in use as a hospital for over five centuries, until it became an old people's home in 1948.

Cruciform plan hospitals were built in the fifteenth century across the continent, with the altar at the cross-point. This plan type slowly developed into a series of wards ranged around internal courtyards. Conditions in many medieval hospitals were frightful, and the fact that an institution where inmates had a bed to themselves was described as a 'model hospital' encourages speculation at the horrors of typical conditions. The infamous Hôtel Dieu in Paris housed at least three patients to a bed without separating diseases – mortality rates were correspondingly horrific. They numbered several thousand in some years (5729 in 1524), in what was a 450 bed 'hospital' with over a thousand inmates. Even in the late eighteenth century observers commented on the cruelty of packing several patients into one bed at this institution.

Military necessity saw the foundation of model institutions, such as the Hôtel des Invalides in Paris (1670), for old or disabled soldiers, the Chelsea Hospital (1682) (Figure 4.2), and the Royal Naval Hospital at Greenwich (1694) (Figure 4.3). The latter institutions were designed by Sir Christopher Wren, largely on the pavilion principle, and Greenwich obviously symbolised Britain's domination of the sea. The cruciform plan also evolved into radial plans, particularly for asylums where constant observation was paramount. British hospital foundations abounded in the eighteenth century, including new institutions such as the London Hospital (1751–57) and rebuilt medieval foundations such as St Bartholomew's, St Thomas' and Bethlehem (Bedlam) in London. The provinces emulated London, mainly in the second half of the eighteenth century, for example Edinburgh (1729);

Figure 4.2 Royal Military Hospital, Chelsea (1682 and later).

Figure 4.3 Royal Naval Hospital, Greenwich (1698).

Dublin (1745); Manchester (1752); Addenbrooke's, Cambridge (1766); the Radcliffe, Oxford (1770); and Birmingham (1779).[1]

War again helped to progress the design of hospitals in the mid-nineteenth century. Florence Nightingale was the superintendent of the Hospital for Invalid Gentlewomen in London when the Crimean War broke out in 1853. Nightingale's influence over conditions in the military hospitals in the Crimea was probably exaggerated for propaganda purposes. She was only in the Crimea for a few months with a small team of nurses, and faced the entrenched attitudes of the Royal Army Medical Corps.[2] However, there is little doubt that her campaign to improve hospitals and healthcare after the war had seminal and far-reaching consequences – many of her principles are still touchstones today. Her ideas on nursing and hospital design resulted in 'Nightingale wards' in most Victorian hospital buildings, many of which still exist. And her writings forged the building form for hospitals, of pavilion wards, for many decades, in the drive to maximise ventilation, daylight and sunlight. The obsession with fresh air was largely based on the Victorian theory of disease spread from 'miasma' or bad air, even in the light of later discoveries that diseases such as cholera were actually water-borne. The death of Prince Albert in 1861 due to 'bad drains' eventually led to sweeping reforms and legislation in the realm of public health.

Although a Public Health Act was passed in 1848, rushed through Parliament by the re-emergence of cholera in the same year, and memories of the devastating effect of the 1832 outbreak, it was relatively ineffective compared to later, consolidating acts.[3] The Conservative party, under Disraeli, used social health legislation to wrest power from the Liberals – best summarised in one of Disraeli's speeches of 1872: '. . . the first consideration of a (prime) minister should be the health of the people'. The final consolidation of legislation was Disraeli's Public Health Act of 1875. This set the scene for further hospital building in the late Victorian era.

The population of England quadrupled from ten million at the beginning of the nineteenth century to forty million at its end. This historically unprecedented growth was made possible by advanced industrialisation, but with inherent social penalties wrought by such rapid development. Some 80 per cent of England's population lived in cities on the eve of World War I. Although national wealth increased several-fold throughout the nineteenth century, *laissez-faire* economics precluded funding for hospitals coming out of the public purse and most Victorian hospitals were funded by public subscription and philanthropic contribution. The general principle was to provide a major health service to those of the middle and upper classes who could afford to pay, which helped to subsidise a minor service for the working classes who could rarely afford healthcare.

The army was again at the forefront of hospital development with examples such as the Royal Victoria Military Hospital at Netley (1856–63). It was typical in terms of contemporary architectural style, a utilitarian Italianate, but not necessarily good clinical practice. Florence Nightingale considered that its 1424 foot long main elevation was merely contrived to appear impressive from the river frontage. She lobbied for pavilion-style hospitals along the lines of the Hôpital Lariboisière in Paris (1839–54). Pavilion-style hospitals followed at Blackburn (1858), Woolwich (1861–65), and Pendlebury (1872–78). The Herbert Hospital at Woolwich is typical of the pavilion plans – it was originally a military hospital designed by Captain Douglas Galton, assisted by the Surveyor of Works to the War Department and various officers from the Royal Engineers. The advantages that this hospital afforded were listed by *The Builder* in 1866:

- Limitation of the number of sick under one roof.
- Complete separation from each other of the wards containing sick.
- Abundance of fresh air and ventilation in every part of the building allotted to sick.
- Complete separation of the ward offices from the wards.
- The use of non-absorbent surfaces in the wards and ward offices.
- Abundance of light, as well as light-coloured surfaces, especially in the ward offices, by which cleanliness is promoted.
- Facility of administration.*

Cruciform plans appeared, after a fashion, with the example of University College Hospital (UCH) by Alfred Waterhouse, built in phases between 1897 and 1906, which had an elaborate system of natural ventilation involving vertical duct risers in the centre of wards (Figure 4.4). The dictates of the pavilion-style plan were somewhat obviated by the beginning of the twentieth century with the moves towards mechanical ventilation and air conditioning. This resulted in a few compromises of previously planned pavilion hospitals which were retrofitted with mechanical ventilation

---

*The Builder. April 14, 1866, pp. 267–271.

Figure 4.4 University College Hospital, London – 1906 and 2005.

systems, for example Birmingham General Hospital (1893) and the Royal Victoria Hospital in Belfast (1903) – the latter operating from waste steam from the laundry.[4] The early decades of the twentieth century ostensibly saw the end of the need for pavilion-style hospitals, due to medical, building and environmental engineering technology advances, and the move to higher-rise hospital buildings, pioneered in America.

4.2 The modern era of hospital building

> . . . in all our plans for the future, we are redefining and we are restating our socialism in terms of the scientific revolution . . . The Britain that is going to be forged in the white heat of this revolution will be no place for restrictive practices or for outdated methods on either side of industry.
>
> *Harold Wilson, Labour Party Conference, 1963*

In Britain, it was only with the welfare state, the 1947 National Health Service Act and the creation of the Ministry of Health that an era of universal and free healthcare was heralded. However, pre-war pioneering precedents, such as the modernist Peckham Health Centre (1935) and the Finsbury Health Centre (1938) (Figure 4.5), stood as pathfinders for the new era. The Peckham Health Centre was a pioneering venture by a husband and wife team of doctors, and focused on preventative rather than curative healthcare. Nearly a thousand families signed up to the 'Peckham Experiment' for a subscription of a shilling a week and partook of various physical exercise regimes with an extensive health check each year. The building was a radical change in hospital planning, by a noted engineer,

Figure 4.5 Finsbury Health Centre – aerial view. Reproduced with permission from John Maltby/RIBA Library Photographs Collection.

who called architects 'decoration merchants'. Sir Owen Williams produced a flexible, open-plan structure with a glass-roofed swimming pool at its centre, and large expanses of curvilinear glazing in its elevations – symbolising light as an antidote to urban squalor. Peckham was overshadowed by Finsbury and closed in 1950 due to funding difficulties.

Finsbury was one of London's poorest boroughs, and economy as well as revolution probably dictated the attempt to provide a range of healthcare on a single site. Facilities included a tuberculosis clinic, foot clinic, dental surgery, and a solarium. Berthold Lubetkin's handling of the complexity arising from the grouping of diverse clinical areas received praise from architectural and medical circles. Critics heralded the building as a radical prototype and it is now a listed building. Among the innovations at Finsbury were elements of prescience that seem to foreshadow the 'patient-focus' developments of the 1990s. Lubetkin designed the Centre to seem like a club so that people were relaxed and welcomed, down to details such as the casual arrangement of furniture in waiting areas, and no reception desk (added later). Interior design included bright colours and the expansive use of glass bricks to advertise the benefits of sunlight.*[5] The building was conceived with flexibility in mind, in an attempt to future-proof it against technological and clinical advances, particularly in the area of environmental engineering infrastructure.

But exemplary new hospitals were rare at the inception of the National Health Service, which included the nationalisation of over 2000 existing, and aging, historic hospitals. They ranged from general hospitals, cottage

---

*There is copious historic evidence to suggest that sunlight therapy can heal and prevent major illnesses.

hospitals, workhouse infirmaries, hospitals for the armed services, specialist hospitals, hospitals for infectious diseases, mental hospitals, through to convalescent homes and hospitals. The need for new hospital buildings was urgent, but in the immediate post-war period housing and school building took precedence over hospitals. Fortuitously, this allowed time to carefully investigate the country's healthcare needs, and the initial outcome in 1955 was the publication of *Studies in the function and design of hospitals.* This document influenced ideas and research on healthcare buildings for the following 30 years. The research was undertaken by a multidisciplinary team including the Building Research and Fire Research Stations. A clear view of the role of research in hospital design was presented, it was accepted that:

> research can illuminate certain aspects of design; it can furnish
> information and can point to profitable methods of approach.
> It must never be thought of as providing definitive answers.[6]

The 1950s witnessed extensive research into hospital design – on scientific principles. The resulting architecture generally followed the Modern Movement principle of 'form follows function'. Along with improved medical and clinical practice, and changing societal aspirations – political, technical and funding factors were major influences on post-war healthcare provision. Architectural innovations included six- and four-bed wards to reduce cross-infection, improved space planning, colour psychology, and central sterile supply departments.

In the 1960s the National Health Service published a series of Hospital Building Notes, alongside valuable building procurement briefing notes, such as activity database sheets, which covered all departments of the hospital. Greenwich District General Hospital, 1963, was seminal in the use of the Building Notes. The Medical Architectural Research Unit (MARU) was set up in 1964, and was directly involved in the design of hospital wards at St Thomas' and other major facilities. The 1960s also saw the birth of standardised solutions for hospital provision, accompanied by the scaling down of the overall programme – such as district general hospitals being reduced from 800 to 550 beds, for reasons of economy. The end of this decade produced the 'Harness' initiative which was a collection of the best hospital designs. Somewhat fortunately, retrospectively, the modular construction dictates of the contemporary school building programme did not directly translate to health buildings. Seminal designs included single storey, rural, campus layouts and several storey urban counterparts – early lessons about the excessive strain on central lifts and service-core were learned.

But the cost of providing and running the ambitious health programme was proving an acute fiscal strain on the country's economic resources. And the world oil shock of 1973 probably helped to precipitate a crisis in confidence in the post-war hospital building programme of the National Health Service. The government was allegedly panicked to admit that the programme was completely out of control in the mid-1970s.[7] There was an overwhelming need to reduce expenditure within the NHS, and particularly the capital expenditure needed for developing healthcare facilities. The Harness programme of hospital building anticipated 70 new hospitals in the 1970s, but only two were built.

By contrast, the 1980s saw a large expansion of new healthcare facilities – particularly district general hospitals based on the 'Nucleus' planning ideas, developed at the end of the 1970s. NHS Estates was created with the imperative of reducing running costs. The drive to achieve economies of scale through standardisation created the 'Nucleus' hospital programme, which eventually saw a total of 130 new Nucleus hospitals (the first was completed in 1983). The model solutions and scale of building achieved under the Nucleus programme were the envy of the world, and specification references to Nucleus became standard in the development of overseas hospitals. Initiatives such as Designing to Reduce Operating Costs (DROC) appeared in the early 1980s, alongside the tail-end of the formerly extensive centralised research and development programme of the Department of Health, in the form of a low energy hospital study (commissioned in 1979 and available in 1982).

Nucleus developed out of the Harness briefing and design system, was aimed at large district general hospitals, and consisted of cruciform-shaped plan templates of about a thousand square metres (Figure 4.6). The templates were up to three storeys, encompassed whole departments, and could be infinitely arranged to form courtyards around central circulation 'streets'. The cruciform shape allowed internal and external courtyards to be formed when adjacent units were arranged, and helped to bring daylight and air into the pre-determined and cost-controlled, but deep-plan, internal layouts. Briefing data packs included individual room data sheets. The Nucleus system was the result of extensive research, briefing and

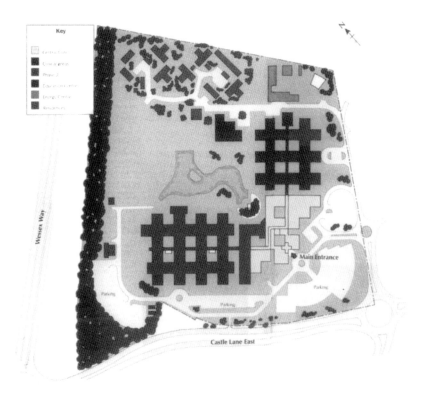

Figure 4.6 Nucleus hospital standardisation plan. Reproduced with permission from Llewelyn Davies Yeang.

Figure 4.7 St Mary's Hospital, Isle of Wight (1990) – a low energy hospital. This figure is also reproduced in colour in the colour plate section.

design time. It became the main principle upon which post-war hospital building was based. By the end of the 1980s 65 district general hospitals were completed, with a further 65 at construction or planning stage. Variations of Nucleus are still used and it was adopted by several overseas countries. Sir Philip Powell summarised the benefits of the system as 'It gave the architects more time to think about the architecture'.[8]

The 1990 NHS reforms started the outsourcing of specialist expertise, such as architects, engineers and medical planners, and the beginnings of an 'internal market'.[9] The introduction of the Patient's Charter in 1991 led to a more commercial approach from medical practitioners, and this was reflected in the procurement of healthcare buildings. Among the technological and design advances made in the 1980s hospital building boom was the move towards energy efficiency. The low energy hospital study required a hospital to be designed that would consume only 50 per cent of the energy used by a conventionally designed hospital, yet delivering an identical service to the NHS. The Nucleus hospital was used as the benchmark, with the model's theoretically calculated energy usage becoming the datum for this ambitious target. The results of the study were embodied in the new St Mary's Hospital, Newport, Isle of Wight (Figure 4.7), which was opened in 1990. A second low energy hospital was designed for the climatic conditions of Northern England, with an even more ambitious target of 60 per cent energy savings over the benchmark model. Wansbeck Hospital in Northumberland was opened in 1993. This was reputedly the last practical demonstration project by the NHS.[10]

4.3 Twenty-first century hospitals

I would like to return to the sense of civic pride when we construct our public buildings. Children learn better in schools that are well-designed, patients can be treated better – indeed recover more quickly – in hospitals that have been built to the highest standard.

Tony Blair, Building, *20 April 2000*

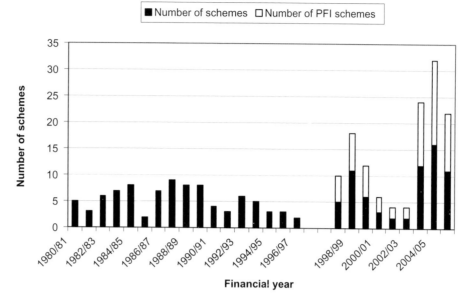

Figure 4.8 Major hospital schemes into the twenty-first century (over £25M).

Rapid medical and clinical advances, together with new diseases such as AIDS, led to the realisation that new health facilities were in danger of becoming redundant by the time they were completed. Fast track procurement methods, such as Design and Build were introduced in the 1990s, with the result that procurement times could be halved when compared to traditional procurement methods. Patient-focused healthcare encouraged the reassessment of therapeutic environments, including the introduction of artwork and the importance of architecture to assist patient recovery. The Private Finance Initiative was mooted by the Conservative Government in 1992, but by the change of administration in 1997 there were no new hospitals procured by PFI. It was left to the New Labour administration to implement the policy (Figures 4.8 and 4.9).

Initial use of the new procurement strategy led the Medical Architectural Research Unit (MARU) to comment that:

> In the NHS there is no coherent research agenda or programme of research studies at present. This confirms a substantial break in what was an established approach. As well as falling behind on functional studies, the new ideas about healthcare buildings that have appeared on the scene from the US and Europe are not being systematically or objectively examined. There appears currently to be an obsession with the process rather than the product, while there is no substantive basis of underpinning research for the current round of PFI hospitals. It seems likely that PFI will discourage innovation and the new hospitals may not respond to the larger agenda of the community and the environment.[11]

There was clearly a feeling that time and fiscal dictates allowed little opportunity to consider the needs of patients, medical advances and architectural quality in the same way that the first half-century of healthcare buildings had done. Research and feedback to inform the process was a

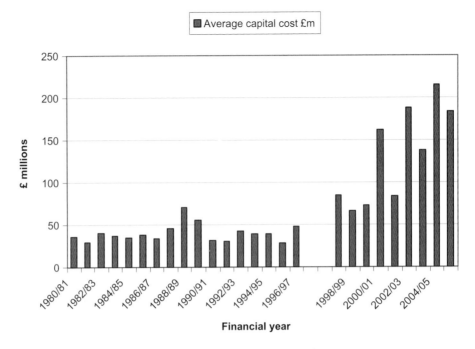

Figure 4.9 Hospitals' average capital cost into the twenty-first century (£M).

telling omission from early implementation. Even laudably entitled guidance focuses more on financial processes, and fails in its stated aim.[12] The commercial sensitivity of PFI consortiums' independently gained data and experiences can act as a barrier to cooperation, unlike earlier centralised initiatives. The immense scale of the current health building programme, while lacking the earlier prescription, is bereft of a mechanism to ensure that successes, and failures, are disseminated to promote healthcare excellence, widely.

A recent MARU research study piloted a framework for design quality to review selected PFI hospital design proposals. They used three key factors to define design quality: function; sustainability; and perception. And three levels at which they could be applied: site; concept; and building fabric. The factors were presented as a series of 40 questions that were addressed to the design teams and consortia. Their responses were analysed to reveal the following findings:

- Ideas about care planning were not particularly innovative.
- Opportunities for developing IT were not well developed.
- The planning diagrams were clever, but space standards may have reduced.
- Issues of sustainability were limited and not new.
- The designs demonstrated neither depth of thought nor innovation in space and form.[13]

Some of these early misgivings were certainly borne out by early reviews of the first PFI procured hospitals. The £87 million Cumberland Infirmary in Carlisle was Britain's first PFI hospital and was opened in April 2000. Media coverage shortly after the opening ceremony reported staff protesting at working conditions and a catalogue of building failures, such as burst water pipes flooding wards; windows that blew in; an atrium that overheated on sunny days; leaking roofs; lack of storage; and excessive charges for minor building alterations. However, Alan Davidson, the NHS Trust's project director described the alleged defects as 'teething problems' and said 'It's a flexible building, with dry-lined walls, wide-span structure, modular wiring and generous floor-to-floor heights'. But Davidson went on to admit that the PFI contract process is inflexible. The later, common complaints about PFI-procured hospitals, of inadequate bedspace numbers and cramped wards were also reported at Carlisle.[14]

4.4 Benchmarking hospitals – Introducing a design quality method

> *Second only to fresh air I should be inclined to rank light in the importance for the sick. Direct sunlight, not only daylight, is necessary for speedy recovery . . . I mention from experience, as quite perceptible in promoting recovery, the being able to see out of a window, instead of looking at a dead wall; the bright colours of flowers; the being able to read in bed by the light of the window close to the bedhead. It is generally said the effect is upon the mind. Perhaps so, it is not less upon the body.*
>
> Florence Nightingale, Notes on nursing, *1860*

The Design Quality Matrices are suitable for completion by professional experts with relevant experience, and can be adapted for any building type. They are robust and powerful tools in the hands of experts. Although the matrix scoring levels are set objectively using published standards, such as British Standards and consensual good practice, there is obviously an element of inherent subjectivity in this system.* Extreme views are ameliorated by group consensus, such as the peer review meetings. The results must be viewed as the expert opinion of a group of experienced consulting architects and engineers – for this reason there are defined levels of significance for the results.†

The Design Quality Matrices measure all aspects of the design quality of buildings, from the architectural strategy of site planning through to the detailed design of junctions of different materials. Each matrix has six sub-factors in columns and scoring levels in rows. The matrices were developed by objectively establishing a fully competent level of performance at the top level of Level 4. Although it is theoretically possible to register a score of Level 5, this would be an exceptional example of the very best practice. Once a top level is established it is a simple matter to cascade lower levels of performance, descending to Level 0. Each descent in performance usually implies a failure to achieve best practice in at least one significant area, or several minor shortcomings.

---

*The basis of the definitions is always linked at the highest level (Level 4, best practice). Level 3, good practice, is considered a minimum acceptable standard.
†Due to uncertainties in the matrix scoring process and the visual nature of the surveys, median results of less than one level apart in small sample groups should be given limited significance.

4.5 Benchmarking hospitals – The Design Quality Matrices

The very first condition to be sought in planning a (hospital) building is that it should be fit for its purpose, and the first law is that fitness is the foundation of beauty.

Florence Nightingale, Notes on nursing, *1860*

Matrix 1 – Architecture

Probably the most subjective matrix in the areas of internal and external architectural merit, but more robust in areas such as site and space planning.* The historic terms of firmness, commodity and delight are used to convey the concepts of robustness or structural integrity, usefulness or functionality, and uplifting of the spirits or beauty. Views of building users were also considered.

Matrix 2 – Engineering

Far more objective in nature, and scientifically measurable (e.g. lighting levels in lux and noise levels in dBA). The integration of services and architectural fabric is often symbolically evident in conceits such as housing boiler flues in architectural-feature chimneys. Maintainability and sourcing of replacement components are critical to continuous quality.

Matrix 3 – User comfort

Comfort conditions are scientifically measurable (e.g. lux, dBA and ambient and radiant temperature) and links between such conditions and user productivity are increasingly empirically evident – excessive noise, too much direct sunlight and poor ventilation degrade internal environments. However, ideal environments are more subtly created by the integration of art and science rather than crudely engineered by actions such as increasing lighting levels. Psychological aspects also play a crucial part in individual comfort and productivity. Successive research has shown that well-designed hospitals reduce patient recovery time and the need for drugs.[15] Recent research also indicates that the psychological benefits of a therapeutic environment also improve patients' perception of the quality of their clinical care.[16]

Matrix 4 – Whole life costs

This matrix concentrates on the potential whole life performance of the building's fabric and environmental services. Also considering ease of facil-

*Benedetti, F. *et al.* (2001) Morning sunlight reduces length of hospitalisation in bipolar depression. *Journal of Affective Disorders.* February, 62(3), pp. 221–3. Bright artificial light improves non-seasonal depression. This study suggests that sunlight could share this effect. Patients on the east-facing side of a hospital ward (morning sun of 15,500 lux) had a mean 3.67 day shorter stay than patients on the west-facing side (morning sun of 1400 lux).

Figure 4.10 Traditionally procured hospital (*circa* 1970) with recent lightweight roof extension.

ities management and the adaptability of the building for future alteration or extension (Figure 4.10). This matrix helps to expose the trade-offs between capital and running costs, which affect future performance.

Matrix 5 – Detail design

Anomalies in building performance are often caused by errors or inconsistencies in detailing, such as architectural junctions of different materials at abutments or incorrectly sized components, furnishings and fittings. The former can lead to leaks or even flooding, while the latter often causes loss of functionality or even serious accidents. Such failures are often attributed to poor detailed design or bad workmanship – or a combination of both.

Matrix 6 – User satisfaction

Initial interviews with facilities managers and staff of hospitals are structured with six questions which they are asked to rank in terms of their satisfaction, on a scale of one to five (five representing maximum satisfaction). Although necessarily subjective, the semi-structured interviews reveal a wealth of anecdotal evidence and help to inform the surveys.

Matrix 7 – Building aspects of clinical safety

This matrix specifically addresses the clinical aspects of building design, such as ease of cleaning and back-up electricity reliability.

4.6 Benchmarking hospitals – Architecture

Architecture is also about the spiritual needs of people as well as their material needs. It has as much to do with optimism, joy and reassurance: of order in a disordered world; privacy in the midst of many; of space in a crowded world; of light on a dull day. It is about quality.

Sir Norman Foster, RIBA Journal, *1983*

4.6.1 Architecture (Matrix 1) – Level 4 definitions

Architectural exterior. Design has obvious firmness, commodity and delight. No features that are obvious architectural excesses. Users like and respect the building. Excellent materials selection and placement. Adequate weathering and maintenance.

Site planning. Functional separation and integration optimises use of site. Good site displacement of built elements and layout. Good solar orientation. Good vehicle access/parking/pedestrian access. Adequate parking provision. Adequate space for future building extension (Figure 4.11).

Interior design. Design has obvious beauty and clarity of purpose. Internal aspects of good scale and ergonomics. Daylight quality and acoustics excellent. Excellent use of colour, finishes and furniture. Interior allows flexibility and potential refurbishment.

Figure 4.11 Dramatic entrance to a PFI-procured hospital.

Space planning. Excellent use of space with good juxtaposition of key clinical spaces. Support spaces, storage and circulation all adequate. Imaginative use of servant to served space.* Good social space.

Specification. Excellent component selection and placement, with adequate input from experienced users and maintenance staff. Excellent detailing and provision for maintenance. No obvious potential design defects at materials' junctions.

Sustainability. Environmental impact minimised by proper consideration of environmental, economic and social factors. Heating, lighting and ventilation systems and components robust, reliable and competently optimised and integrated with passive counterparts. Potential for an excellent BREEAM rating.

4.7 Benchmarking hospitals – Environmental engineering

> *Hospital acquired infection is the cause of around 5,000 deaths a year in the UK. Recent research has shown that ventilation practice and design is a significant contributor.*
>
> *Nick Cullen and Stewart Boyle,*
> Building Services Journal, *2002*

4.7.1 Environmental engineering (Matrix 2) – Level 4 definitions

Integration. Services design empathetic to and optimises all aspects of the architecture. Good consideration of thermal and lighting issues. No intrusion of services into occupied space. Appropriate user control of environment.

Mechanical systems design. Robust best practice utilising the most appropriate components integrated into efficient reliable systems. Covers heating, ventilation, cooling and plumbing. No acoustic intrusion from services into the use of the building.

Electrical systems design. Robust best practice utilising the most appropriate components integrated into efficient reliable systems. Covers internal and external lighting, communications, cables, conduits and ducts – no unintended visible intrusion of services.

---

*This phrase is used in the sense intended by the American architect, Louis Kahn (1901–1974). Served space represents the essential purpose of the building, such as wards, consulting rooms and laboratories in a hospital – places where people are. Servant space represents areas such as circulation space, environmental engineering voids and risers, and storage spaces.

Maintainability.   Maintenance and access designed to minimise loss of use, and avoid need for specialised access for replacement. All components and service data widely available.

Sourcing.   All components selected for wide availability and compliance with well-known standards. Design has avoided use of specially manufactured items that could incur delays in sourcing and high replacement costs.

Sustainability.   Services components, system arrangement and controls selected and commissioned to minimise environmental impact. Comprehensive and easily useable data available for maintenance. Minimal use of materials deleterious to the environment. Potential for an excellent BREEAM rating.*

4.8 Benchmarking hospitals – User comfort

The architecture of healthcare must surely be one that provides reassurance, comfort, welcome, and human scale alongside clinical excellence.

David Hutchison MBE, Hospital builders, 2004

4.8.1 User comfort (Matrix 3) – Level 4 definitions

Summertime overheat.   Building interior unlikely to experience more than 30 hours per year above environmental temperature greater than 27 °C, and occupants have controlled sunlight.

Visual environment.   Daylight and artificial lighting sources entirely appropriate for task and promote a cheerful but non-distracting atmosphere. Full compliance with workplace regulations.

Heating comfort.   Internal air temperatures within −1.5 °C to +2.0 °C of target temperature. No reason for occupant discomfort from asymmetric thermal radiation.[†]

---

*NHS energy targets were outlined in a letter dated April 2001, from John Denham, the Minister of State for Health. The letter outlined a mandatory target of 35–55 GigaJoules/100 cubic metres for the healthcare estate for all new capital developments and major redevelopments or refurbishments; and that all existing facilities should achieve a target of 55–65 GigaJoules/100 cubic metres. The minister went on to remind recipients of '... the importance of environmental issues, including achieving energy efficiency and whole life costing to encourage best use of resources over a sustained period'.
[†]Research suggests that the temperature of a space's enclosure (e.g. floor, walls and ceiling) should be measured in addition to ambient air temperature to determine optimal thermal comfort limits in a space.

Audible and visual intrusion. No interference to space functions from continuous, intermittent or impulsive background noise within interior or exterior occupied spaces. No unwanted or noticeable visual intrusion.

Acoustics quality. All occupied areas free of acoustic features that act to the detriment of efficient working and use of the building. Covers reverberation time and intelligibility of speech.

Air quality, internal. No noticeable odour, dust, noticeable allergic or health symptoms from any contaminants such as micro-organisms, organic or non-organic compounds. Humidity satisfactory in all spaces. Carbon dioxide levels below 1500 parts per million.

4.9 Benchmarking hospitals – Whole life costs

> It's unwise to pay too much, but it is worse to pay too little. When you pay too much you lose a little money – that is all. When you pay too little you sometimes lose everything, because the thing you bought was incapable of doing the things it was bought to do. The common law of business balance prohibits paying a little and getting a lot. It can't be done if you deal with the lowest bidder, it is well to add something for the risk you run, and if you do that you will have enough to pay for something better.
>
> *John Ruskin, 1819–1906*

4.9.1 Whole life costs (Matrix 4) – Level 4 definitions

External materials. All components selected and installed to achieve lowest cost of ownership. All have good resistance to vandalism, sun, wind, rain. Graceful degradation of appearance with wear. Detailing to best practice.

Internal fabric and finishes. Fabric and finishes chosen for lowest cost of ownership. Properties include ease of routine and special cleaning, graceful degradation of appearance with wear, easy repair and replacement.

Building services capital items. All components selected for minimum cost of ownership. Adequate space for minor and major maintenance. Design enables most service activities to be undertaken during occupation.

Building services revenue maintenance. All components selected for minimum cost of ownership. Component arrangement and availability

Figure 4.12 External sun shades (PFI) – brise soleil to southerly orientated elevations.

good. Easy maintenance access. Most service activities possible during occupation.

Facilities management: fitness for function.   All architectural fittings, fitments, furniture and furnishings selected for minimum cost of ownership, and average repair time is short. All items eminently suitable for purpose (Figure 4.12).

Flexibility for layout change and extension.   Building plan, positioning within site, construction and materials facilitate easy future adaptation and extension without excessive cost or disturbance to occupiers.

4.10 Benchmarking hospitals – Detail design

God is in the details.

Popular aphorism

4.10.1 Detail design (Matrix 5) – Level 4 definitions

External detail.   Good resistance to vandalism sun, wind and rain. Graceful degradation of appearance with wear and tear. Detailing to best practice. Good functional and aesthetic detailing to all roofs, walls, plinths, e.g. damp-proof courses at least 150 mm from the ground.

Internal detail.   Ease of routine and special cleaning, graceful degradation of appearance with wear, easy repair and replacement. Good functional and aesthetic detailing to all floors, walls, ceilings, e.g. shadow gaps to suspended ceilings.

Junction details.   Architectural junctions of different materials, such as roof/wall abutments, detailed to good practice with good workmanship. Good functional and aesthetic detailing to all door and window openings and thresholds, e.g. crafted flashings rather than mastic excretions.

Furnishings.   All furnishings selected for ability to retain good appearance and for minimum cost of ownership. All seating comfortable for expected occupancy – anthropomorphically suitable to BS 5873. Correctly sized, robust and solid.

Fittings.   All architectural fittings eminently suitable for purpose. Anthropomorphically suitable to BS 5873. Correctly sized, robust and solid. Suitable provision for disabled persons' use/access.

Safety and security.   Detailed architectural disposition to good practice and avoiding potential hazards. External and internal hazards controlled by design, such as minimum entrances, which are capable of observation and/or CCTV and/or fencing.

4.11 Benchmarking hospitals – User satisfaction

The real bottom line is this – there are all these things that you the taxpayer is paying billions for and you'll have to suffer the results if they are wrong.

Hilary Cotton, Director of Research, Design Council

4.11.1 User satisfaction (Matrix 6) – Questions to be asked

Initial interviews with facilities' managers are semi-structured with six questions, which they are asked to rank in terms of their satisfaction, on a scale of one to five (five representing maximum satisfaction). The six questions represent the 'sixth matrix' which adds a user satisfaction dimension to the BRE Design Quality Matrix (DQM). The questions are used to obtain anecdotal evidence of problems and success, and help to focus the subsequent survey. The responses are necessarily subjective and usually score at higher levels than the experts' opinion. The six questions are:

(1) Does the building work well?

(2) Does the building lift the spirits?

(3) Will the building weather well, withstand wear and tear, and be easily maintained?

(4) Is the building flexible?

(5) Is the building secure?

(6) Is the indoor environment of the building fit for purpose, in terms of daylighting, heating, ventilation and acoustics.

4.12 Benchmarking hospitals – Building aspects of clinical safety

Heath depends on a state of equilibrium amongst the various factors that govern the operation of the body and the mind: this equilibrium in turn is reached only when man lives in harmony with his external environment.

Hippocrates, 460–377 BC

4.12.1 Building aspects of clinical safety (Matrix 7) – Level 4 definitions

Building services. Compliance with all services related to clinical safety performance requirements. Includes separation of mechanical ventilation intake and exhaust (and proximity to opening windows). Carbon dioxide levels acceptable; adequate air flows everywhere; acceptable lighting levels.

Furniture, fittings and equipment selection. Selected for easy cleaning and the avoidance of dust and dirt traps to hygiene standards appropriate to use. Minimal degradation with wear and tear.

Internal finishes and junction details. Floor, wall and ceiling materials selected for safety in use. Design detailing and installation minimise difficult to clean corners and ledges etc.

Standby plant. Covers standby electrical generation, ventilation services, lifts etc. All essential services and utilities without supply failure or interruption to hospital business.

Hazardous waste. All hazardous waste and dirty utensils effectively separated from medical and clinical processes. Includes competent ventilation levels, airflow paths, and minimisation of cross-contamination in transit.

Architectural aspects. All internal and external architectural features, such as parapet walls and stairway dimensions etc., comply with building regulations and health and safety legislation.

4.13 Benchmarking hospitals – Recommendations

There has been progress in new hospitals, with one or two excellent schemes, but innovation remains hard to find and some designs are mediocre.

Jon Rouse, then Chief Executive, CABE

4.13.1 Recommendations

- The current massive programme of hospital procurement needs to be accompanied by a central experience-sharing system, similar to those instigated in the post-war era.
- There is no substitute for an informed client to achieve design quality and optimal functionality – this is a particularly acute issue in the health building sector.
- The briefing process is at the core of delivering better buildings. If insufficient time, effort and budget are afforded at the critical early stages when the brief is formulated between designers and informed clients, the results will haunt all parties for decades to come. Time for design, and design leadership is crucial at the early stages.
- Design quality metrics, or performance indicators, should be laid down as part of the briefing process, and design quality should be monitored at all subsequent stages – such as each of the RIBA Plan of Work stages. Post-occupancy assessments will complete this cycle and provide feedback for future projects.
- Architectural design competitions create a forum for the emergence of new ideas and approaches. Combined with staged selection processes they can discern appropriate solutions and allow for balanced selection criteria.[17]
- Demonstration projects were a core element of the post-war hospital building programme and we would benefit from similar approaches in the current round of investment. These could be architectural competition winners and provide exemplars, ideas for standardisation where appropriate, and a test-bed for innovation. The medical profession should be thoroughly involved as informed clients.
- Environmental sustainability and energy efficiency needs to be addressed with appropriate benchmarking tools. The exemplar model was used before – it needs to be reinstated.
- Case studies from across Europe, and other continents, should be investigated to glean the lessons learned from wider experience.
- The vision for future healthcare environments should be addressed in an appropriate forum, reviewing worldwide case studies, demonstration projects, and medical and clinical advances.
- Further research into the patient experience is required to deliver truly patient-focused architecture. This may represent a change of direction in healthcare provision.[18]

4.14 Environmental sustainability

The concept of environmental sustainability is closely allied to that of whole life costing as both require a long-term understanding of buildings, taking into account not only present needs, but the need for future changes and the cost and performance in use and over time. The minimum design life of a building is often considered as 60 years, and the minimum design life-cycle of a civic building as 120 years.* The need for sustainability has many consequences for building design, not least in the use of land, space and environmental services. The main criteria of sustainability are characterised by the 'triple bottom line' of social, economic and environmental (global, local and internal) aspects. An holistic approach is clearly required that takes into account all areas of a development's 'eco footprint'.

For example, a new low-energy hospital sited in an out-of-town location will have disadvantageous transportation energy implications, and as such will rarely be an ideal sustainable solution.† Hospitals are also particularly high users of water, so water conservation becomes another important area of an holistic approach. Hospitals are also perceived as optimum candidates for Combined Heat and Power (CHP) systems, due to their 24-hour occupancy – such systems may also fit in well with the obvious need for emergency standby generation in hospitals. However, the general uptake of CHP in the health sector is not particularly impressive, with only 208 examples out of a potential total of several hundred general hospitals.‡ There seems little doubt that CHP can generate major energy savings for hospitals. Anecdotal evidence from a traditionally procured hospital, with its earliest building dating from the 1960s, suggests that they save approximately £220 000 a year in energy costs as a result of their CHP plant. Renewable energy is also a partial solution to reducing energy costs (Figure 4.13).

Other widespread opportunities for improving sustainability include competent commissioning of variable speed drives on air handling fans and heating pumps, use of lighting controls, and reduction in standing losses of boilers. Architectural design needs to take account of displacing artificial lighting by daylight, or fabric aspects of summertime overheating. Frequently, these items are viewed solely on an initial capital costs basis, being an easy target at budget meetings and contract financial close to achieve capital cost constraints. Experienced hospital engineers are fully aware of the impact on operational costs, and the frequent lost opportunities to minimise whole life costs due to constraints on capital cost. A widespread view is that the capital to achieve minimum cost of ownership should be ring-fenced. Public Sector Comparators must include all environmental sustainability requirements, and a champion for sustainability is appointed to

*British Standard 7543: 1999 (ISO 15686).
†Planning guidance which aims to encourage local access and limit unnecessary travel, especially car journeys, specifically refers to hospitals. *Town centres and retail development* PPG6 (1996), Department of Environment UK, London: The Stationery Office.
‡*Digest of UK Energy Statistics*, Dukes (2004), London: The Stationery Office. p. 147. The leisure sector recorded 426 CHP installations and the hotels sector recorded 299 installations.

Figure 4.13 Antrim Hospital, Northern Ireland – retrofitted wind turbine.

ensure that sustainability is not overlooked during final negotiations with preferred bidders. There is evidence that some health trusts are aiming for flagship, environmentally sustainable hospitals.[19]

Sustainability and energy efficiency are prominently linked to whole life costs and often serve as a key indicator of the commitment, or lack of it, to a whole life costing approach, generally – as opposed to capital cost solely dictating procurement decisions. Most PFI hospitals are sited on out-of-town, green-field sites which lead to increased transportation energy usage, leading to increased carbon dioxide emissions, pollution and often inconvenience to staff and patients – negative impacts on all the bottom-line sustainability measures.

Causeway Hospital in Coleraine, Northern Ireland, is in many ways the best hospital we had experience of, which was likely to score at good practice levels (Level 3), across all columns of the matrices. This hospital was traditionally procured a few years ago and includes innovative features, such as a pneumatic air distribution system for dirty laundry and a CHP installation. Causeway also appears to have taken an holistic approach to whole life costing; one example is the inclusion of permanent gantries to the extensive rooflights, to facilitate easy cleaning, maintenance and repair.

The Royal Institute of British Architects (RIBA) recently urged architects to boycott PFI projects that do not meet high design quality criteria. RIBA Councillor, Sunand Prasad stated that the criteria could include a PFI proposal being properly researched and with sufficient emphasis on design. The RIBA believes there should be an end to competitive tendering practices which waste resources and minimise the time for design. RIBA President, Jack Pringle, vowed to devote his term of office to improving the PFI process as 'PFI is here to stay . . . we are about to rebuild the public estate – this happens once in every two generations'.[20] Among suggestions to improve the process is the idea of the public-sector client appointing a design team to work with them directly, to develop the design to an appropriately detailed stage to ensure high design quality, before the project is put out to competitive tender. This should ensure that the winning consortium inherits the risk, a design which is truly fit for purpose, and a healthy level of client involvement.* The designers could be retained in a consultant capacity (novated) to help the client nuance the brief, the lack of which is the main source of problems on existing PFI projects. Such suggestions could reduce waste in the bidding process, bring down barriers to entry to smaller and perhaps more innovative businesses, and put the client and the building user back in control, again.[21]

4.15 International case studies

> Hospitals and big infrastructure buildings are examples of architecture where the meaning of the old Vitruvian 'utilitas' still pertains. I rejoice that such a category is still entrusted by society to architects. The complexity of the programme (of the Madrid Maternity Hospital) is present in its architecture, with its system of courtyards that produces a porous plan, ready to receive disparate uses. The courtyards also help to establish a clear grid of movement – a very important feature in buildings of this nature.
>
> Raphael Moneo, RIBA Gold Medal acceptance speech, 2003

4.15.1 Bronson Methodist Hospital, Michigan, USA

Internal landscaping, daylighting, wayfinding, evidenced-based design, 2000

Bronson Methodist Hospital, Kalamazoo, Michigan, USA, is $181 million new-build, 343-bed hospital which was opened in 2000. The designers were briefed to produce a state-of-art facility with 'nature integrated into a technical environment'. An internal garden is at the heart of the building, and natural light is used extensively. Wayfinding is intuitive, guided by landmarks and daylighting. Roger Ulrich, using evidence-based design methods, benchmarked statistical outcomes from the move from the old hospital into the new one. The new building resulted in an 11 per cent decrease in 'hospital acquired infection' (HAI); the turnover of nurses reduced by half; and increased staff and patient satisfaction (over 95 per cent satisfaction from surveys). Major financial savings are gleaned in the new facility due to fewer patient room transfers. The new building has also resulted in a large increase in market share.

4.15.2 Causeway Hospital, Coleraine, Northern Ireland

Innovation, CHP, whole life costs, traditional procurement, 2002

The town of Coleraine in Northern Ireland is located about 12 miles away from the Giant's Causeway, an International Heritage Site. Design work on a new hospital started in the mid-1990s with a brief that sought an alter-

---

*The RIBA also launched the Client Design Advisor register in October 2005, in an attempt to increase client involvement in non-traditional methods of building procurement.

native to the Nucleus plan template. Ultimately some features from the Nucleus system were retained, such as the structural grid and internal courtyards, as they provided optimal bay widths, and natural lighting and ventilation, respectively. The new Causeway Hospital has a maximum capacity of 250 beds, 34 departments and over 1000 staff. A central street, on an east–west axis bisects the departmental templates for easy wayfinding. The central wedge-shaped block forms a focal point, or hinge, for the main entrance and reception, including an atrium restaurant.

The designers introduced an innovative technology to combat one of the causes of hygiene problems – the cost and practicality of handling the daily flow of dirty laundry. A large-bore pneumatic system moves surgical waste and dirty laundry through tubes in the ceiling void, taking it from each ward and the theatre directly to a terminus in the energy centre. This reduces porter workload and keeps infectious material away from people. It is the first installation of this technology in the UK and was supplied by an American specialist firm. Other special features include a $3 \times 300\,kWe$ diesel engine-based CHP (Combined Heat and Power) system, and bed-head trunking systems which incorporate both uplighting for general ward illumination and medical gases outlets (Figure 4.14).

4.15.3 Madrid Maternity and Paediatric Hospital, Madrid, Spain

Urban site, courtyards, daylighting, wayfinding, acoustics, 2003

The new Madrid Maternity Hospital, by architect Raphael Moneo, is part of the Gregorio Maranon Hospital which covers three city blocks – some existing buildings are incorporated in to the new maternity block. It comprises a pair of hospitals, one for maternity and the other for paediatrics, which include 9 delivery rooms, 11 operating theatres and 313 beds. The architect's response to a harsh urban environment was to turn the plan inwards around eight large courtyards, placing support function spaces on the perimeter. These service spaces also serve as an acoustic buffer zone, which combine with a dense superstructure (reinforced concrete floor slabs and external walls) to isolate the inward-looking wards and courtyards from city noise levels. Wards are detailed to give 'isolation, tranquillity and domestic character', using maple window frames and Majorca shutters, which contrast with the steel, aluminium and glass facades. Internal partitions are plasterboard studwork for flexibility of layout and engineering services, while high specifications of marble and ceramic tiles are used in circulation spaces, with coloured linoleum in the wards.

4.15.4 Basel University Hospital, Basel, Switzerland

Refurbishment and extension of exemplar 1930s hospital, daylighting, 2003

Basel University was founded in 1460 and is the oldest university in Switzerland. Basel University Hospital is now a teaching hospital for 1050 students of medicine and dentistry. The original hospital was built between 1939

Figure 4.14 Causeway Hospital, Coleraine, Northern Ireland – atrium, rooflight gantries and water feature. This figure is also reproduced in colour in the colour plate section.

and 1945 and was considered exemplary for its time. It was recently refurbished to improve performance and update it in line with contemporary clinical needs. An extension was also added to house an operating theatre and gynaecology unit. The new building continues the modernist architectural style of the original hospital, but creates less utilitarian interiors using colour and natural light. Flexibility of internal layout is achieved by repeating plan configurations and using moveable partitions. The fact that a 60-year-old hospital was successfully refurbished to satisfy modern clinical requirements demonstrates the principles of adaptive reuse and long life/loose fit.

4.15.5 Evelina Children's Hospital, Guy's and St Thomas' Hospital, London

Urban site, innovation, wayfinding, daylighting, natural ventilation, traditional procurement, 2005

The NHS trust's aim was to create 'a hospital that does not feel like a hospital' so that children's visits to the building were not intimidating. Hopkins Architects won a RIBA architectural competition in 1999 and the hospital was opened in October 2005. The 140-inpatient bed facility was part funded by a charity fund from the parent hospital and NHS funds – the construction budget was slightly over £40 million. The facility also includes three operating theatres; kidney dialysis unit; full imaging service; cardiac unit; outpatients department; and a school within the hospital. The architects cite 'fun and efficiency' in their brief, and part of the fun is an (optional) helter-skelter between the first floor, atrium level and the ground floor. Wayfinding is facilitated by themed floors ranging from 'Ocean' at the bottom, all the way through to 'Sky' at the top, via 'Forest' and 'Mountain', among other habitats. The themed floors are colour coded with inlaid floor patterns which depict relevant symbolism. Vacancies for nurses' posts in the hospital have fallen from 30 per cent to 2 per cent, while applications for consultants' posts have doubled. The client's representative, Alastair Gourlay, hopes that they have '. . . set the bar higher in our aspiration to provide a quality healthcare environment and shown that design is a catalyst for improving the patient experience'.*

4.16 Further international case studies

- **Oslo National University, Norway** – competition, patient-focus, 1991.
- **Rijnstate, Arhem, The Netherlands** – flexibility and expansion, 1994.
- **Santa Clara, San José, USA** – government-owned, patient-focus, 1999.
- **Atsumi, Aichi, Japan** – general hospital, wayfinding, privacy, 2000.

*Just what the doctor ordered, *RIBA Journal* (2005), December, pp. 36–44.

- **St Vincent's, Sydney, Australia** – teaching, high-rise, efficiency, 2000.
- **Boulder, Colorado, USA** – first hospital to get LEED certification, 2003.

4.17 Chapter summary

Hospitals are ancient religious building types which have evolved into secular institutions, largely state-funded in the UK after the middle of the twentieth century. Medieval plan-type precedents included cruciforms and courtyards, with many early examples of external treatment areas which presage modern tuberculosis sanitaria. However, unsanitary conditions in medieval hospitals and limited medical understanding of the spread of disease dictated bleak prospects for most patients. Many early hospitals were more a means of separating diseased inmates from the general population, than genuinely curative institutions. This stark fact probably continued into the mid-Victorian age, until reforms in healthcare and increased clinical understanding began to show clear functional architectural needs in the form of maximising exposure to fresh air and sunlight. Even today, with outbreaks of hospital-acquired infections such as MRSA,* hygiene continues to play an important and often basic role in hospital design, a requirement which suited the 'clean lines' and 'clutter-free' aesthetic of modernist architecture but has now highlighted behavioural and architectural aspects, such as the move to increasing single-room occupancy.

Pavilion-style 'Nightingale' wards, which revolutionised the form and scale of hospital design in the late nineteenth century are still at the heart of much of Britain's health infrastructure, although now increasingly refurbished. The post-war hospital building programmes rivalled Victorian attempts in scale and ambition, despite economic constraints in the mid-1970s. This centralised NHS programme allowed scientific research and standardisation in hospital design, with concurrent economies of scale and consistent good practice. Nucleus hospitals continue in use and compare favourably in many aspects to more recent building procurements. The system also continues to inform aspects of planning and briefing for new hospitals and international examples of good practice warrant further study in our current drive to modernise the health infrastructure of the UK. The Private Finance Initiative was introduced in 1992 and the first PFI hospital was opened in 2000, with mixed reviews.

A series of seven matrices, that make up the BRE Design Quality Method, can be used to score hospitals. The matrices contain several sub-factors and scoring levels are objectively set for completion by construction or property professionals. They cover the following main areas:

- **Architecture**. The relatively subjective area of aesthetic merit, and also the more prosaic qualities of specification, site and space planning.

---

*Methicillin-resistant *Staphylococcus aureus*.

- **Environmental engineering**. More objective and supported by scientifically measurable lighting, noise and temperature levels. Sympathetic integration with architecture is crucial, not to mention maintainability and replacement sourcing.
- **User comfort**. Internal comfort conditions are also scientifically measurable and links between them and clinical aspects are increasingly empirically evident. Integrating art and science creates ideal environments, e.g. the quality of daylight is just as important as the measurable quantity. Psychological aspects also play a crucial part in individual comfort and productivity. Successive research has shown that well-designed hospitals reduce patient recovery time and need for drugs.[22]
- **Building cost of ownership**. Covers the occupancy costs of hospitals and the potential whole life performance of building fabric and services. It provides an analysis of the trade-offs between capital and running costs that affect future building performance.
- **Detail design**. Failures in building performance are often caused by poor detailed design or bad workmanship. Rectifying and coping with such failures will increase maintenance and occupancy costs.
- **User satisfaction**. Semi-structured questions are used to assess users' satisfaction with the building. Each aspect is scored on a scale of one to five (five representing the highest level of satisfaction). The results are necessarily subjective.
- **Building aspects of clinical safety**. This matrix specifically addresses the clinical aspects of building design, such as ease of cleaning and back-up electricity reliability.

The last major hospital building programme in the UK followed the 1947 National Health Service Act, was centrally instigated, and attended by complementary investment in shared research, feedback, and demonstration projects. Drives towards economic efficiency led to standardisation, such as the Nucleus system of hospital procurement, including briefing data packs and standard plan–layout templates. Sir Philip Powell summarised the benefits of the Nucleus system as 'It gave the architects more time to think about the architecture'. The ambitious proposals to rebuild and extend hospital provision in this country went through fits and starts, largely due to economic conditions and the cost of running facilities. Only two new hospitals were built in the 1970s. The oil shocks of this decade stimulated the creation of energy efficient hospitals such as St Mary's on the Isle of Wight, with a target of reducing energy use by 50 per cent compared to a typical DGH. The introduction of the Patient's Charter in 1991 led to a more commercial approach and experimentation with fast-track building procurement methods, such as design and build. Patient-focused healthcare was also introduced in this decade. PFI was mooted by the Conservative government in 1992, but the Labour administration procured the first hospitals using PFI after the 1997 elections.

The overall design quality of contemporary hospitals probably has significant room for improvement. The post-war hospital building programme was accompanied by a comparable effort and investment in design research and systems thinking, which led to the efficiency of the Nucleus system. The immense scale of the current health building programme, while lacking the earlier prescription, is bereft of a mechanism to ensure that successes, and failures, are disseminated to promote healthcare excellence, widely.

Shared experience, architectural competitions, and demonstration projects with the full involvement of the medical profession should lead to innovation and efficiency in healthcare design. Case studies, both from an architectural and economic point of view, from across Europe and the world, should allow us to benefit from wider experience. The future provision of healthcare buildings is at a crossroads and requires further research.

4.18 References

1 Pevsner, N. (1976) *A history of building types.* London: Thames and Hudson.

2 Farwell, B. (1981) *For queen and country: A social history of the Victorian and Edwardian Army.* London: Allen Lane.

3 Ley, A.J. (2000) *A history of building control in England and Wales 1840–1990.* Coventry: RICS Books.

4 Banham, R. (1969) *The architecture of the well-tempered environment.* London: Architectural Press.

5 Hobday, R. (1999) *The healing sun: Sunlight and health in the twenty-first century.* Forres: Findhorn Press.

6 Nuffield Provincial Hospitals Trust (1955) *Studies in the function and design of hospitals.* London: OUP.

7 Owen, D. (1976) Hospital building: Dr Owen reviews the prospects. *The hospital and health services review.* January, pp. 26–29.

8 Monk, T. (2004) *Hospital Builders.* London: John Wiley & Sons.

9 Francis, S. *et al.* (1999) *Fifty years of ideas in healthcare buildings.* London: Nuffield Trust.

10 Francis, S. *et al.* (1999) *Fifty years of ideas in healthcare buildings.* London: Nuffield Trust.

11 Francis, S. *et al.* (1999) *Fifty years of ideas in healthcare buildings.* London: Nuffield Trust.

12 Treasury Taskforce (1997) *How to achieve design quality through the PFI process.* Partnership for prosperity, Technical note number 7. London: HM Treasury.

13 MARU (2000) *Design quality in selected PFI hospitals.* Unpublished. Commissioned by NHS Estates. Cited in Francis, S. *et al.* (2001) *Building a 2020 vision: Future healthcare environments.* London: The Nuffield Trust.

14 Spring, M. (2003) We've got your results, *Building Magazine,* 30 May.

15 Ulrich, R. (1984) View through a window may influence recovery from surgery. *Science,* vol. 224.

16 Lawson, B. (2004) Assessing benefits in the health sector. In Macmillan, S. (ed.) (2004) *Designing better buildings: Quality and value in the built environment.* London: Spon.

17 NHS Estates (1994) *Better by design: Pursuit of excellence in healthcare buildings.* London: HMSO.

18 Francis, S. *et al.* (2001) *Building a 2020 vision: Future healthcare environments.* London: The Nuffield Trust.

19 Blake, D. and Hall, C. (2005) Redevelopment of Whipps Cross University Hospital. *The PFI Journal*, Issue 50, September.

20 Bennett, E. (2005) RIBA urges boycott of bad PFI. *Building Design*, 8 July.

21 Booth, R. (2005) A commonsense solution to PFI debacle. *Building Design*, 8 July.

22 Ulrich, R. (1984) View through a window may influence recovery from surgery. *Science*, vol. 224.

Chapter 5

Housing

5.1 Historical evolution of housing

> *I find it incredible that there will not be a sweeping revolution*
> *in the methods of building during the next century. A few ener-*
> *getic men might at any time set out to alter all this.*
>
> *H.G. Wells,* Anticipations, *1902*

The population of England quadrupled from 10 million at the beginning of the nineteenth century to 40 million at its end (Figure 5.1). This historically unprecedented growth was made possible by the prosperity of advanced industrialisation, but with inherent social penalties wrought by rapid urbanisation, such as overcrowding and squalor. Some 80 per cent of England's population lived in cities on the eve of World War I. Agricultural decline, exacerbated by policies of free trade with consequent cheap imports of prairie wheat, caused a rural exodus to the cities. The spread of the railway network enabled cheap and swift migration from rural areas to new industrial employment opportunities in towns and cities. Conversely, systematic suburbanisation allowed the emergent middle classes to escape city centres, contrary to trends in continental Europe.

Political emancipation began with the First Reform Act of 1832 and was then compounded by subsequent Acts. Continental socialism was gradually imported, but at first in an idealistic guise when compared to the bloodshed in mainland Europe – in the form of practical Liberalism. But, utopian socialism proved a strong cultural and artistic catalyst among the artists and architects of the Arts and Crafts movement in the late nineteenth and early twentieth century. The rise of the middle classes, coupled with economically competitive education spurred on the rise of the professions. Political reaction to the consolidated success of the Liberal Party found cogent form in two speeches by Disraeli, who was the undisputed leader of the Conservatives by 1872. These tellingly concentrated on social health legislation and the first compared the biblical quotation 'Vanitas vanitatum, omnia vanitas' with his contemporary adage 'Sanitas sanitatum, omnia sanitas'.*

---

*'Vanity of vanities, all is vanity' (Ecclesiastes 1:2), thus 'Sanity of sanities, all is sanity' – or 'sanitation'.

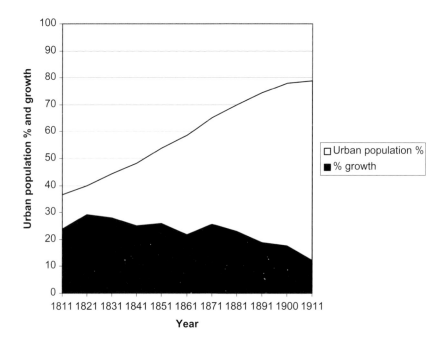

Figure 5.1 The extent of urbanisation in England and Wales, 1811–1911.

Pure air, pure water, the inspection of unhealthy habitations, the adulteration of food – these and many kindred matters may be legitimately dealt with by the legislature . . . the first considera-tion of a minister should be the health of the people.[1]

This Latin analogy heralded the political acceptance of the new 'religion' of sanitation and the gradual recognition of the dire social consequences of *laissez-faire* capitalism. Although a Public Health Act was passed in 1848, allowing the creation of local bye-laws, the legislation was relatively inef-fective compared with later consolidating acts, such as Disraeli's 1875 Public Health Act. The political importance of sanitation was symbolically emphasised by 'The Great Stink' of 1858, during which the stench of the open sewer that the Thames had become, emptied the House of Commons – not to mention deaths from widespread diseases such as cholera which peaked in mid-century.[2] Snow's evidence for the water-borne transmissions of disease was reinforced when Prince Albert died of typhus in 1861, attributed to 'bad drains', a fact which undoubtedly helped to stimulate concentration on improved sanitary legislation.*

National wealth in the United Kingdom increased six-fold in the nine-teenth century, but by 1900 Britain's policy of Free Trade, complementing her *laissez-faire* economics, was beginning to turn against her – as nascent foreign industries, protected by tariff barriers, reached maturity. British industrial capacity was overtaken by the emerging industrial powers of both

---

*Dr John Snow (1813–58) graduated MD from London University in 1844. He was a pioneer anaesthetist and administered chloroform to Queen Victoria for the birth of two of her children. He first advanced his theory in 1849. The site of the water pump, near his surgery off Carnaby Street, where he studied the spread of cholera-infected water, is now marked by a granite stone, and, given his teetotalism, ironically, by a pub called the John Snow.

America and Germany by 1914.[3] But middle-class wealth was always comparatively modest and rented accommodation was the norm, preceded by significant investment in their children's education.[4] The terrifying social price of Britain's earlier industrial domination was all too tangibly evident in the streets of her capital and other industrialised cities by the last decades of the nineteenth century. This was poignantly illustrated by the simple statistic that average working-class individuals were several inches shorter than their counterparts higher up the social scale.[5] Social philanthropy came of age with sound intellectual underpinnings as exemplified by Thomas Hill Green at Oxford, a pioneer of the welfare state, and continued by those who came immediately under his influence – including William Morris, by association with Charles Faulkner, with whom he later founded Morris, Faulkner and Company.[6]

Architecture displayed a polarity similar to other fields of Victorian endeavour, notably symbolised by the battle of the styles between the Gothic Revival and Classicism. This was exemplified on one side by Pugin's moral and spiritual crusade for the true Christian pointed style. This war of aesthetic attrition was increasingly played out in competitions for public buildings by mid-century.[7] The Goths were largely, and unsurprisingly, victorious in the spiritual sphere, but the Classicists had more or less won in the field of secular buildings apart from, notably, Street's Law Courts in the Strand. Even celebrated Goths such as George Gilbert Scott, who had cut his teeth on utilitarian new building types such as poor houses,* reverted to Italianate Classicism rather than lose the commission when his original Gothic scheme for the Foreign Office in Whitehall was rejected. Neither the Gothic Revivalists nor the Classicists could postulate suitable historical models for economic middle-class domestic architecture – possibly the Goths' only model was the Vicar's Close at Wells in Somerset? This absence of historical precedent opened the way for the Vernacular Revival, pioneered by George Devey (1820–86), and popularised in the form of the 'Queen Anne' and 'Old English' styles by Richard Norman Shaw (1831–1912). Shaw operated mainly at the top end of the market, in mid-century, when suburbs were still exclusive collections of villas, reminiscent of the initial suburban experiments several decades earlier. But his stylistic approach was equally, if economically, turned to higher density semi-detached villas in burgeoning garden suburbs, such as Bedford Park in the late-1870s.[8]

The new battle for the domestic, suburban market was a fierce one between speculative builders and the rapidly increasing ranks of professional architects; by the 1870s architects were using the new religion of sanitation as a major weapon in their armoury. Even architects of the artistic calibre of Shaw were also technically proficient in matters such as plumbing, and indeed took a keen interest in all aspects of domestic environmental servicing.† The RIBA advised the Local Government Board

---

*Poor Law Act, 1832.

†Shaw sent a detailed drawing of an unpatented, simplified water closet drainage system to the building press in 1877, after a year of testing the design in one of his houses. The drawing was published by various journals the following year and later published as a technical pamphlet. Saint, A. (1976) *Richard Norman Shaw*.

on the drafting of Model Bye-Laws* dealing with sanitation among other matters, such as structural and space standards, which were published in 1877. Such collaboration was thought to inspire public confidence in professionals and resulted in a technical handbook rather than basic pre-scriptions, also, presumably, to the loss of the speculative builders in general.[9]

The battle was further exacerbated by the fact that the majority of middle-class suburbanites were tenants[†] rather than owners, which meant that landlords were responsible for many estate developments, though many architects also became their own developers. While the assault on speculative builders had focused on unsafe structural matters earlier in the century, the impetus of the public sanitation movement in latter decades placed the emphasis on the overall 'healthy home' and increasing pros-perity enabled the luxury of the 'artistic house'. The increasing complexity of late nineteenth-century building services, allied with architectural issues such as plan layout and detailing, allowed architects to assert their inte-grated, professional approach as the only safe way to build and architects promoted themselves as 'house doctors' and 'guardians of family health'.[10] Such technical matters as ventilation and plumbing became equal to aes-thetic preoccupations, leading another famous artist–architect, Philip Webb (1831–1915) to say 'Now this is so beautiful I don't like it to be covered up', upon inspection of a new domestic drainage system.[11] But, unscrupu-lous builders were never completely ousted, as there were always those seeking to save on professional fees, often with ultimately dire conse-quences, if half of the architectural propaganda is to be believed. But, the promotion of the 'artistic house' garnered the middle to higher end of the suburban market for architects, and builders sought to superficially emulate the aesthetics and styles of these vanguard dwellings in cheaper, mass-housing schemes.

The reliance on architectural historicism and revivalism throughout most of the Victorian era entered a cul-de-sac in the last decade or so of Victoria's reign. While technological and scientific knowledge increased, the largest Imperial power in the world could not find a complementary architectural expression. Frenetic experiments which were euphemistically called 'freestyle' emerged. Paradoxical attempts were made to imitate craftsmanship through mechanical means. There was a sentimental hankering after hand-craftsmanship allied to a fascination and will to experiment with new technology, which often resulted in some strange hybrids – craft culture achieved through state-of-the-art technology and manufacturing.[‡] However, by the end of the century British domestic archi-tecture, at least, reached an apogee recognised by the rest of Europe, and

---

*Forerunners of modern building regulations.

†Approximately only 14–23 per cent for owner occupation in 1914. Swenarton, M. (1985) The scale and nature of owner-occupation in Britain between the wars, *Economic History Review*.

‡For example, Edward Prior's patented Early English Glass – a random manufacturing process to imitate the inconsistent quality of medieval glass. And the concrete panels imitating stone produced with Norman Shaw, Lascelles' patent cement slab system – published in Earnest Newton's *Sketches for country residences* (circa 1882–84).

Figure 5.2 'The Barn', Exmouth – designed in 1896 by Edward Prior with local stone, pebbles from the beach and reed thatch. Reproduced with permission from RIBA Library Photographs Collection.

confirmed in Herman Muthesius' *Das Englische Haus* in 1904.* This domestic cultural peak was undoubtedly enabled by middle-class prosperity at the height of Empire, and virtually all of Muthesius' illustrated houses were far from modest (Figure 5.2). He reported that:

> *There is nothing as unique in English architecture as the development of the house . . . no nation is more committed to its development because no nation has identified itself more with the house.*

Ultimately, the trinity of sanitation, planning, and artistic aesthetics was adapted to lesser budgets and pervaded burgeoning middle-class suburbia.† Architects also became increasingly involved with speculative estate developments, such as Shaw's emblematic aestheticism at Bedford Park in Chiswick, and many became speculative developers of artistic houses in their own right.[12] The nineteenth century heralded a series of royal

---

*Muthesius was working as a cultural attaché for the German Embassy in London when he first encountered the contemporary English domestic architecture which inspired his volume. His infatuation continued to the extent that he built a butterfly-plan house based on Edward Prior's 'Barn' when he returned to Germany.

†Prout cites examples of architects' increasing success within middle-class suburbia, where their use increased four-fold between 1876 and 1896 (from 20 per cent to 80 per cent) in areas around London and Birmingham. Prout, D.M. (1991) *The architect and domestic architecture in the urban and suburban environment in the nineteenth century in England,* unpublished PhD thesis, Courtauld Institute of Art, London University.

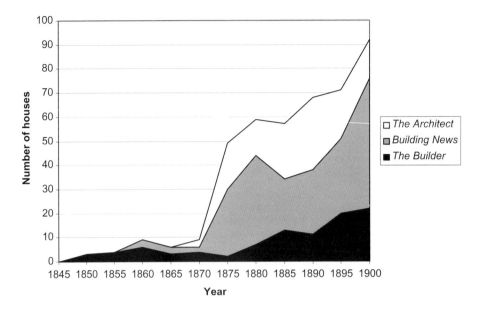

Figure 5.3 Number of houses illustrated in the building press, 1845–1900.

commissions into all aspects of society which resulted in the overhauling of many cherished institutions, sometimes in the name of elitism rather than progress. But, generally, the investigations sought to bring anachronistic practices, such as religious admission tests at the ancient universities, into line with an increasingly secular and modern society. Industrialisation and burgeoning urban population also brought expressions of civic pride, such as town halls and other public buildings, but it was the domestic market which provided most opportunities for architects after 1870 (Figure 5.3).

About a third of Britain's dwellings were erected between 1800 and 1911 (several million houses), and a third of them between 1870 and 1911. Traditional domestic construction techniques did not change significantly over the period 1840–1919, apart from obvious improvements due to improved building regulations, sanitation and local bye-laws. The large amount of Victorian housing that has survived has done so not just because it is flexible, but because it is popular with the general public. Strong local building and materials traditions continued until late in the nineteenth century. It was only in the early twentieth century that brick-making became a national industry and regional production petered out. In architectural terms local materials gave us the variety of brick colours such as Luton 'purples', Reading 'silver-greys', Staffordshire 'blues'. The construction quality of Victorian housing was not immune from bad workmanship, but the stock that has survived for well over a hundred years must be the best. No age is free from construction mistakes, but at the end of the nineteenth century there were frequent comments about improved construction, even in small houses. Building regulations and local bye-laws did not eradicate bad construction, but they seemed to reduce the scope for it. In terms of materials, Portland cement (patented in 1824) was universally used for all foundations and drainage pipe joints by the late nineteenth century. Damp-proof courses were introduced from around 1850, and from 1890 all new housing in Manchester used them – by 1900 new buildings included them

Figure 5.4 Greenore Village, County Louth, Ireland – railway workers cottages, school and shop (1873).

almost invariably. Floorboards were no longer permitted to lie on the ground, even in small houses, from the 1860s to 1870s onwards, heralding ubiquitous perforated 'air bricks' to ventilate suspended floors.[13]

Housing standards generally improved over the nineteenth century, led by model housing prototypes such as those exhibited at the Great Exhibition in 1852, and funded by Prince Albert, and successful industrialists such as George Cadbury's model village at Bourneville near Birmingham. Such enlightened industrialists realised that productivity could be increased by providing decent dwellings for their employees, alongside new factories sited on the edges of conurbations (Figure 5.4). These early schemes led to the 'garden city' concept championed by Ebenezer Howard and realised in Welwyn and Letchworth in the early twentieth century. Social, technological and legislative progress also generally improved the housing stock, with improved bye-laws and mandatory measures such as damp-proof coursing and cavity walls.

5.2 The modern era of housing

> *There has been altogether too much buncombe associated with the factory-built home. Publishers everywhere have accepted too freely the idea of pre-fabrication and have given it much publicity. Students of the problem should consider critically what has been proposed . . . .*
>
> *John Burchand,* The evolving house, *1936*

World War I provided the catalyst for mass social housing in Britain. Lloyd George promised 'homes fit for heroes' for returning combatants, after the generally poor health of the working population recruited to fight the war was publicised. The Walter's report in 1918 recommended that local authorities should be subsidised to build housing for rent, at lower density than the average in Victorian terraced housing. Over four million dwellings were built in council estates during the inter-war years. Due to the shortage of skilled labour and essential materials, about a quarter of a million dwellings of this new housing stock were constructed by non-traditional methods. Among the new methods of construction that were developed were more than 20 steel-framed housing systems, along with other systems based on pre-cast and *in situ* concrete, timber, and occasionally cast iron. Some of these were more successful than others, resulting in varying levels of building performance over the years, and there was usually a switch to traditional techniques whenever the labour supply allowed. The use of non-traditional techniques was, however, more extensive in Scotland, due to widespread supply-side problems. This led to the formation of the Scottish Special Housing Association (SSHA) in 1937, which could build houses by non-traditional methods only.

The Building Research Station was firmly established in 1925, following on from the pioneering work done by the architects Edwin Sachs and Raymond Unwin. From 1895 to 1910, the former, an Anglo-German architect, exhausted himself advocating the objective: scientific testing of building materials. Unwin worked towards understanding the technical imperatives surrounding post-war housing demands, while chairing the Building Materials Research Committee, which turned into the Building Research Board in 1920. BRS was initially a testing house with strong engineering and contractor links which employed only one architect, P.W. Barnett,* before 1933. Other staff at BRS were mainly young chemists, engineers and physicists.[14] However, links were steadily built up with technical architects, and E.A.A. Rowse of the Architectural Association persauded BRS to test the welded-steel system of construction proposed for the Quarry Hill flats, Leeds, in 1936. This system appeared to be at the scientific vanguard of the answers to social housing, but BRS's experts were cautious. The building was later demolished due to technical faults. Robert Fitzmaurice joined BRS in 1933 and promoted the idea of monitoring 'building performance' rather than using draconian legislation to improve building and buildings. The idea was certainly ahead of its time and probably remains unrealised today. Fitzmaurice was keen on turning the research at BRS into an applied science to create a 'modern vernacular' in building technique. To this end, he published his first volume of *Principles of modern building* in 1938. The reaction was mixed in some quarters, as the young Canadian architect, Bill Allen, who joined BRS in 1937, relates:

> *It was a sort of bible to a certain group of modern architects at the time. F R S Yorke and Wells Coates I met through Fitz at the station. These young chaps said that they saw BRS and the Bauhaus as two branches of the same idea.*
>
> *Fitzmaurice, incidentally, in writing* Principles of modern building *was heartily disliked by every major scientist and BRS. They thought that he was popularising what they were creating as a*

---

*Barnett, or PWB as he became known, was a lynch-pin in the early history of BRS. He served in the army throughout the 1914–18 war and trained at the Bartlett School of Architecture at University College London. He was a very early authority in architectural acoustics, and dealt with the Station's external contacts and special investigations until his early death in 1933.

new branch of science. He was very popular among builders, and becoming influential among architects. Although his book is scientifically very good, it was essentially applied science. The other boys had some confused ideas about science and publication in archival journals and things of that sort. Even the people who didn't read Principles *were influenced by it, if you know what I mean.**

BRS was the first organisation of its kind in the world and presaged similar establishments in many other countries. World War I had exposed many deficiencies in British industry that arose from inadequate application of science. The mission of the Station was and has remained an essentially practical one – the improvement of building. Building remained an empirical art until the nineteenth century. The classic structures of the past are the successes, the failures remain buried or were rebuilt. The towers of no less than eight of England's early cathedrals collapsed during, or not many years after, construction. While tradition and craft have an undeniable place in the building industry, obviously and particularly in the area of historic building conservation, tradition explains how something should be done – it does not ask why. The Station set about answering such questions related to building physics and the performance of materials over the course of its first half-century, a time when Britain generally led the world in the broad field of building research.

Inter-war private housing developments were usually of a lower density, causing problems of 'ribbon' and 'pepper pot' development, made possible by low petrol prices. Ribbon developments, along arterial roads, exacerbated the perception of housing incursion into rural areas, among other problems. Pepper pot developments, on the other hand, made vehicular access more difficult, as they were isolated houses in rural locations. The sprawling, suburban housing boom of the 1920s and 30s invaded the British landscape like the tentacles of an octopus, which inspired the title of an influential book by Clough Williams-Ellis. The architect of Portmeirion created the catalyst for new legislation with his book *England and the octopus*, published in 1928. The provocatively argued book started a polemic that led to the passing of the Prevention of Ribbon Development Act and the London Green Belt Act, shortly afterwards. They were the precursors of the modern planning system.[15]

The aftermath of World War II created an even greater need for mass housing development, not to mention the need to rebuild housing damaged by enemy aircraft. The Ministry of Health predicted the future housing demand in early 1943, and a strategy to cope with estimated post-war demand was devised at the beginning of 1944. The Reconstruction Committee's proposal involved a three-staged timetable, starting with an emergency period for the first few years to try and house all those who needed accommodation; the following five years would concentrate on new housing construction; and the final period of ten years was aimed at

---

*Quoted in Saint, A. (1987) *Towards a social architecture: The role of school building in post-war England.* New Haven: Yale University Press, p. 14.

replacing sub-standard and slum housing. In the initial emergency period of two years it was hoped that nearly half-a-million permanent dwellings would be provided; it was belatedly agreed that this would include around 200 000 dwellings with a short and finite design life. The Burt and Dudley Committees were convened in 1942 to consider non-traditional construction techniques to overcome labour and skills shortages, and planning and space standards to reflect lifestyle changes, respectively. Social surveys revealed that a small, detached house or bungalow was preferred over a flat by the vast majority of the population.

The Building Research Station came into its own during the post-war reconstruction, liaising with the RIBA and the Birt committee, to become a driving technical force in British building. The Architecture Physics Division of BRS combined architects and scientists who pioneered work in the environmental sciences, heating, ventilation, lighting and acoustics. Principles of 'psychophysics' and 'ergonomics' were applied to determine subjective responses to physical phenomena in the performance of buildings. More prosaically, the only possible answer to the sheer scale and scope of post-war housing demand was seen as prefabrication. The problems were different from those faced after the first war, in that material shortages were less crucial than the supply of skilled labour. Additionally, the surplus of steel and aluminium production caused by the war effort dictated housing experimentation with materials such as these. The most ubiquitous type of steel-framed house was the British Iron and Steel Federation (BISF) house designed by Frederic Gibberd, while the Airey and Wate's houses were typical of the concrete systems. The aircraft industry contributed lightweight, aluminium framed and clad systems, such as the AIROH* bungalow and the ARCON house (Figure 5.5).

The decades following World War II saw the philosophy of house construction changing towards that of industrialised building, with as much work as possible transferred from the site to the factory. However, public confidence waned after the Ronan Point collapse, which involved large panel, off-site construction. High-rise housing buildings were already controversial for social reasons, but Ronan Point raised technical doubts as well. Ronan Point was a 22 storey point-block with an inherently strong structure, but it was not designed to withstand the large gas explosion that caused its partial collapse. The explosion occurred in a corner flat on the eighteenth floor and caused the floors above to lift, as they were unrestrained without vertical loading – the panels were blown outwards leading to progressive collapse. There were rumours of poor workmanship and an absence of restraint ties, but the design codes of the time only required limited horizontal ties – the vertical panels were normally assumed to be restrained by gravity and the weight of the panels above (Figure 5.6). The collapse obviously caused a revision of the design codes and remedial work to all remaining large panel structures. Other construction problems were found in some of the other large panel buildings. Volumetric systems, using a series of prefabricated 'boxes' that were connected on site, were also

---

*Aircraft Industries' Research Organisation on Housing

Figure 5.5 The aluminium temporary house: the last of the four sections being swung into place. Reproduced with permission from RIBA Library Photographs Collection.

Figure 5.6 Ronan Point, London: after building collapse in May 1968. Reproduced with permission from RIBA Library Photographs Collection. This figure is also reproduced in colour in the colour plate section.

used during the 1960s and 1970s. For obvious reasons, these usually involved lightweight timber or metal frames – following on from earlier volumetric aluminium bungalows from the immediate post-war period.

Timber-framed construction was popular in the early 1980s, and dominated prefabricated housing to the extent of approaching one-third of the market, until an infamous television episode of *World in Action*. This programme was severely critical of a small group of timber-framed houses in the west of England, and alleged that they were not watertight, causing the beginnings of structural decay. The programme went on to imply that these dwellings were typical of all timber-framed construction. The Building Research Establishment was commissioned to investigate new timber-framed dwellings in the late 1980s, as the Government was concerned about the negative effect the claims in the programme could have on the 'Right to Buy' scheme. BRE surveyed more than 400 houses, including many in regions of severe weather exposure, and found no evidence of decay that supported the predictions made by the programme. These predictions did not subsequently come true.[16] About a million dwellings were constructed using non-traditional techniques, and BRE has listed over 500 systems that were in use from 1919 to 1976.[17] Condition surveys by BRE in the 1980s and early 1990s revealed serious corrosion to some steel-framed houses and condensation problems in some of the steel-clad systems, but many steel houses remain in good condition. The BRE report concluded that most of the steel-framed houses had generally performed in a similar manner to many traditionally built dwellings of the same vintage.[18] Similar conclusions were reached in a sister report on timber-framed housing:

> ... the performance of timber-frame dwellings built between 1920 and 1975 is generally similar to that of traditionally-built dwellings of the same age. Provided that regular maintenance is carried out ... a performance comparable with traditionally-constructed dwellings of the same period should be maintained into the forseeable future.[19]

5.3 Twenty-first century housing

> I do think we haven't done enough on the design. There's not enough imagination. Design is equally as important as the quality of construction. That's a major area for improvement ....
>
> *Deputy Prime Minister John Prescott*, Building Design, *2005*

Modern methods of construction (MMC), including off-site manufacture (such as panellised or volumetric pod construction) have arrived on the UK construction scene. They are expected to revolutionise the way housing is designed and built over the next decade. Government policy, among other factors such as shortage of skilled building operatives, is influencing these developments. The Egan report and the recent Barker review of housing have recommended greater take-up of modern methods of construction, and off-site manufacture in particular (Figure 5.7).

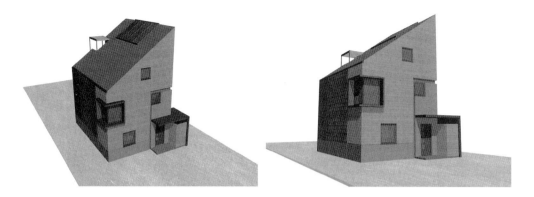

Figure 5.7 Concept proposals for an MMC house on the BRE Innovation Park, using Structural Insulated Panel Systems. This figure is also reproduced in colour in the colour plate section.

BRE is developing a technical standard to set performance requirements for new building systems for dwellings. These should address the concerns of mortgage lenders, insurers and others, to tackle some of the perception problems around the new systems, and encourage the development of high-quality products. MMC is heralded as the answer to twenty-first century problems of housing supply. But, as David Hylton, of Nationwide, claims:

> *At the moment there is a lack of confidence in non-traditional systems . . . they don't have an entirely successful history! Mortgage lenders want to be satisfied that a building has been well-designed and constructed . . . and able to last a good long time. There are currently several standards, but we what we need is just one that we can rely on, in conjunction with more general inspections.*

The Standard for Innovative Methods of Dwelling Construction, LPS 2020, has the support of the Council of Mortgage Lenders and the Association of British Insurers, and of construction sector interests. An extensive programme of development and stakeholder consultation workshops, resulted in the launch of the draft standard at the ODPM Sustainable Communities Summit in Manchester in January 2005. It should provide a route to certification for innovative building systems, sub-assemblies and elements, which are not wholly covered under current recognised standards and codes for dwelling construction, and have a limited track record of service in dwelling construction in the UK.

The LPS 2020 Standard was designed to meet the variable needs of different approval bodies, regulators and warranty providers, which currently result in manufacturers going through several testing and assessment procedures. The LPS 2020 standard aims to:

- Provide a single and consistent method for assessing the design and performance of innovative building systems that do not have an adequate track record in service in the UK.
- Ensure that the manufacture and factory production of innovative systems is controlled.

- Complement the control and inspection functions of existing warranty providers and building control.
- Check buildability and produce a checklist of key items for site inspection, to ensure adequate performance in the final dwelling.
- Give confidence to insurers, lenders and owners that innovative systems will perform adequately.
- Achieve equal treatment for insurance and lending purposes as conventional dwellings under normal insurance and lending terms.
- Enable manufacturers to demonstrate optional enhanced performance of specialist systems, e.g. enhanced flood resistance or fire performance or reduced environmental impact.
- Maintain a database of approved innovative systems and their location, for future maintenance purposes.

5.4 Benchmarking housing – Introduction

BRE was appointed by Quintain Estates to conduct a technical due diligence exercise on the Quintessential Homes Consortium bid to the London Wide Initiative (LWI) in 2004. The bid involved three 'competition sites' around London. BRE's role was one of independent technical assessor of overall design quality. The Design Quality Method (DQM Housing) was used to assess overall design quality of the three schemes. The Housing Quality Indicators (HQI) were used to underpin DQM matrix definitions. The HQI system is a measurement and assessment tool designed to evaluate housing schemes on the basis of quality rather than simply of cost. The HQI assesses the quality of a housing project using three main categories: location, design and performance. These are subdivided into ten sections – the Indicators:

(1) Location
(2) Site – visual impact, layout and landscaping
(3) Site – open space
(4) Site – routes and movement
(5) Unit – size
(6) Unit – layout
(7) Unit – noise, light and services
(8) Unit – accessibility
(9) Unit – energy, green and sustainability issues
(10) Performance in use*

BRE assessed the overall design quality of the three schemes comprising the Quintessential bid and concluded that they all achieved good practice levels (Figure 5.8). BRE interrogated all available design documentation on

---

*An HQI assessment generates separate scores for each Indicator producing a profile of the scheme, and an overall HQI score. A free spreadsheet version of the HQI is available from the Office of the Deputy Prime Minister's (ODPM) website. A priced, software version of the HQI is available from BRE.

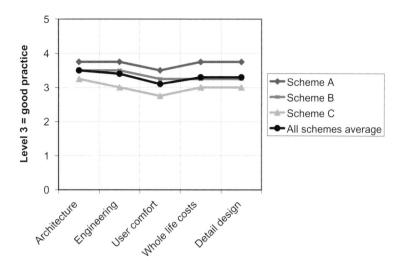

Figure 5.8 BRE DQM Summary Matrix prediction for Quintessential's LWI bid.

the extranet system and used HQI software to assess matrix rating levels. BRE experts in the various individual topic matrices also proffered their professional opinions on the schemes. Each scheme, and the average of all schemes, scored at good practice level (Level 3). The difference between schemes, of less than one matrix level, is considered statistically insignificant.

5.5 References

1 MacArthur, B. (ed.) (1995) *Historic speeches*. London: Penguin.

2 Halliday, S. (1999) *The great stink of London*. London: Sutton.

3 Dearlove, J. and Saunders, P. (1991) *Introduction to British politics*. Cambridge: Polity Press.

4 Harris, J. (1993) *Private lives, public spirit: Britain 1870–1914*. London: Penguin.

5 Floud, R. and McCloskey, D. (1994) *The economic history of Britain since 1700*. Cambridge: Cambridge University Press.

6 den Otter, S. (1990) *The search for a social philosophy: The idealists of late-Victorian and Edwardian Britain*, unpublished DPhil thesis, University of Oxford.

7 Harper, R. (1983) *Victorian architectural competitions: An index to British and Irish architectural competitions in The Builder*. London: Mansell.

8 Fishman, R. (1987) *Bourgeois utopias*. New York: Basic Books.

9 Gaskell, M. (1983) *Building Control: National Legislation and the introduction of Local Bye-Laws in Victorian England*. London: Bedford Square Press.

10 Prout, D.M. (1991) *The architect and domestic architecture in the urban and suburban environment in the nineteenth century in England*, unpublished PhD thesis, Courtauld Institute of Art, London University.

11 Lethaby, W. (1935) *Philip Webb and his work*. London: Oxford University Press.

12 Girouard, M. (1977) *Sweetness and light: The Queen Anne Movement, 1860–1900*. New Haven: Yale University Press.

13 Muthesius, S. (1982) *The English terraced house*. New Haven: Yale University Press.

14 Lea, F.M. (1971) *Science and building: A history of the Building Research Station*. London: HMSO.

15 Golland, A. and Blake, R. (eds) (2004) *Housing development: Theory, process and practice*. London: Routledge.

16 Covingaton, S.A. *et al.* (1995) *Timber frame housing systems built in the UK between 1920 and 1965 (BR283)* and *Timber frame housing systems built in the UK between 1965 and 1975 (BR284)*. Garston: BRE.

17 Harrison, H.W. *et al.* (eds) (2004) *Non-traditional houses: Identifying non-traditional houses in the UK, 1918–75*. Garston: BRE.

18 Harrison, H.W. (1987) *Steel-framed and stell-clad houses: Inspection and assessment (BR113)*. Garston: BRE.

19 Covington, S.A. *et al.* (1995) *Timber frame housing systems 1920 and 1975: Inspection and assessment (BR282)*. Garston: BRE.

Appendix
BRE's Design Quality Matrices

BRE DQM	**Architecture** *Generic*		NB: This form must be adapted to appropriate building type before use		Design Quality Method	MATRIX ONE **1**
Level	Architecture – exterior	Site planning	Interior design	Space planning	Specification	Sustainability
5	*Exemplary*					
4 best practice	Excellent firmness, commodity and delight without architectural conceit or excess. Excellent materials selection with provision for weathering and maintenance. Users respect the building.	Excellent displacement of built elements optimises site geometry. Good orientation and access. Space for extension.	Excellent design with clarity with appropriate scale and size. Excellent daylight, acoustics and colour. Robust finishes.	Excellent use of space with good juxtaposition of key spaces. Imaginative use of servant to service space. Good social space. Sound ergonomic design.	Excellent component selection and abutment. Excellent detailing and maintenance provision. Long-life materials selected for low maintenance.	Minimal impact on the environment, in balance with social and economic factors. Excellent energy efficiency in components and materials. Excellent BREEAM rating.
3 good practice	Good design with minor shortcomings. Good use of all materials. Some maintenance difficulties and weathering discrepancies.	Good site planning but some failures to achieve best practice. Constrained site reduces extension.	Good design, but with compromised proportions. Minor problems with daylight, acoustics and finishes.	Good space planning. A few departures from best practice in terms relationships of served to servant space.	Good specification in general, but with a few minor deviations from best practice. Some access difficulties.	Good consideration of environmental issues, and related social and economic aspects. Good energy efficiency. Very Good BREEAM rating.
2	Design is mediocre and uninspiring, but functional. Adequate materials, but poor weathering and maintenance.	Site plan is competent, but uninspired. Access and extension difficulties.	Interior design is competent, but uninspired. At least one major failure in daylight, acoustics etc.	Adequate space plan, but with clear relationship problems in at least one space. Circulation space problems.	Adequate spec, but with deficiencies immediately obvious to informed users. Some short life materials.	Some sustainability issues addressed in an ad hoc way. Little consideration of energy efficiency. Good BREEAM rating.
1	Mundane design with some functionality problems. Short-life materials and predictable weathering and maintenance problems.	A few significant operational difficulties due to poor site planning. No possibility of extension.	A few significant, or several minor failures in daylighting, acoustics, colour, or finishes.	A few significant, or several minor operational difficulties due to inadequate planning. Lack of consideration for intended use. Inadequate circulation space.	A few significant, or several minor specification deficiencies – obvious to informed users. Many short life materials and components.	Token sustainability. Energy efficiency not apparent in operating data – e.g. typical consumption figures. Pass BREEAM rating.
0	Banal architecture with many functionality problems. Use of inappropriate materials e.g. school that resembles an industrial shed. Weathering and maintenance very poor.	Major operational difficulties arising from poor site planning, inadequate space and difficult access.	Internal finishes and materials utilitarian, inappropriate for use, or inadequate. Poor acoustics, lighting etc.	Substantial difficulties obvious in use, due to inadequate planning, or consideration for intended use. Wholly inadequate circulation.	Specification deficiencies obvious to users. Design life of most components and materials inadequate to ensure minimum design life of building.	Sustainability not on the agenda or in the brief. Energy consumption above typical levels for the building type. No energy management apparent. No BREEAM rating.

BRE DQM	**Environmental Engineering** *Generic*		NB: This form must be adapted to appropriate building type before use		Design Quality Method	MATRIX TWO **2**
Level	Integration with architecture	Mechanical system design	Electrical system design	Maintainability	Sourcing of repairable items	Sustainability of bldg services
5	*Exemplary*					
4 **best** **practice**	Environmental engineering design is sympathetic to, and optimises, all aspects of the architecture. Consideration of thermal, lighting and acoustic issues. No intrusion of services into occupied spaces.	Robust best practice using the most appropriate components, integrated into efficient and reliable systems. Includes heating, ventilation, cooling and plumbing. Nil acoustic intrusion.	Robust best practice using the most appropriate components, integrated into efficient and reliable systems. Includes internal and external lighting, communications and any other systems. Component selection supports architecture.	Maintenance facilities and access are designed to optimise use, and time to clean and repair. Specialised access for replacement avoided. All service data widely available.	All repairable and replaceable items are selected for wide availability and compliance with well-known standards. Design has avoided the use of specially manufactured items with long future order times and high replacement costs.	Environmental engineering components, system arrangements and controls selected and commissioned to minimise environmental impact. Equivalent to BREEAM Excellent rating.
3 **good** **practice**	One or two minor departures from ideal as defined in Level 4. No deficiencies related to thermal and lighting issues.	One or two minor departures from ideal as defined in Level 4. No deficiencies related to efficiency of heating, lighting and cooling.	One or two minor departures from ideal as defined in Level 4. No deficiencies related to lighting control or adequate ICT provision.	One or two minor departures from ideal as defined in Level 4. Limited revenue maintenance to some items can be excepted.	One or two minor departures from ideal as defined in Level 4. No deficiencies related to essential services, such as back-up generation in a health facility.	One or two minor departures from ideal as defined in Level 4. Equivalent to BREEAM Very Good rating.
2	Good design at a visual level. Some minor technical deficiencies related to ventilation, thermal and lighting aspects. Component location in occupied spaces is not good.	One or two minor departures from Level 4. Minor departures from good practice related to efficiency and operation of heating, lighting and cooling.	One or two minor departures from Level 4. Some deficiencies related to lighting control or ICT provision. Visible components do not clash with environment.	Some significant cost and availability impacts due to inadequate design consideration. Access equipment and specialist tools needed for maintenance.	One or two minor departures from Level 4. Some deficiencies related to selection and specification of components. Some spare parts are difficult and/or costly to obtain.	Some obvious failures by designers and cost consultants to properly consider long-term environmental impact. Equivalent to BREEAM Good rating.
1	Component selection, positioning, safety, thermal, and lighting issues not thought through. Services noticeably intrude into occupied spaces.	Design approach is compliant with design codes, but not optimised for efficiency. Component selection is not good for noise and reliability.	Design approach has one or two major deficiencies. Compliant with design codes but obviously uses lowest cost components.	Significant cost and availability impacts due to inadequate design consideration.	Many deficiencies related to selection and specification of components. Many spare parts are difficult to obtain. Sourcing of spares a significant problem.	Widespread minor and some major failures to consider environmental impacts. Equivalent to BREEAM Pass.
0	Frequent and obvious clashes between services and architecture. Significant failures on thermal and lighting issues.	Design marginally sized. Concerns over component suitability. Not properly commissioned. Users aware of problems.	Arbitrary design approach that has obviously failed to consider users' views. Components and fittings under-specified in many cases.	Minimal consideration given to maintenance at design stage. Maintenance costs higher due to access costs.	Widespread use of components with limited availability. Maintenance staff have to spend considerable time to obtain replacement items.	Widespread major failures to consider environmental impacts. Equivalent to no BREEAM rating.

BRE DQM	**User Comfort** *Generic*		NB: This form must be adapted to appropriate building type before use		Design Quality Method	MATRIX THREE **3**
Level	*Summertime overheating*	*Visual environment*	*Heating comfort*	*Audible and visual intrusion*	*Acoustics quality*	*Air quality (internal)*
5	*Exemplary*					
4 best practice	Building interior unlikely to experience more than 30 hours/year above internal environmental temperature 27 °C. Occupants have very limited beam radiation from sun. Adequate summertime ventilation.	Daylight and artificial lighting sources entirely appropriate for task and promote a cheerful but non-distracting atmosphere. Full compliance with Work-place.	Internal air temperatures within −1.5 °C to +2.0 °C of target temperature. No 'Monday morning' discomfort with intermittent heating. Adequate ventilation – no noticeable draughts in winter.	No interference to work or leisure from background noises in interior or exterior occupied spaces. No unwanted or noticeable visual intrusion.	All occupied areas free from acoustic features that act to the detriment of efficient working and enjoyment of the building. Covers, reverberation time, intelligibility of speech and music.	No noticeable odour, dust, allergic or health symptoms from contaminants such as micro-organisms, organic or non-organic compounds. Satisfactory humidity in all spaces.
3 good practice	Same as Level 4 with the exception that not more than 50 hours/year above 27 °C. No hot air pockets at ceiling level, e.g. high-level opening lights in fenestration.	Few minor departures from Level 4 standards. Daylighting sensibly even over whole usable area, Good use of colour. Very few reflections on VDU screens.	A few areas non-compliant with Level 4 standards. Minimal problems from asymmetric radiation. Occasional underheat on Monday mornings.	Very occasional slight intrusion to internal activities from background noise. Occasional visual intrusion from passing pedestrians and vehicles.	Most large and/or heavily used areas compliant with Level 4. Compliance with relevant acoustics good practice guidance.	Minimal problems due to non-compliance with Level 4. Most occupants unable to recall any problems related to air quality.
2	Occupants report summertime overheat as an occasional problem. Possibly some discomfort from beam radiation from the sun. Ceilings trap hot air.	Significant departures from Level 4 standards in one or two spaces. Daylighting sensibly even. Good use of colour. Very few VDU screen reflections.	Majority of areas compliant with Level 4 temperature control. Occasional reports of discomfort from uneven heating and cold Monday mornings.	Occupants notice noise and visual intrusion. Insufficient to disturb activity. Either due to insufficient isolation or inappropriate planning adjacencies.	A noticeable number of spaces are not ideal acoustically – to the extent that speech levels have to be raised occasionally, and/or words repeated.	Some occupants can recall air quality related issues when questioned. Probably no noticeable impact on occupant health or productivity.
1	Summertime overheat a frequent problem. Users known to move away from sun path. Fans in use. Ceilings 'hot'. Inadequate ventilation.	Many instances of departure from Level 4 standards. Inadequate daylighting. A number of dark corners. Veiling reflections in VDUs.	Some obvious failures to control temperatures. Building noted as cold on Monday mornings when cold outside. Some cold draughts.	Noise and visual intrusion occasionally disturbs task in hand, e.g. rain drumming on metal roofs in a school, suspending teaching.	Many spaces are not ideal acoustically, to the extent that speech levels have to be raised occasionally, and/or words repeated.	A few occupants comment on indoor air quality. Noticeable odour on first entering building. Some complaints of nasal and throat irritation.
0	Summertime overheat a major problem. Users try to avoid use of hot areas. Hot areas have fans, some permanently fixed.	Many instances of poor daylighting, distracting glare, veiling reflections in VDU screens, poor colour coordination.	Widespread overheat/underheat. Users report cold feet. Monday morning heating timed early to avoid heating problems.	Noise and visual intrusion frequently disturbs task in hand. Building functionality severely impaired.	Much of building has unsatisfactory acoustics that obviously impact on efficiency of working or on social conversation.	Obvious problems. If asked, many occupants note that the building seems 'sick'. Some occupants link health problems to air quality.

BRE DQM	**Whole Life Costs** *Generic*		NB: This form must be adapted to appropriate building type before use		Design Quality Method	MATRIX FOUR **4**
Level	*External materials*	*Internal fabric and finishes*	*Building services – capital items*	*Building services – revenue*	*Facilities management – fitness*	*Flexibility – change and extension*
5	*Exemplary*					
4 best practice	All components selected and installed to achieve lowest cost of ownership. All have good resistance to vandalism, sun, wind and rain. Graceful degradation of appearance with wear. Detailing to best practice.	Fabric and finishes chosen for lowest cost of ownership. Properties include ease of routine and special cleaning. Graceful degradation of appearance with wear – easy repair and replacement.	All components chosen for minimum cost of ownership. Adequate space for minor and major maintenance. Design enables most service activities to be undertaken during occupation.	All components selected for minimum cost of ownership. Component arrangement and availability good. Easy maintenance access. Most service activities possible during occupation.	All architectural fittings, furniture and furnishings selected for minimum cost of ownership and support to organizational objectives. All items eminently suitable for purpose. Average repair time is short.	Building plan, site planning, construction and materials make future adaptation and extension easy. Extension possible without excessive cost and disturbance to occupiers. Long life, loose fit, low energy.
3 good practice	Level 4 requirements largely satisfied. But a few minor shortfalls leading to the appearance of premature aging in some limited areas.	Level 4 requirements largely satisfied. But a few minor failures leading to the appearance of premature aging in some limited areas.	Level 4 requirements satisfied for all major components. All components selected for highest appropriate operating efficiency. Some minor shortfalls.	Level 4 requirements satisfied for all major items. Some minor shortfalls, possibly involving long order periods for replacements.	Level 4 requirements satisfied for all major components. Some minor shortfalls, possibly involving costly replacement, e.g. scaffolding needed for access.	Level 4 requirements satisfied in most areas. Some minor shortfalls. Balance between functionality and flexibility achieved.
2	Level 4 requirements satisfied for most but not all major components, and for most minor components. Some obvious failures to achieve good practice.	Level 4 requirements satisfied for most but not all major components, and for most minor components. Some obvious failures to achieve good practice.	Level 4 requirements satisfied for most but not all major components. Some failures to specify and properly install components with the appropriate efficiency. Some areas less than good practice.	Level 4 requirements satisfied for most but not all major components. Some failures to specify components with optimum running and replacement costs.	Level 4 requirements satisfied for most but not all major components. Some under-specification and less than optimum running costs. Some obvious failures to achieve good practice.	Level 4 requirements satisfied for most but not all major areas. Minor difficulties identified on less important items. Minor impact on future costs and functionality.
1	More than a few obvious failures to specify suitable materials and install them with good detailing.	More than a few obvious failures to specify suitable materials. Service life impaired.	More than a few obvious failures to specify suitable components. Service life impaired. Notably high costs of ownership.	More than a few obvious failures to specify and install suitable components. Impact on costs of ownership.	More than a few obvious failures to specify and install suitable components. Impact on costs of ownership.	Future adaptation and extension may be limited by site planning and space planning. Major impact on costs and functionality.
0	Many obvious failures to specify and properly install robust materials. Frequent and obvious examples of unsatisfactory details.	Many obvious failures to specify and install suitable materials. Many obvious examples of unsatisfactory details.	Many obvious failures to specify and install suitable and efficient components. Service life significantly impaired with associated costs.	Many obvious failures to specify and install suitable and efficient components. Service life significantly impaired with associated costs.	Many obvious failures to specify and install suitable and efficient components. Service life significantly impaired with associated costs.	Future adaptation almost rendered impossible, or severely limited and potentially very costly, due to plan configuration, construction.

BRE DQM	**Detail Design** *Generic*		NB: This form must be adapted to appropriate building type before use		Design Quality Method	MATRIX FIVE 5
Level	**External detail**	**Internal detail**	**Junction details**	**Furniture and furnishings**	**Fittings**	**Safety and security**
5	*Exemplary*					
4 **best practice**	All materials and components selected and installed for good resistance to sun, wind, rain and vandalism. Graceful degradation of appearance with wear, aging and use. All detailing to best practice.	Good functional and aesthetic detailing. All internal materials and components appropriate for function. Easy maintenance and replacement. Minimal need for access equipment. Graceful degradation.	All architectural junctions detailed to best practice with good workmanship. Aesthetically pleasing and unlikely to suffer premature failure during predicted life or from vandalism.	All furniture and furnishings selected for ability to retain good appearance and minimum cost of ownership. All seating comfortable for expected occupancy – and with low VOC emission.	All architectural fittings suitable for purpose and aesthetically pleasing. Anthropomorphically acceptable. Correctly sized, robust and solid. Suitable provision for disabled persons use and access.	Detailed architecture to best practice and safe. Design accords with *Secure by design* guidance. Security management and operating costs minimised. All significant safety hazards competently addressed.
3 **good practice**	Level 4 requirements satisfied for all materials and major components, and for most of the minor components. Minor discrepancies.	Level 4 requirements satisfied for all materials and major components, and for most of the minor components. Minor discrepancies.	Level 4 requirements satisfied for all materials and major components, and for most of the minor components.	Level 4 requirements satisfied for all widely used furniture, and furnishings, and for most of the other furniture and furnishings.	Level 4 requirements satisfied for most widely used fittings, and for most other fittings. Minor discrepancies.	Level 4 requirements satisfied for all most major issues, and for most of the less significant issues. Minor discrepancies.
2	Level 4 requirements satisfied for most, but not all, major components, and for the great majority of minor components.	Level 4 requirements satisfied for most, but not all, major components, and for the great majority of minor components.	Level 4 requirements satisfied for most, but not all, important material junctions, and for the great majority of minor details.	Level 4 requirements satisfied for most widely used furniture and furnishings, and for the great majority of other items.	Level 4 requirements satisfied for most widely used fittings, and for the great majority of other items.	Level 4 requirements satisfied for most major issues, and for the great majority of less important issues.
1	A few obvious failures on major materials and components, and/or multiple failures on minor details.	A few obvious failures to specify suitable major materials and components, and/or multiple failures on minor details.	A few obvious failures to specify and install suitable details on widely used junctions, and/or multiple failures on minor details.	A few obvious failures to select widely used items compliant with Level 4 requirements, and/or multiple failures on less widely used items.	A few obvious failures to satisfy Level 4 requirements on widely used and/or important fittings. Multiple failures on less widely used items.	A few obvious failures to satisfy Level 4 requirements on important issues. Multiple failures on less important issues.
0	Many failures to properly specify and detail materials and components.	Many failures to properly specify and detail materials and components.	Many failures to specify and install suitable details on widely used and on minor junctions.	Many failures to address Level 4 requirements on widely used and/or other items.	Many failures to address Level 4 requirements. Many failures on less widely used items.	Many failures to address Level 4 requirements on important issues. Many failures on minor issues.

Index